Understanding The Difference Between Democrats And Republicans

(A Republican Perspective)

Understanding The Difference Between Democrats And Republicans

(A Republican Perspective)

By Edward Baiamonte

The American Political Press
215 Henry St.
Stamford, CT 06902
(203) 327-3832

Copyright @ 1991 by Edward Baiamonte

*All rights reserved. No part of
this publication may be reproduced or
transmitted in any form or by any means
electronic or mechanical, including photocopy,
recording, or any information storage and retrieval
system, without permission in writing from the publisher.*

*Requests for permission to make copies of
any part of the work should be mailed to:*

*The American Political Press
215 Henry St.
Stamford, Ct. 06902
(203) 327-3832*

Set in Linotype Times Roman

Printed in the United States of America

Library of Congress Cataloging in Publication Data

*Baiamonte, Edward 1951-
Understanding The Difference Between Democrats And Republicans*

ISBN 0-9631799-0-X

to justin edward and cristen april,
or vise versa

THE FIRES OF HELL ARE RESERVED FOR THOSE WHO PASS THROUGH LIFE WITHOUT FORMING OPINIONS ABOUT THE MAJOR ISSUES OF THE DAY.

- DANTE

I KNOW OF NO SAFE DEPOSITORY OF THE ULTIMATE POWERS OF THE SOCIETY BUT THE PEOPLE THEMSELVES, AND IF WE THINK THEM NOT ENLIGHTENED ENOUGH TO EXERCISE THEIR CONTROL WITH A WHOLESOME DISCRETION, THE REMEDY IS NOT TO TAKE IT FROM THEM BUT TO INFORM THEIR DISCRETION BY EDUCATION.

- THOMAS JEFFERSON

I KNOW YOUR DEEDS, THAT YOU ARE NEITHER COLD NOR HOT, I WISH YOU WERE EITHER ONE OR THE OTHER, SO, BECAUSE YOU ARE LUKE WARM-NEITHER HOT NOR COLD-I AM ABOUT TO SPIT YOU OUT OF MY MOUTH.

- REV. 3:16-19

TABLE OF CONTENTS

INTRODUCTION	-	1
FOREIGN POLICY	- LETS HELP RUSSIA NOW	5
POVERTY	- DEMOCRATS AFFECT POVERTY	14
THE RECESSION	- CAPITALISM VS. SOCIALISM	22
S & L SCANDAL	- $500 BILLION WASTED BY DEMOCRATS	33
ABORTION	- PRO-CHOICE FOR THE FETUS	40
ABORTION	- EMOTIONS AND THE SUPREME COURT	48
CAPITAL GAINS	- THE DEMOCRATS HATE THEM	53
HEALTH CARE	- DEMOCRATS WANT SOCIALISM	61
FREE TRADE	- DEMOCRATS DON'T LIKE FREEDOM	69
CRIME	- REPUBLICANS REDUCE CRIME	77
MEDIA	- BIAS AT ABC NEWS	85
EDUCATION	- FREEDOM OR CONTINUED DECLINE	91
ENERGY CRISIS	- SOLVED BY THE REPUBLICANS	99
CLARENCE THOMAS	- A MAN WHO SCARES THE DEMOCRATS	104
RAPE	- A SPECIAL DILEMMA FOR DEMOCRATS	112
WOMEN & FREEDOM	- BREAD LINE OR FREE MARKET	118
CIVIL-RIGHTS	- THE SELF-RIGHTEOUS DEMOCRATS	122
GULF-WAR	- REPUBLICAN IMMORALITY	128
DEREGULATION	- THE DEMOCRATS HATE IT	132
EDUCATION	- REPUBLICANS WANT FREEDOM	139
IDENTITY CRISIS	- A HUGE DEMOCRATIC PROBLEM	147
MEDIA BIAS	- DEMOCRATS AT NBC NEWS	154
MEDIA BIAS	- NBC WANTS YOU TO RECYCLE	156
THE DRUG PROBLEM	- A FREE MARKET SOLUTION	164
FREE SPEECH	- POLITICALLY CORRECT DEMOCRATS	172
TAXES	- NO END TO DEMOCRATIC TAXES	180
VOTING RIGHTS	- DEMOCRATIC DECEIT	186
RACISM	- DEMOCRATS ACCUSE AMERICA	194
ELITE DEMOCRATS	- THE INTELLECTUALS PANIC	200
PHILOSOPHY	- DEMOCRATS RUN FOR COVER	207
FEDERALISM	- WELFARE FOR THE STATES	213
CONSUMERISM	- DEMOCRATIC CONTEMPT	220
QUOTAS	- AFFIRMATIVE ACTION & DEMOCRATS	227
PACIFISM	- THE DEMOCRATIC SOUL	233
ATOM BOMBS	- DEMOCRATS TOO SCARED TOO THINK	237
RALPH NADER	- CONSUMER ADVOCATE AND DEMOCRAT	242
FREE PRESS	- REPUBLICAN GENERALS IN THE GULF	247
RACISM	- DEMOCRATS REMIND REPUBLICANS	251
SOCIALISM	- THE MANY FACES	255
A NEW TERM	- DEMOCRATS RENAME SOCIALISM	258
POVERTY	- DEMOCRATS ENLIST REPUBLICANS	261
H. ROSS PEROT	- MANAGEMENT WITHOUT PRINCIPLE	263

INTRODUCTION

After 10 million years of human history and 200 years of American History, the Democrats and Republicans have emerged as the single most important inheritors of that part of humankind's legacy which is discernable and controllable. Crime, poverty, war, health care, education, economics, social security, and much of world history are all intimately tied to the outcome of the battle between Democrats and Republicans. Oddly enough, Americans have never learned to appreciate the differences between the two groups that, in many ways, rule and shape their lives, and determine their country's destiny. Polls consistently indicate that upwards of 70% of voters cannot identify differences between Democrats and Republicans. This explains why Barry Goldwater was crushed in one Presidential election, while Ronald Reagan won a landslide victory in another, even though both were contemporaries and had identical views. This explains why Lyndon Johnson won a landslide victory while George McGovern suffered a landslide loss, even though both had virtually identical views. Landslides on the Presidential level are contradicted on the Congressional level. Successive Republican Presidents and successive Democratic Congresses have led to political gridlock. If America is to regain her past stature, the gridlock must be broken; voters must learn the common philosophy behind Republican and Democratic faces so they can vote a party line with consistency and purpose; so that majorities with real legislative clout can finally emerge; so that failures and successes can be accurately laid at the door of those responsible.

Isn't it odd that in the biggest, best, and oldest Democracy in the World, American's split and squander their vote as if faces meant more than philosophy. Our Founding Fathers were at once optimistic and pessimistic about the value of democracy. Too much democracy, they feared, would lead to petty squabbling and eventual civil war; too little democracy would lead back toward totalitarianism. George Washington was so fearful of democratic fighting that he urged both Jefferson and Hamilton, the trenchant leaders of the opposing political parties of the day, to patch up their mortal differences and simultaneously assume cabinet posts within his administration. It was a noble attempt to avoid the acrimony and potential instability of democratic politics, and it failed abruptly, thus ushering in the birth of seriously partisan politics.

INTRODUCTION

Owing to our Founding Father's contagious fear of democracy, however, the birth was something of a grudging still-birth. This can be seen in our educational system where it has always been possible to go through high school, college, and graduate school, taking numerous courses or majoring in history, political science or economics, and never be asked to write one single paper about why, for example, the Democrats are better than the Republicans or about the millions of lives that might have been saved if Republican foreign policies had been followed in the Twentieth Century. First our gov't, and now our culture has asked of us that we never juxtapose, analyze, and then decide between the two parties, that have largely inherited human history, except when we get in the privacy of the voting booth. But, a voting booth without an experienced voter is no more useful than an airplane without a experienced pilot.

Politics is like sex. It is too hot an issue for our major institutions to handle without the grave risk of offending major portions of their constituencies. As a result, we are left to pick up tainted knowledge on the street, or from subtle hints that overly exuberant parents, teachers, or media personalities drop. America is at once intensely proud and fearful of its democracy.

The secret ballot was a well-intended democratic innovation designed to provide voters with enough privacy to vote their true convictions without fear of reprisal. Unfortunately it is an innovation that also manifests a concomitant desire to think and even learn about politics in private so as to, again, avoid possible reprisals from a public revelation of political positions and, additionally, the acrimony that often accompanies adversarial democratic politics. With such an attitude, it is no wonder that 60-70% of us don't know the difference between Democrats and Republicans and that by default we send equal numbers of Democrats and Republicans to Washington where they proceed to divide and grid-lock the governmental process.

As if to compensate for our gross inability to learn about politics, and our contradictory love of democracy, great emphasis has always been placed on the hallowed business of extending the voting franchise. Our schools and major media tend to encourage faith in and allegiance to basic

INTRODUCTION

democratic principles and institutions, but not partisan political debate. Such debate, they inherently and condescendingly feel, would lead to growing instability and eventual civil war. Some of our democratic traditions are so non-democratic that modern political elections have degenerated to become mere beauty contests with too many judges, rather than realistic democratic elections. This book, then, is devoted to the general reader who has no fear of democracy or of bringing into sharper focus his or her understanding of the political parties that govern this country.

Thousands of years ago Plato developed the dialectical method of posing brief but intense questions and answers, as the best method for finding the truth; this became the basis for determining quilt or innocence in our criminal and civil courts of today. All could agree that it is a method far superior to the comparatively meaningless soapbox monologue method that has emerged as the mainstay in the political arena. By directly rebutting the specific words that Democrats are writing and speaking, I have employed the dialectical method in the modern political arena, although more with the combative tone and rhetoric of an 18th Century pamphleteer than a polite 20th Century columnist. Simply speaking, this book is a rigorous debate or trial about the central ideas and issues behind both of our major political parties.

My specific approach has been to refute a wide variety of representative, current, and mostly written, Democratic opinion. It was my hope that by offering a pointed rebuttal to ideas commonly held by many of the most important Democratic writers and thinkers of the day, that the book would automatically have a context and relevance that otherwise would be lacking. Further, such an approach should serve to build on the modest and restrained debate that already does go on in this country. That I personally have held the Democrats responsible for virtually everything that has gone wrong, or is about to wrong, should only serve to provoke the reader toward further exploration designed to find out whether I and the Republicans, are, indeed, correct. It is certain that with absolutely opposite approaches to gov't, both parties cannot, for example, save or destroy the same number of lives with their policies. It is a cowards dream to pretend

INTRODUCTION

that our opposing parties can continually, and by default, split the popular vote, share gov't power, and somehow reverse, rather than exacerbate, all the negative trends in America.

Please keep in mind as you read that it is neither simplistic nor impolite to find so much fault with the Democrats. By sharply breaking with mainstream tradition to openly, directly, and rationally define the parties, and then blame one party, the Democrats, for most of the serious ills in our society, I hope to, at the very least, make the case that voting is indeed a very serious undertaking that has too long been treated in a very cavalier fashion. The Democrats have, in the Republican view, unfairly exploited the political process by promising the moon to acquisitive voters. They have thereby managed to achieve a false and mistaken respectability by virtue of their long standing and popular presence on the American political scene; not because their ideas have improved the lives of so many people. The Democrats have become a respected institution whose competition with the Republicans is now thought of with great legitimacy. A political election is now merely a sanctioned rivalry between Team A and Team B. It must finally occur to us that there is no Team C upon which we can passionately blame the long-standing deterioration in such areas as family values, education, crime, economics & business, poverty, health care, and race relations. The fault must lie with one of our two major parties.

Each article in this book deals with one of the major issues of our time in a manner designed to detail how the general principals of both major political parties consistently cause them to approach seemingly disparate issues in a predetermined way. The net effect from all of these highly tendentious articles should be a markedly enhanced ability to see the common thread in all the words spoken by Democrats and Republicans so that party philosophy will become more important to the reader than the glamorous faces and false promise of new ideas that cause so many voters to aimlessly swing back and forth between parties.

FOREIGN POLICY-LET'S HELP RUSSIA NOW

Dear Sen. Bill Bradley,

In watching your brief televised debate against Sen. Daniel Patrick Moynihan, during which you assured all of America that they need have no fear of Russian nuclear weapons, it seemed incredible that you could be so confident about what the future holds, especially as regards something as life threatening and planet threatening as Russian nuclear weapons.

Your remarks seem a little less bizarre when considered in light of your Democratic Party affiliation. Indeed, "have no fear" could be the slogan used by modern, purblind Democrats to describe their approach to all foreign policy matters. In 1961 President Kennedy marked the apogee of aggressive Democratic thinking on foreign policy when he said, while standing virtually on the Berlin wall, deep inside communist Germany, "America will go anywhere, pay any price, and bear any burden in defense of freedom." From that point on, Democrats were badly soured by the self-inflicted wounds received from the bungled Bay of Pigs invasion and the Vietnam War. They have been extremely reticent to make any foreign policy commitments since those two disasters. By the time of the recent Persian Gulf War, the Democrats were almost unanimously opposed, except for a notable exception or two. The brief war turned out to be a breath taking heart stopper that galvanized the nation behind the military in a way that most people, especially the Democrats, failed to anticipate. Today, only a tiny percentage of the electorate can imagine a Democratic President as Commander in Chief.

Your remarks, Sen. Bradley, about ignoring the Soviet nuclear threat, fit very well into the standard Democratic foreign policy tradition that has cost the U.S. so dearly in the past. It has always been difficult for many Americans, and most Democrats, to imagine that war and death could really come.

FOREIGN POLICY

Before World War I, America was warned by Germany that Atlantic Ocean passenger shipping would be regarded as military in nature and subject to attack. Despite warning advertisements placed in American newspapers, The Lusitania, primarily a passenger ship, was loaded with munitions and passengers for a trip across the Atlantic; it was sunk with virtually all of the 1200 passengers, including 128 Americans, drowned or killed. President Wilson and most Americans strangely assumed that they could grow rich while supplying munitions to the Allies, and traveling the high seas on armed passenger ships that had orders to attack Germany ships on sight; all with absolute impunity. According to international law, at that time anyway, ships with offensive weapons could be sunk as legitimate combatants, and, accordingly, the Lusitania was promptly sunk. The sinking made U.S. entry into the war all but inevitable, just as the preposterous sinking of the USS Maine had made entry into the Spanish-American War all but inevitable.

Despite years of World War I in Europe, and the obvious possibility that the U.S. might become involved, there was no significant standing American Army for General Pershing to command when America entered the war. It was not until a year after war was declared by the U.S. that any significant military assistance was available for the Allies. In the end, the huge American economy was unlimbered on an unprecedented scale just as the War was ending. Virtually none of the material was ever used. A skilled and equipped standing U.S. Army, with stated international objectives, might well have averted WW I, but Americans chose not to worry; to hope and pretend that war would not touch them. It can reasonably be argued that millions of people died in WW I while waiting for America to act.

After the War, America was severely divided about the rationale for having participated, and again became isolationist. General Patton, Hector C. Bywater (THE GREAT PACIFIC WAR-1925), and others, noted that Japan was attacking all over China and the South Pacific; that America was poorly defended in the region, and particularly in the Pearl Harbor area. Despite years of war beforehand, America hoped and pretended that involvement could be avoided; that a solid defense was unnecessary. The American military was allowed to shrink until it was 19th in the World, almost as if it had nothing of importance to defend. The tiny American,

LET'S HELP RUSSIA NOW

Pacific fleet was then badly mauled as it slept in Pearl Harbor. Had it not been for a fortuitous victory shortly thereafter, at Midway, the American Navy would have been virtually wiped from the Pacific.

The Japanese Zero was the dominant fighter aircraft of the time. Only after the War had long been in progress did Grumman develop the Hell Cat, and Chance-Vought, the Corsair, both of which were superior to the Zero. Only after the War got started did America start the development of the B-29 long range bomber so that Japan could be reached with conventional and the newly developed atomic bombs that ultimately were to end the war.

The European theater was much the same. The War was fought and 60,000,000 people killed as the world waited for America to produce the weapons needed to end it. The Germans began hostilities years before America entered the war, but America did little besides hope that war wouldn't touch them. The Germans had the V-1,2,3, and 4 while the Allies had the V-nothing. The Germans had the first long range cannons, the first long range night vision rifle scopes, the first long range guided missiles, and the first jet fighters. The American B-17 and B-24 heavy bombers were sent on countless missions deep inside Nazi Germany, without fighter escort, because long range fuel tanks had not yet been developed for the fighters. Close to one third of the bombers and crews never came back. The Germans and Japanese initially scored major victories all over Europe, Africa, and Asia. The American economy finally came to the rescue with huge quantities of men and materiel pouring into Africa, Italy, England, Russia, Asia and the Pacific. It is not an exaggeration to say that if the U.S. had started war production in earnest, even one year sooner, tens of millions of lives could have been saved.

When the Korean War started, the ability of the U.S. to project power at great distances was again very weak. America flew into the war with WW II style, propeller planes, and was greeted by Communist jet fighters that used American planes and pilots as target practice. Only afterwards, was the superior fighter, the American Sabrejet, introduced, and only afterwards were the Allies able to get an Army into Korea just in time to rescue the country, which had staged a full scale retreat into the very tiny Pusan Perimeter area, as the Communists advanced immediately behind.

FOREIGN POLICY

The aftermath of WW II, and the Korean War, got the cold war started in earnest. Americans were scared, and they maintained a military that was generally equal to or superior to the Soviet Military. For example, when the Russians developed the Bearcat Bomber to strike American Navel vessels from a distance of 40 miles, the U.S. developed the F-14 and the Phoenix Missile to strike the Bearcat at a range of 75 miles. This balance of power represented a dramatic and intelligent reversal of the flat footed, isolationist foreign policy which had previously been employed. Still, despite the seemingly obvious lessons this century has taught, Democrats are always encouraging the U.S. to let down its guard on defense. They apparently believe that each war is, as Woodrow Wilson said about World War I, "the war to end all wars."

Without commenting about whether the U.S. should have been in Vietnam, it is fair to say that it was a Democratic disaster, just as for opposite reasons, the Persian Gulf War was a Republican success. Presidents Kennedy and Johnson tried to fight the Vietnam War just as their Democratic predecessors tried to fight previous wars-by not fighting them. American involvement grew very slowly with the fervent hope that the next escalation would be sufficient to end the War. The escalation was always half-hearted and designed to provoke a surrender rather than to provide the men and materiel necessary for a crushing military blow. In the end, the effort was a humiliating failure; America finally lost a war to a vincible enemy, and concomitantly, a belief in its ability to aggressively project a moral foreign policy.

The Persian Gulf War came after 10 years of a fortuitous and unprecedented Republican military build up that reversed a trend encouraged by both the Democrats and the general disillusionment that followed the Vietnam era. Nevertheless, the showdown between Russian made Scud and American made Patriot missiles showed how easy it is to get caught off guard even when you have tried to be fully prepared. The Democrats traditionally oppose spending on major weapons projects, and the Patriot was no exception. It was an outgrowth of the Star Wars plan proposed by President Reagan and widely ridiculed by the Democrats. The Patriot worked fairly well in shooting down incoming Scud missiles, according to most media reports, but not nearly so well according to Israeli

LET'S HELP RUSSIA NOW

citizens, many of whom seemed to count several more Patriot misses than officially reported. Regardless of what the exact numbers are, it is alarming that the U.S. was not thoroughly capable of shooting down a missile that was originally developed by the German rocket scientist who developed the Nazi V-2 rocket in the 1940's. Hitler's Germany used essentially the same missile to bomb London in WW II that Iraq used to bomb Israel and Saudi Arabia in 1991. If Iraq had had a missile marginally more sophisticated than the Scud, and there are numerous such missiles in the arsenals of many countries, the U.S. would have had no defense, and the war would have taken a dramatically different and tragic turn. If a few more Scud missiles had hit Israel, it is certainly within reason to assume that Israel would have been very inclined to launch theater nuclear weapons at Iraq.

During the recent Russian coup, it was widely reported that the briefcase, which contained the codes to launch Soviet nuclear missiles, was taken from Gorbachev and placed in unknown hands. This was obviously an extremely grave situation that can re-occur, regardless of who is in power, unless and until the situation is eventually resolved in the West's favor through the establishment of a stable, democratic and free society. As of this writing, the briefcase has gone back to Gorbachev and then to Yeltsin, a man whose future has to be regarded with great skepticism until the very volatile situation there is somewhat stabilized. The current situation is certainly not a safe or desirable one. Further, by the end of the Century it is anticipated that 15-24 more nations will add nuclear missiles to their arsenals. National defense, then, is something about which the U.S. will always have to be vigilant. Looking back over the horror of this Century, could anybody conceivably argue that the U.S. has been too vigilant; that we could have let down our guard a little more than we did?

In light of this, it is impossible to imagine, Sen. Bradley, how you can assure America not to be vigilant about the Soviet nuclear threat. Can't you see what a lack of vigilance has already cost us this century. Isn't it better to be vigilant than risk destruction?

At one point in the debate you say, "The fact of the matter is, the Soviet Military has the capacity and the determination to control nuclear weapons. They have the command and control system; they have nuclear security that's aimed at unconventional threats, both civilian and military."

FOREIGN POLICY

"Second, you say, the Republics have already stated their willingness to cooperate in the control of nuclear weapons, both Russia, Ukraine, and even some of the Baltics. The nuclear forces are overwhelmingly Russian and they are overwhelming located in the Soviet Union. I don't think we should exaggerate this fear."

Your first paragraph about the Soviet military capacity, and the determination to control nuclear weapons, is awful. Now that the country is crumbling, you assume, for some unstated reason, that they have more capacity, determination, command and control, than they had years ago at the time of, say, the Chernobyl disaster. You then say, "the fact of the matter is." I wonder how you are so sure of the facts regarding the Soviet Union. Do you expect us to believe that as a U.S. Senator you have accurate sources that the rest of America doesn't have. The CIA was the best, and virtually the only source of information on the Soviet Union and they, as Senator Moynihan is fond of pointing out, overestimated the size of the Soviet economy by about four times. They knew every little detail about Russia except that it was about to collapse. Did the facts you learned from your special sources indicate to you that the Soviet Union was about to collapse? Did you tell us in the past about your presentiments? Even the Democratic "New York Times" pointed out, in a June 14th editorial, that 22% of those called to military service in Russia do not respond; that the officer corps is severely divided and cannot be counted on to obey orders. This seems highly plausible given the current state of affairs in Russia. Time magazine reports, "officials in Moscow talk of instability, possible civil war and a potential tidal wave of refugees clamoring to enter Western Europe. Some of them suggest that chaos in the USSR could lead to nuclear war among the Soviet Republics." Again, this is plausible, certainly more plausible than the collapse of the country looked two years ago.

Boris Yeltsin, the newly elected president of the Russian Republic, suggests that the Communist Party is so opposed to the loss of power they are experiencing, particularly through a program called "departizatsiya," that they might be very tempted to attempt a old fashioned military coup, just like we have seen, literally hundreds of times, all over the world. The Soviet military leadership is currently content to work within the

LET'S HELP RUSSIA NOW

crumbling system to slow down the pace of the Gorbachev \ Yeltsin reforms. If Yeltzin should gain power, relative to Gorbachev, and the pace and scope of reforms quicken, all without a drastic improvement in the economy, who can say with assurance how the military will react over the long term? In fact, who can say what the disposition of the Soviet people and military will be in five years? Who new in advance how volatile Iran and Nicaragua were? Did you know Sen. Bradley? The authoritarian path is the only path the Soviet people have ever known, and it is certainly likely that they may resort to it again. In the June issue of "FOREIGN AFFAIRS" magazine, probably the most prestigious publication of its kind, there is the warning that, in the worst case, "chaos and civil war could cause nuclear and chemical weapons to fall into the wrong hands." Lawrence Eagleburger, of the State Department, talks of a "situation akin to 1914" that led to World War I.

Boris Yeltsin may have won the recent election, but in third place was Vladimir Zhirinovsky, widely believed to be representing the traditional Communist Party. He is a Russian nationalist who believes that minorities within the Soviet Union can be blamed for the current problems. He offered cheaper vodka and praise for Stalin, the only dictator in this century responsible for more deaths than Hitler. Zhirinovsky predicts that total economic and political collapse will force Russians to turn to him in the coming months and years. Zhirinovsky managed to get six million votes his first time out, which coincidentally, is the same number that Hitler received in the 1930 elections. Rationality prevents an understanding, Senator Bradley, of what sources you have that can assure America to relax in the face of Russian nuclear weapons.

Next, you go on to say that the Russian Republics have already stated their willingness to cooperate in the control of nuclear weapons. Then you qualify your statement by saying, "Russia, Ukraine, and even some of the Baltics." Firstly, a statement about a willingness to cooperate, is almost meaningless given what we know about history. Remember how Hitler seemed willing to cooperate with Chamberlain, or how the U.S. agreed to cooperate with Iraq prior to the recent war. Secondly, you say, "even some

FOREIGN POLICY

of the Baltics." Well, what about the others. Do you need to be reminded that just one MIRVED ICBM can wipe out the East Coast of the U.S. It may seem unlikely that these weapons would be used that way, but it also seemed even more unlikely that Iraq would get U.S. weapons and threaten to use them against the U.S. in the recent war. Thirdly, do your sources really indicate that there are no Saddam Husseins lurking in the Republics; do they also indicate that none of the Republics would use the nuclear weapons, that they may have, to help secure their independence from the Russian Republic or to resolve the very grave internal problems that many of them face.

Lastly, you note that the nuclear arsenal is overwhelming Russian and overwhelmingly located in the Soviet Union (presumably you meant, not in the Republics). This is very different from saying they are 100% Russian and 100% located in the Soviet Union. The implication you leave is that it's fine if a few of the 30,000 ICBMs are left scattered around the Republics, so long as most of them are on, supposedly, very stable and secure Russian soil. Of course, this does not even consider the 500 ship Soviet Navy and all its weapons. Tom Clancy's recent book, "The Hunt For Red October," detailed the potential threat from just one renegade Russian submarine. The book was taken seriously enough that Clancy was asked to run for the Senate and hired as a foreign policy consultant by NBC News.

Your assurances that American policy should be to relax and do nothing, as the Soviet situation develops, completely ignores the potentially, deadly problems that the U.S. can and should act to head off. The Russians have declared that socialism is a failure and they are ready to give it up for Western style free markets. This outcome has been the single most important goal of American foreign policy since the middle of World War II. Now that the Russians have made the correct intellectual recognitions, the single most important goal of U.S. foreign policy must be to help them translate their discoveries into the practical development of a free society. A failure to follow through could result in a Soviet enemy worse than the one which was feared for so long.

Now that the euphoria from the first failed military coup is passing, the Soviet people must again direct their attention to building the free market

LET'S HELP RUSSIA NOW

economy that many say they want. The Soviet mind set is still very socialist, and Gorbachev himself has just re-stated that he is still a socialist; this would seem to indicate very clearly that the road ahead for the Soviets, whichever direction it goes, will be rocky, indeed.

For the time being, at least, the Russians have come to us, hat in hand, begging for economic aid to help them make the transition from socialism to capitalism. This aid must be given while the blessed chance exists. Certainly it should not be given for use in ways that are deemed likely to fail. When you were asked, Sen. Bradley, whether we should extend MFN (most favored nation) status to Russia as we have done for China, you replied, "that would depend on how they do on immigration." Firstly, the Russians have done extremely well on immigration, lately. As compared to the past, the world is now flooded with Russian immigrants beyond its capacity to absorb them. Secondly, while the immigration issue may once have been an important lever to use against Soviet idealogy, it is now grossly irrelevant as compared to the imminent realization of our most important foreign policy goals.

Every McDonald's hamburger bought in downtown Moscow represents the efflorescence of American values and free markets. The more the Russians get to experience the riches the American economy and culture has achieved, the less likely they are to accept anything like their previous system. Instead of cautioning us to sit back and relax in the face of 30,000 Russian nuclear weapons, why not spend your time figuring out the most efficient ways for the U.S. to help the Soviets toward free markets and institutions, while we still have the chance. Oh well, I suppose this is too much to ask of a Democrat who would rather sit back and pretend that the future, for the first time in human history, is safe.

Republicans will obviously disagree among themselves about exactly how big the defense establishment ought to be in the wake of the Persian Gulf War and the failed Russian coup, especially if Pat Buchanan is successful in reviving the Taft-wing of the party, but they will always favor a stronger defense than the Democrats in a Century that has witnessed the bloody wartime deaths of upwards of 200 million people. Republicans realize how essential it is that the world's mightiest moral power also have the world's mightiest military.

POVERTY - DEMOCRATS AFFECT POVERTY

Dear David Broder,

I have just read your editorial in which you speak turgidly of the Democratic glory days when Lyndon Johnson started to build his "Great Society." Your article was very useful in that you identified and labeled the good guys and the bad guys. The good guys, as you pointed out, were Lyndon Johnson and the Democrats, while the bad guys were and are, Reagan\Bush and the Republicans. Since voters only have two major choices when they enter the voting booth, it was good strategy for you to define your position with enough actionable concision to enable your readers to make the correct choice when they next visit the voting booth. From the Republican point of view, however, your reasoning was so weak that your presentation of the poverty issue is more likely to have the opposite affect as intended, and encourage Republican votes.

The picture that accompanied your article suggests that you are old enough to have been reporting during the "Great Society" years. For Democrats, they were undoubtedly years of great exhilaration; years when liberals finally fulfilled the promise of FDR that had been so badly interrupted by WW II and the Eisenhower Presidency. Democrats got more than they ever dreamed possible. In the space of less than two years, they got The Civil-Rights Act, The Voting Rights Act, and The Economic Opportunity Act. These were the cornerstones on which the "Great Society" was to be built. Democrats, like yourself, who were reborn during this exciting period are understandably having a hard time letting go, but those who came of age a little later, as it was becoming clear that the programs were failing, aren't finding it nearly so hard.

In fact, the cadaverous Democrats are rapidly becoming a party of old people, something that makes the future very threatening for them. According to the Roper Center at the University of Connecticut, the highest concentration of Democrats is now in the 69-77 age group, while the highest concentration of Republicans is in the candescent 18-25 age group. Older Democrats tend to be attracted to the FDR/LBJ tradition, while younger ones tend to recognize that the old programs weren't successful and that they need to be eliminated or substantially reworked. The Democratic Leadership Counsel (DLC), for example, to which all the Democratic presidential hopefuls, except Jesse Jackson, belong, would

DEMOCRATS AFFECT POVERTY

consider it a grave political liability to speak in the FDR/LBJ tradition. When Gov. Bill Clinton, perhaps the strongest presidential contender, began his speech at the DLC by saying, "every welfare mother who can work must work," it was hard for many in the audience to believe how far this group of Democrats was backing away from their long cherished positions. The cautious message to Democrats, from Presidential candidate Paul Tsongas and others was, "lets be careful not to appear as Republican wannabes." He might have more honestly said, "we're still proud Democrats even though we enacted our entire program and then some, and we're worse off now than ever before."

So, while you did identify the good guys and the bad guys in your editorial, you did nothing more to expand the context of the debate. For you, and most Democrats, the only problem is to compare statistics about poverty from Democratic and Republican administrations and then determine the winner. For Republicans the issue is much more heavily nuanced. They don't believe that the Federal Gov't should be in the anti-poverty business any more than it should be in the Post Office business. Republicans are generally so busy trying to resist the extensive anti-poverty machinery which the Democrats have put in place that it is easy for them and us to forget that their real objective is to dismantle the machinery so that all involved will be forced to try other approaches that actually may work.

Republicans believe that the poverty issue, like many others, is a local issue which cannot be addressed effectively from Washington; that Federal intervention adds a huge layer of incredibly expensive bureaucracy to the anti-poverty effort; that the Federal dole desensitizes non-poor people to their moral obligation by assuring them that the distant Federal Gov't will take care of their neighbors, friends, and family so they won't have to, and that it seduces the poor into feeling that the money they receive is manufactured in Washington as an entitlement for them, rather than taxed from the people who work painfully hard for it.

Democrats recognize none of these arguments. They turn to the Federal Gov't as a matter of expediency, not as a matter of philosophy. As it turned out, the consensus for anti-poverty legislation existed in Washington in the 1960's; so the Democrats took advantage of it. It was just as likely

POVERTY

that an evil or opposite consensus could have existed on the Federal level. In fact, the expectation of this evil or opposite consensus on the Federal level was of primary importance to the Founding Fathers as they developed the Constitution in a way designed to limit the size, power, and scope of the Federal Gov't. Even with the Bill of Rights added to the Constitution, there was no reason to assume that the Federal Gov't would become more moral than State and Local Gov't. When it does become so, it is mere coincidence; there is no historical reason to anticipate that it will continue to do so. The more the Federal Gov't is relied on and empowered, the more powerful and potentially corrupt it is apt to become. Power is a nice thing when it's on your side, but only when it's on your side. Power spread out and balanced among the States is the safer, and wiser, long term alternative.

The tendency for all people and all branches of gov't to gather as much power as conceivable, out of a belief in their own goodness, is fairly obvious. Democrats do it; socialists do it; we all do it. Mr. Broder, you want even more legislative power in Washington to increase the governments role in the War on Poverty. The mere fact that Federal social welfare expenditures rose from $52 Billion in 1960 to $834 Billion in 1987 should cause you to reconsider. The fact that the Supreme Court, after 200 years discovered a Fifth Amendment privacy right to an abortion, or found capital punishment to be cruel and unusual punishment, even though it is explicitly referred to twice in the Constitution, should make you reconsider what the limits of Federal judicial and legislative authority ought to be. Needless to say, these issues are at the heart of Republican thinking which has always manifested a well founded and historically derived fear of federal gov't.

Conceptual issues aside, since Democrats seem to be motivated exclusively by a sort of quasi-maternal instinct to help or care for those in need, the dwindling but still powerful "Great Society" wing of the party, to which you belong Mr. Broder, does still make some arguments that deserve to be taken seriously. Firstly, you are very critical, in a non-specific way, about a recent speech in which President Bush proposed to seek a "Good Society," rather than the "Great Society" of LBJ. LBJ was a bumptious, lusty, Texas-sized New Dealer with a legendary ego; he wielded power with the self-assurance of a dictator. He honestly believed that he could create a great society from Washington. The programs he put

DEMOCRATS AFFECT POVERTY

in place, remain in place today, and are funded at increasingly higher levels than even LBJ would have dared dream about. Every year LBJ loyalists seemed to hope that a little more funding would compensate for the failure of the programs to work at previous, lower funding levels. Yet, it would seem obvious, after listening to the way Democrats still scream, that poverty today is about as serious, or worse than it was in 1964. When Bush spoke of a "good society," he was recognizing why poverty had not declined, and that it is not philosophically desirable or technically possible to create or engineer a "Great Society" from Washington. Bush knows that the rise of laissez-faire capitalism from 1750 to 1950 did more to alleviate poverty than the combined affect of everything else that had transpired over the entire course of human history. Central planning to create a "Great Society" does not work, according to Republicans, no matter where or under what variation it has been employed, and the numbers are now available to prove it.

Your next big argument goes as follows: "Isn't it better to try, to fail and to learn from failure, than to sit and do nothing." Your thinking, I suppose, is that if you can just keep tinkering with peoples lives from Washington, eventually you will find the formula to eliminate poverty. This is like trying to get to the moon by tinkering with a Model A Ford, when you have a Saturn 5 rocket fueled up and ready to go. Capitalism is the modern weapon of choice that has actually worked and transformed life on this planet.

Next, you get very serious while pretending that you are going to show the numbers which make your point in an irrefutable mathematical way. Your first and most damning numbers point out that from 1965-1970, youth poverty was slashed from just over 20% to just under 15%, while in the Reagan/Bush years it has gone back to just under 20%. To you, these numbers mean that the Reagan/Bush policy was a failure. In truth, for all the complaining Reagan did about Federal programs, they were so well entrenched and supported that he was not able to do anything put fund them at record high levels. In fact, in 1970, when you say Democratic policies had reduced poverty to just under 15%, total Federal and State expenditures on all programs were $145.8 Billion; at the end of the Reagan

POVERTY

years when poverty went up to the 19% level, spending was $834.4 Billion. In sum, poverty got worse, not because Reagan/Bush has been stingy with Federal money, but, in large part, because Democratic programs just didn't seem to work no matter how much funding they received.

A closer look at youth poverty reveals that in 1970, 12% of America's 63,000,000 children lived in single parent homes, while in 1987 the number had doubled to 24%. The poverty rate in single parent households is five times higher; for obvious reasons. The reasons for the rising number of single parent households are as follows: 1) social welfare expenditures were given mostly to women so that the economic dependency aspect of marriage and family was greatly reduced, 2) the decline of physical labor in the work place made jobs and independence more possible for women, 3) traditional religious values which proscribed a rigid set of principals on which to conduct family life suffered an accelerated decline in the aftermath of the Vietnam, Civil-Rights enlightenment, 4) the rise of feminism encouraged the legitimacy of single adult lifestyles.

While everyone has a tremendous sympathy for the children of poor single women, there probably always will be a bias against them owing to the reluctance of two parent families, non-parent families, and single adults without children, to compromise their life styles to support the reproductive habits of poor single mothers. When the "New Deal" addressed this problem in the 1930's, widows with children were the only single parents considered for Welfare because they were looked upon as legitimate victims. This author recalls growing up in the early 60's when the shame of a pregnant unwed mother and her parents was so great that a family would often feel compelled to move out of town. Today, condoms are handed out routinely and free of charge as if to signal that the centuries old battle to promote civilized and familial sexual customs has been lost, leaving instead, a full scale retreat with only the minimal hope that a death from AIDS can be avoided in the process. The cultural degradation that occurred in the sixties and seventies may have permanently reversed a positive historical process that was literally thousands of years old. Bringing discipline to human sexual practices was no easy job. Today the world is a vastly different place; it is doubtful that a simple comparison of numbers from 1970 with those of 1987 is sufficient to indicate anything.

DEMOCRATS AFFECT POVERTY

Next, you speak of Welfare or AFDC (AID TO FAMILIES WITH DEPENDANT CHILDREN). Closing in for the kill, you note that the "Great Society" lifted benefits to $168 per capita, while in constant dollars the program declined to $131 last year, under the bad influence of Reagan/Bush. This is your complete argument; you close it by asking, "this is common decency?" as if to say that Reagan and Bush aren't decent men, while you are.

Firstly, as Reagan once said, "isn't welfare a kind of slavery." If Reagan really did reduce AFDC, it could easily be regarded as a decent thing to do by Democrats and Republicans alike who often now agree that it is desirable to shorten rather than lengthen the welfare rolls. Conservative Democrats, primarily those who participate in the DLC, are only now beginning to talk of the need to cut welfare dependency, but no plan with even a moderate consensus has yet emerged. Whatever decent and well-intentioned approach they choose, it will ultimately involve reduced expenditures. What reasoning process could lead you to evaluate programs by simply gauging the amount spent, rather than the results achieved?

In truth, by using your definition of decency, Reagan and Bush are very decent guys; spending actually went way up, but not in the tiny little program you chose to argue about. In 1987, the $16.4 Billion AFDC budget was exactly 1.96% of the total social welfare expenditure budget. Overall social welfare spending went up from $1947 in 1970, measured in per capita constant 1987 dollars, to $3364 under Reagan in 1987. If money and decency correlate directly, as you say, then Reagan/Bush are very decent guys.

Maybe, Mr. Broder, you are tempted to argue that all the people served by social welfare expenditures aren't relevant to you for one reason or another; just the millions served under the category referred to as Public Aid, of which AFDC represents 24%. In this category, per capita spending went up from $221 dollars in 1970 to $447 in 1987. This is a 102% increase during the Reagan/Bush years, over the glory years of the "Great Society."

If you want to argue that all poor people are irrelevant to you, except those that are on just AFDC, you are being silly because efforts to help

POVERTY

have always been much more comprehensive to include, for example, housing, health care, and food programs. But, if you insist, the Dept. of Commerce-Bureau of the Census reports that in 1970 total AFDC expenditures were $4.853 Billion, and $16.8 Billion in 1987. It would seem that even by your standards, Reagan was a very decent guy. If benefits per person in the program leveled off, it is because 3 times more people were in the program. To allow this to happen, when Federal and State Gov't was running record high deficits, was certainly very decent, at least if money and decency are so closely related as you claim.

Your next argument, Mr. Broder, represents one of the most fraudulent uses of statistics possible. You note that in the year 1964, when Johnson gave the "Great Society" speech, the poverty rate was 19% and that it declined to 12% when he left office 5 years later. You then close your turbid argument by saying the rate was never that low under Reagan/Bush. This is a point that Democrats love to make, but it is wholly deceitful. Firstly, from the time LBJ left office in disgrace, after one unfortunate term, his programs stayed, and, as mentioned above, were funded at record levels that Johnson couldn't have imagined; this high spending continues until today. In 1970, at which time all of Johnson's programs were implemented and in operation, spending was $145 Billion; it rose every year thereafter so that today it is approaching $1 Trillion. The obvious fact is that poverty hit a historic low in 1970, on virtually the same day that the "Great Society" became fully operational; from that day on poverty never declined in America; this is obviously because the programs didn't work.

Even more important, though, is what you omitted. On the very same chart from which you selectively pulled your poverty numbers, you chose not to see what happened to poverty from 1950 to 1970, when Republican free markets were virtually the only mechanism to control poverty. I will allow for the possibility that perhaps your chart was prepared by someone who didn't include the years 1950 to 1970. It turns out, according to the complete version of the chart you used, poverty declined from 28% to 12% in the 20 Republican years prior to the "Great Society." It is absolutely horrible to think of the tragedy this represents. The Democratic "War on Poverty" turned out to be a War on the Poor.

DEMOCRATS AFFECT POVERTY

Next, you mistakenly pay a complement to President Reagan by noting that the number of poor was cut to 27.6 million, from 49.1 million, by gov't programs in 1989, when he was President. You ask your readers, "Is that a failure of social policy." The answer: yes, it is a failure, because as a compassionate people our objective should be to reduce the number of poor, the way Republicans did from 1950 to 1970, not maintain them, at or near the poverty line, as the Democrats did between 1970 and 1990.

None of this is to say that Republicans are against Federal anti-poverty programs for either philosophical or practical reasons, but merely to say they are against all programs that don't work and actually do damage. Democrats remain politically viable on this issue, and many issues, only because they have convinced those who cannot intellectually understand freedom and capitalism that being opposed to Federal programs means being uncaring about those who are supposed to benefit from the programs.

THE RECESSION - CAPITALISM VS. SOCIALISM

Dear Newsweek Magazine,

I have just read your article in the National Affairs section titled: "Straight Talk." The article was designed to find out from each of the presidential candidates what they would do to end the current recession. The introduction closed with a note that said, "the six Democratic candidates responded, but most managed to avoid answering the question." This is exactly what would be expected from a party that doesn't like Republicans or capitalism, but has watched its own alternative philosophy fail for the last 25 years.

The subject of economics is one that humbles voters and politicians alike; it requires more background than other subjects before a person can easily distinguish the difference between Democrats and Republicans. Nevertheless, when all is said and done, the two parties divide in exactly the same way, on economics, as on most other subjects. The Republicans emphasize limited gov't as the political\economic approach to end the recession, while the Democrats emphasize gov't action. The labels fly hot and heavy in this area, and they are very useful so long as they are attached to the correct political party. Republicans, favoring limited gov't and individual liberty, are generally and with some purity attached to labels such as: capitalism, conservatism, laissez-faire, free enterprise, supply side, and monetarism. The Democrats are attached with less purity, but nevertheless attached to: socialism, liberalism, Keynesianism, eclectic Keynesianism, the demand side, industrial policy, wage price controls, and fiscal policy. All the variations on the Republican side are designed to limit gov't and promote individual liberty; the variations on the Democratic side are designed to have the opposite affect.

In 1789 the Constitution started the U.S. off very close to the capitalist model-but, bank panics, recessions, Karl Marx and socialism, the Great Depression, World War II, and John Maynard Keynes all conspired to argue for gov't or Democratic intervention, in an attempt to smooth out the

CAPITALISM VS. SOCIALISM

road. From the end of World War II, to the 1970's, Democratic thinking was promoted with elegant scientific models that successfully converted most of the economics profession. Keynes founded the basic theory, with publication of his seminal work, "The General Theory of Employment, Interest, and Money." His lead was built on by many others, perhaps most notably, Paul Samuelson, who reached the height of his influence in 1970 when he won the Nobel Prize. At that time, the Republican economists were being treated with little respect and were unable to mount any serious opposition.

In the 70's, the situation changed dramatically. Milton Friedman had battled heroically against the Democratic mainstream all his life, and finally, his scientific theories became persuasive enough to turn the tide back toward the Republican belief that the economy would function best if the gov't role was severely cutback and rigidly defined. Friedman's battle to superannuate liberal economics was one of the great ones in academic and political history; it may go down with Copernicus' battle to convince astronomers that the earth was not the center of the universe. All tolled, twelve economists from the conservative, University of Chicago, (Friedman's original home base) have now won the Nobel Prize in economics.

It would seem that while Samuelson and Friedman were both very distinguished scientists, they were both motivated by more than pure science as they pursued their disparate areas of inquiry. Friedman was a conservative across all fronts; opposed to gov't involvement in everything from education to interstate commerce. Samuelson was the opposite; for him, gov't was the solution; individual liberty was the problem, and his economic theories were designed to prove it.

Those who think it is simplistic or naive to see a conterminous relationship between modern Democratic beliefs and basic socialist beliefs, should consider what Samuelson had to say about Russia in the thirteenth edition (1989) of his economics textbook, which is still the bible in most college economics courses. "The Soviet economy, according to Samuelson, is proof that, contrary to what many earlier skeptics had believed, a socialist command economy can function and even thrive. That is, a society in which the major decisions are made administratively, without profits as

THE RECESSION

a central motive force for production, can grow rapidly over long periods of time." Samuelson was, one hundred and eighty degrees, wrong about the Russian economy because he was possessed of an abiding faith that gov't control of the individual is the solution. Somewhere in his philosophical\psychological past he adopted this basic belief that led him to always look favorably on gov't.

Republicans, conversely, always thought of Russia as an economic basket case; they were never inclined to believe that such a system could work. Each of us, it would seem, has a world view that we bring to the study of economics. Samuelson's respect for Russia is not unique among Democrats. W. Averill Harriman, a close friend and advisor to FDR, who was the most successful Democratic politician of the Twentieth Century, has said that his friend, FDR, was openly jealous of Stalin because he had the authority to communize virtually everything in an effort to help the Russian people. This was obviously before the World and FDR knew of the millions that Stalin was quietly murdering. It seems that while there are significant differences between the technical labels which can be attached to Democrats, the philosophical\psychological difference is considerably narrower; the same thing could be said of Republicans. Emboldened, from the new opportunities presented by Professor Friedman's success, and then by Ronald Reagan's more populist success, Republicans sought to extend the economic battle by openly and aggressively reselling capitalism in an effort to give it back the good name which Democrats had long since taken away. Supply side economics became the new label that was designed to counter the long popular, Keynesian label.

Keynesians had long held that the GNP (all the goods and services produced by an economy) and employment were controlled by aggregate demand, which in turn could be controlled from Washington with, mostly, fiscal policy, and, to a lessor extent, with monetary policy. As the Soviets had a "command" economy, the Keynesians envisioned a modified command economy for the U.S., in which Americans were hooked up like puppets to Washington so their aggregate demand for goods and services could be manipulated within specified boundaries. Supply siders argued that it hadn't worked, was un-American, and, what was really needed to make

CAPITALISM VS. SOCIALISM

an economy grow and yield greater prosperity for all, was traditional and natural, capitalistic incentives for suppliers to supply more goods and services.

It seemed like basic common sense to Republicans. After all, the Industrial Revolution, which had transformed a million years of static economic life in just 200 years, was essentially a capitalistic revolution. The most fundamental incentives in an economy, they thought, should encourage the production of more and better, goods and services. In a theoretical, capitalistic, supply side economy, people are encouraged to supply goods and services or labor, to those who voluntarily find them of value. The primary benefit or reward comes from supplying or giving; the money received later, and in return, is secondary, and serves primarily as a good measure of the value of the gift. This measure can then be used by the supplier\gift giver to determine how to direct his future production. The Judeo\Christian, capitalistic emphasis was on giving-first, and receiving-second.

In a theoretical, socialist, Keynesian, demand side economy, people are encouraged to show up feeling entitled; to demand or consume goods and services-first, and to supply them-second or not at all. The Russian economy didn't work, Republicans argue, because it encouraged demanding and receiving, rather than supplying and giving.

When Republicans explain that capitalism was naturally a part of early American religious values, Democrats argue that this runs counter to everything they feel in their hearts; that capitalists are motivated by greed; not by a Judeo\Christian obligation to gift giving. Republicans then explain that if capitalists were really motivated just by the money they receive from the products they sell, they would quit their jobs once they had accumulated several million dollars. In fact, this almost never happens, even when capitalists acquire more than they can possibly spend, they rarely quit; this is because they, like all humans, are more motivated by giving than receiving, as God would want. The modern, Marxist interpretation of the economic process, that has been diluted and popularized by Democrats, promulgates a negative, and self-defeating view of man's nature which assumes basic economic motives are evil and must be controlled by gov't, which is somehow less evil.

THE RECESSION

Economic anthropologists teach that primitive economies evolved according to the capitalist model, even without money. Gifts were given to family members, friends, and neighbors, for survival, and to promote a sense of community. Tremendous pressure was felt by those who received gifts, to return gifts of similar or greater value. Status within the community accrued to those entrepreneurs most skilled at producing and supplying gifts. In fact, survival often depended on the skills of the entrepreneur\gift givers. Today, such people are the enemy of the Democrats. The most recent proposal, to stimulate the economy from the Democratic Congress and Rep. Dan Rostenkowski, is to tax the rich more and the middle class less. This is the opposite of supply side economics; it represents exactly the kind of negative and perverse view of mankind and the way the world works, that makes economic recovery so slow. The rich save and invest more than the middle class; to tax them is to harm savings and investment(supply)in favor of short term, stimulative middle class spending(demand). The net economic affect would be neutral or negative; the hoped for political affect would be to trick the middle class into voting Democratic.

To end the recession, and encourage long term economic growth, it is necessary to unleash natural, capitalistic impulses to supply goods and services; this means the attenuation of the constraints which Democrats have used to recess the economy in their vain efforts to cater to the demand side. Recessions do not happen because workers lose their interest in working, or because businesses lose their interest in selling. Recessions happen because Democrats interfere with people who want to do the things they are naturally inclined to do. The geniuses in gov't cannot supply one single computer, automobile, or medicine; they don't have one bit of expertise to offer those who invent and improve the goods and services that maintain and improve the standard of living. The one and only thing those in gov't can do, is throw a monkey wrench into the work of those who do know how to supply and contribute, and then garner votes by promising to remove the wrench.

Republican supply siders have always had a long laundry list of approaches to gently push the economy back toward freedom and capitalism; these include: 1) Personal Taxation-15% flat tax on all personal income; no deductions. This is a simple way to raise more money for

CAPITALISM VS. SOCIALISM

the treasury; remove the penalty for increasing levels of productivity; force thousands of tax related workers to seek employment in economically productive jobs, and discourage billions of dollars from flowing to where the tax benefits are greatest, rather than to where the economic benefits are greatest.

For example, prior to the 1986 Tax Act, the gov't provided numerous incentives to avoid high personal income tax rates by offering real estate shelters. Therefore, billions and billions of dollars went into real estate, and was not then available for high tech design and manufacturing. The Japanese were investing in products that improve the quality of life, while the Democrats were forcing Americans to stupidly invest in real estate. The Democrats second guessed the free market and may well have made a huge mistake with the entire American economy.

2) Business Taxation - 100% elimination. These are phoney taxes that have no affect on gov't revenue; the tax is merely another cost to a business that is passed on; often to the consumer. However, no business decisions are made in modern America without careful attention to the tax consequences. The senseless mergers and buy outs of the 1980's, which involved much of America's corporate base were made possible by the double taxation of corporation profits. As an unintended consequence of the business tax, it become wiser to divert what would have been corporate profits, to pay junk bond interest expense. In this way taxable earnings were eliminated, but America's economy was tossed around like a toy. Similarly, much of America's real estate was tossed around and devalued by the 1986 Tax Act as it affected business; this was tremendously wasteful, and precipitated the S & L scandal, which in turn greatly aggravated, or perhaps caused, the recession.

The wide ranging patchwork of shifting business taxes, from the capital gains tax to the corporate income tax to the depreciation tax, do nothing but encourage management to avoid free market decision making in consideration of tax consequences; over the long term this spells disaster for the economy. Free markets are specifically designed to improve

THE RECESSION

the standard of living through continuous fine tuning as millions of consumers make voluntary economic decisions on a daily basis which reflect their ideas; not the gov'ts. Business taxation throws a monkey wrench into the process that, at best, represents an immature, socialistic guess at which way the economy ought to be directed, and, at worst, a vain attempt to raise gov't revenue by taking it from organizations that cannot vote.

3) Gov't Spending - Limit Federal Gov't spending to $750 Billion. The Federal gov't now spends about 25% of the GNP; State and Local gov't, with revenue from income taxes, sales taxes, and property taxes, more than double total gov't spending. This means that gov't collects about $25,000 per year from every person who holds a job in America. The drag on the economy is tremendous as this huge pile of money is torn from those who earn it and mostly wasted by gov't as it is spent on things that taxpayers wouldn't buy if they were free to make their own decisions about how their money was spent. A recent example is the scandal at HUD where $100 Billion ($1000 for every job holder in America) was waste on housing projects, most of which will never be occupied. Or, consider that gov't spends about $750 Billion per year through the social welfare expenditure budget, and the number of poor is higher than it was before the Democrats got involved. When you consider that poverty went up despite the $10 Trillion,(over 20 years) and, 20 years of rapid technological progress, it is hard to escape the conclusion that 75% of gov't spending is pure waste.

4) Regulations - Eliminate gov't regulation of business. Business must be free to pursue economic opportunities. The banking industry is central to any economy. Stupid and unnecessary regulation of the S & L industry, for example, caused most of it to go bankrupt at a cost of close to $500 Billion ($5000 for every worker in America). The commercial banking industry which is many times larger than the S & L industry is now suffering from many of the same problems that originally beset the S & L industry. The Democratic tendency to re-regulate the industry is exactly the opposite of what is needed; if it happens and it fails, the result could easily be sufficient to cause a depression.

Insane regulation of the grain and dairy industries, drives up the cost

CAPITALISM VS. SOCIALISM

of food in America-20%. As in the case of banks, the gov't should simply get out of the way so farmers will devote their resources toward economic ends rather than toward such things as getting gov't subsidies and price supports. Consumers pay $80 Billion Dollars extra per year because of so called "fair trade" regulations. The list of gov't regulation and control, and the damage it does, goes on and on; in each case the cost to the supply side of the economy is enormous. The modern businessman employs only some of his energy trying to supply high quality, low priced products; the rest is spent trying to avoid, evade, ignore, profit from, or circumvent, socialist interference with the free market.

In each one of the above cases, it is apparent that the Democratic gov't has gotten so big and become such an integral part of the economy that supply side functioning is largely cut off; this is why the economy is in recession. The gov't has grown to a size that the Democrats of 25 years ago wouldn't have dared to dream about; the result is stagnation and recession, but the Democratic solution is still to call for even more and better control and strangulation of the supply side.

Each of the Democratic candidates has numerous demand side proposals which they listed in the Newsweek article as follows:

Jerry Brown, who was often called Governor Moonbeam, somehow wants to expand trade with Eastern Europe so it can become the engine of economic growth; he wants to employ young people who he says are currently "lost", and he wants to examine a cut in payroll taxes. Actually, Brown's proposals are neither demand nor supply side, they just have nothing to do with basic issues pertaining to the general functioning of the economy. Examining a cut in payroll taxes is ok, but it is far better to actually support a cut and then back it up with a similar spending cut to make up for the lost revenue. His very recent call for a simple, efficient, flat, 13% income tax is an old Republican idea; his flaky, value added tax and interest in Jesse Jackson represents standard leftist Democratic thinking. His belief that he can make Detroit produce a 100 MPG car is pure moonbeam. Brown defies description and common sense.

Paul Tsongas recently said at the New Hampshire Democratic Convention, "American's want hope; they don't care if it comes from a

THE RECESSION

Democrat or Republican." He's trying hard to be a middle of the road Democrat, despite his liberal credentials. He wants to cut the capital gains tax for the rich, but raise their income tax. This is fine tuning and nothing more. The capital gains cut is a good supply side idea; the income tax like is a good demand side idea; the combined affect would be about zero.

Tsongas is perhaps the most original and cunning of the lot. He has adopted an approach that must please his pollsters greatly. He goes around claiming to be the best of both worlds: a conservative (Republican) on business issues and a liberal (Democrat) on social issues. In truth, it is generally impossible to be both since it is liberalism that has rendered the economy in recession in the first place. Secondly, Tsongas wrote a little campaign book in which he revealed that he doesn't believe in conservatism at all, but rather in socialism or industrial policy, as he calls it.

Tom Harkin, is the most socialist of the bunch. His plan is to invest in America: infrastructure, new energy systems, better schools and health care, and job training. None of these proposals has anything to do with reviving the economy. Investing in these areas might stimulate some activity, but taxing to get the money to invest would have the opposite affect; there would be a net loss since the money would be more efficiently spent if left in the private sector. The rapacious Harkin says he will get the money from a reduction in subsidies to the defense of Europe and Japan. This must be discounted since any president will realize this savings as the Soviet threat recedes, and it will not be enough to even marginally reduce the Federal deficit, let alone pay for new spending initiatives. Further, it is very important to note that defense cuts will hurt those workers and industries connected with defense. Spending the money elsewhere will have a stimulative affect, but the net affect on the recession will be a big Democratic zero.

Doug Wilder, politically the weakest of the candidates, has a three part initiative. Part One calls for a $50 Billion (3.6%) cut in the Federal Budget. This is too tiny to have any affect. Part Two calls for a $35 Billion tax cut. This is about 2.5% of the Federal Budget and less than 1% of the total gov't budget. Even if he got it all, it would be trivial. Part Three calls

CAPITALISM VS. SOCIALISM

for a new $15 Billion initiative to "reduce bureaucracy." At about 1% of the budget it would amount to nothing.

Bill Clinton, dared to say nothing specific. He wants what everybody wants; i.e., incentives to make long term investments, rewards for people who produce goods and services, more money in new technologies, less emphasis on defense spending, and a tax cut for the middle class. Like Tsongas, Clinton is a little embarrassed to be a Democrat, and therefore pretending to be middle of the road, in this case he sounds a little like a Republican supply sider, but he mentions nothing specific, and he has an impeccable Democratic history. Mere words should not serve to expiate past transgressions, especially around election time. Clinton should not be trusted until we see if he sticks with the rhetoric of the conservative DLC, which he founded, or reverts to standard tax and spend Democratic programs.

Bob Kerry, the last candidate to speak with Newsweek, wanted to revive the economy by investing everywhere. Tax dollars, he feels, should go to "investments in people, businesses, our country, new technologies, American entrepreneurs, and infrastructure." And, while all this spending is going on, he wants to cut the budget deficit and encourage savings. In short, Kerry wants to invest and save at the same time; this is a childlike contradiction. The best measure of Kerry is his Senate voting record which shows him to be one of the top three tax and spend liberals in gov't just behind second place Sen. Edward Kennedy.

Mario Cuomo, as yet a non-candidate, did not speak much to Newsweek, but in late November 1991, he did appear on ABC's, "This Week With David Brinkley." To Newsweek, when asked about whether he had heard any Democrats sounding ambitious economic themes he said, "Well, not yet, but they will." The Newsweek reporter described this complete lack of serious thought from the Democrats as, "mysterious." When Cuomo was asked for his economic plans on the Brinkley show, he said "why don't we all sit down together and take some ideas from the Democrats and some of those from the radical right." What this translates to, is a clarion call for the status quo. Then Cuomo implied that he could offer nothing specific, but that he would fine tune the spaghetti like, mixed economy, with a group of socialist geniuses, once he got into the White House to see all the data. This is something that defies credibility. This is 1992 A.D.; if Cuomo, who has a long history as a very liberal Democrat, and the others, don't have a well

THE RECESSION

defined alternative to the status quo, then they have no business being in gov't.

None of the Democratic presidential candidates are proposing anything that might be considered, moderately significant; this is because they have strategized that it is safer, albeit deceptive, to say nothing, rather than to reveal the extent of their continued socialist leanings to a Republican world which is now rediscovering the value of economic freedom and capitalism. Clinton, though, is the probable nominee. Owing to the exigencies of a long campaign he will undoubtedly waffle between the conservative positions of the (DLC) Democratic Leadership Conference and traditional, liberal, tax and spend Democratic policies. But, through it all he will confuse everybody by talking a 10 mile long, Ivy-League blue streak, but not manifest the slightest concern that increased taxes and diminished individual liberty have enabled the gov't to grow to almost three times the size it was just 10 years ago without any sign of improvement in the economy, education, health care, drugs, crime and urban decay.

The demand side appeal of the Democrats is based purely on the deceptive, Santa Claus image they have managed to project. If a Democrat were to be honest; to publicly say, "I'm proud to see gov't taxing $30,000 from each of the 93 million households in America; he would be instantly impeached. If honesty further compelled him to say, "The taxation process is such a meaningful and important part of gov't that I want tax day (April 15) changed to election day (the second Tuesday in November) so that Americans will further appreciate the relationship between Democrats and taxes; he would be in even worse trouble. If he were further compelled to help Americans understand the reality of taxation by recommending that the relatively painless withholding taxes be replaced with a standard billing process so that Americans would have to write a check to pay the monthly tax bills just the way they have to write a check to pay the monthly food, clothing and shelter bills; he would be in still worse trouble. These slight, symbolic changes would all but destroy the Democratic Party. Demand side, Democratic tax and spend programs are everywhere a failure, but Democrats have still managed to install a system wherein they often get paid before the people who provide us with real benefits such as food, clothing and shelter. Under the current system the Democratic spendthrifts get our money before we know we've earned it; thus their is no pain and no resistance.

THE SAVINGS AND LOAN SCANDAL

Dear Mr. Riegle,

I have read your recent UPI syndicated article on HR 354, a House Bill which, in theory anyway, reflects what the Democrats in Congress have learned from the on going Saving and Loan Scandal. To a Republican who generally believes in capitalism and free enterprise, the bill and the thinking behind it, is very irrational, and likely to exacerbate the banking industry's problems, rather than ameliorate them.

To begin with, Republican purists interested in economic growth and safety, most notably Ronald Reagan, knew the Savings and Loan Industry had to be eliminated or merged with the general banking industry. Those banks were the exclusive creation of the Federal Gov't. They were allowed to pay higher interest than commercial banks in return for making mortgage money available to would-be homeowners. It was a classic Democratic scheme in that it quietly took from people with one hand (high mortgage rates) and loudly gave back to them with the other, (high interest on savings) thus making them think they were better off. In this case, the banks had to get higher mortgage rates to compensate for the higher artificial interest rates that they had to pay depositors. In truth, there was no non-political benefit to anybody; just a ton of wasted time, money and energy.

Certainly, Reagan deregulated the banks too quickly and in a haphazard way by allowing, if not forcing, the bankers to invest in other areas beyond the safe, simple, and secure, single family home mortgages with which they were so familiar. Inexperienced bankers, who were more gov't bureaucrats then entrepreneurs, were instantly cut loose from gov't regulation and forced to compete with more experienced commercial bankers by investing in commercial real estate, and, to a lessor extent, other commercial ventures. These investments frequently went bad because the Saving and Loan executives had no experience in the very specialized world that they

S & L SCANDAL

prematurely entered. To be fair to the S & L Industry, it must be pointed out that the situation was badly aggravated by The 1986 Tax Simplification and Reduction Act, which instantaneously reduced the value of real estate by removing the tax subsidies which had artificially inflated its value. This meant that many of the bad loans which precipitated the S & L Scandal were more caused by the 1986 Tax Act, than by the bad judgement of S & L executives.

The culpability of the S & L executives is further reduced, but by no means eliminated, by the Federal Govt's mismanagement of interest rates. The Savings Banks made many mortgage loans when it was assumed long term rates would stay at the 5 to 6% level. When, gov't mismanagement of the economy (inflating the currency, rather than raising taxes) caused great insecurity about the future, long term interest rates shot up to double digits; the Savings and Loan Industry found itself earning half what its newer competitors were earning, and no longer able to pay competitive interest rates. To help, a posture the Feds always take, even though they almost never can deliver, the Reagan administration quickly cut the banks loose so they could save themselves by going after the higher return investments that they desperately needed to stem growing losses from the old 5 to 6% mortgages. Being inexperienced and financially desperate, they made bad loans that were made worse by the 1986 Tax Act.

This was exactly the kind of experience that Republican philosophy warns about. Gov't management, regulation, manipulation, and control was involved every step of the way. When gov't finally made too many mistakes, the whole country was almost thrown into depression because virtually total control of the whole country's banking system was entrusted to a few men in Washington. If control had been left in numerous private hands; spread out all over the country, any mistakes would have been localized, containable and of educational value to the rest of the country. Further, the govt's totalitarian involvement in the industry encouraged consumers, the ultimate and best regulators of any industry, not to pay attention as the situation developed, but rather to sit back and trust in their government.

$ 500 BILLION WASTED BY DEMOCRATS

Republicans were intimately involved in the 1986 Tax Act and the S & L Scandal, but their involvement came in the course of deregulating the industry and the economy so that it would not be prey to exactly the kind of upheavals that occurred.

If consumers knew they were the protectors of their money once it had been deposited it in a bank, the industry would be as secure as possible. Democrats will say, once again, "people are stupid," only those in gov't know how to manage something as complicated as the banking industry, and how to protect consumers. Republicans counter that a bank is no different than any other business; before consumers buy the product they must seek assurance that it is a good product. In the case of a bank, a customer would want to know that the money deposited, would be there when it was needed. If a bank could not assure depositors that the money would be safe, depositors would simply go elsewhere. On balance, it would be an easier job than convincing a customer that a computer, or a car, or a stereo was a good product.

When the S & L's were deregulated by the Garn-St. Germain Depository Institutions Act of 1982, bankers were given the vastly extended lending authority that was to be their undoing; depositors were, miraculously, given nothing. They should have been warned a year ahead of time that their money was going to be used for many things other than single family home mortgages; that it would be essential for them to monitor the safety of their savings, and the investments made by their banks. Instead, savers were told nothing; they found out nothing, and did nothing, except assume the gov't would protect them. If the nation's savings is ever to be invested safely and wisely the scrutiny of savers will be the essential control that makes it possible. No matter how wise and well intentioned gov't regulators may be, the job is too large and too difficult for them alone. If only Washington is in control; one major conceptual mistake, in the rapidly changing banking environment, could endanger the whole system. Accordingly, savers must get involved and their savings must be, at least partially, at risk, so they will force bankers to invest with the maximum amount of discipline.

A bank might advertise, for example, that it invests 80% of its money

S & L SCANDAL

in single family home mortgages in the State of Ohio; at variable rates averaging 10%; keeps 20% in reserve at all times; anticipates that 10% of its loans will go bad, and will always pay depositors 1 percentage point below the mortgage rate. If a competitor wanted to compete by offering higher rates to depositors that came from mortgages for more risky, multi-family homes, he would be free to do so. Presumably, the original competitor would quickly point out, in advertising, that he provided more safety, although a lower interest rate. In this way, the free market would force a competition to develop, the purpose of which would be to provide the maximum safety to depositors that was consistent with the interest rate they wanted to receive.

If some money center banks wanted to invest in LBO's and international interest rate swap contracts, they would be free to do so, but they would have to convince depositors or other investors that the money was being safely and well invested. This is an infinitely preferable system to the ever growing concentration of financial power in the hands of the Federal Gov't, where one mistake, just a little bigger than the S & L mistake, can plunge the whole country toward depression.

HR 345 does not recognize any of this, it merely represents the contravening socialist belief that eventually the gov't will learn how to manage the banking industry, and, for that matter, all other industries. Like children, Democrats always want just one last chance. HR 345 does not recognize that for America's standard of living to increase, businesses must evolve according to the dictates of consumers as they search for price, quality, convenience, service, security, etc. HR 345, instead poses the same old refrain about a series of new, tighter regulations that, next time, will catch a problem before it has a chance to become serious. No regulation, except free market regulation, can provide the kind of intense scrutiny that is necessary to monitor the vast savings of an entire nation as it is invested in thousands and thousands of different places.

Free market regulation forced the computer industry to decrease price 1000% and increasing speed 1000%, in just the last 10 years. HR 345 represents the opposite Democratic approach, it attempts to impose new

$500 BILLION WASTED BY DEMOCRATS

regulations that prevent future bankers, who will be operating in a new and unanticipated environment, from running off with, or badly investing the money entrusted to them. The banking industry, from the creation of the Federal Reserve Bank in 1913 until today, is among the most heavily regulated in the country; this didn't stop the Saving & Loan scandal from wasting more real money than it cost to fight all of World War II. When gov't mismanagement allows that kind of money to be wasted, HR 345 has to be greeted about the same way as a cancer diagnosis. Tragically, Democrats exist on the notion that the next time, they are going to hit on a regulation scheme that works, or at least one they can make us think works. Democratic contempt for consumers is so great that it is not possible for them to consider the Republican alternative. They continue to propose gov't regulation, and get away with it, because voters have not yet developed an ability to appreciate gov't actions for their ideological origins. The Savings & Loan scandal has now come and gone, and neither party was made to pay a price. It is as if somebody else's philosophy was running the industry.

When a third party issues risky corporate bonds to finance a risky corporate merger, the bonds are widely derided as junk bonds because there is a reasonable possibility that they will not be paid off. When the gov't issues $250-500,000,000,000 in bonds to cover S & L deposits that were mostly used to buy gold toilets and build unoccupied office buildings, they are the safest bonds in the world because the gov't gave itself the power to legally obligate every man, women and child in America to pay them off over time. If the cost from the S & L Scandal does reach $500 Billion, as some predict, that will require $4000 in interest and principal from each person in America. Because of the insidious way the gov't operates, nobody really feels a thing. The expense for the S & L scandal, the HUD scandal, and the numerous other acts of gov't mismanagement, has been quietly and deeply buried in inflation and creeping taxation. When the public gets suspicious of these tactics, the Democrats pass the problem off to our children in the form of long term budget deficits which will have to paid off, but only in the distant future when they will not be running for office. In the course of paying for inflation, taxation, and budget deficits, the Democrats have found a way to make the American standard of living level off or go down, in spite of the amazing technological progress that business makes each year.

The solution, Mr. Riegle, is to let consumers regulate the industry and the economy. They will be infinitely more thorough and rigorous than you have been. The industry is changing very rapidly all around the world and no one knows which way it should develop to maximize the U.S. standard of living, any more than they knew which way the computer industry should have developed 10 years ago. Banking is a diversified industry that now creates only 25% of the country's credit, competes with brokerage firms, and in the commercial paper market, derives significant income from off balance sheet items like interest rate swap contracts, and international monetary futures. The whole banking industry, of which the S & L's are a small part, is being strangled by gov't regulations that define what aspects of the business they may participate in, and even where they can operate. Meanwhile, other industries are now free to compete against the banks. The insurance, brokerage, commercial paper, and credit industries take huge chunks out of the banking industry, which is largely prohibited from competitive response. So far about 20% of the entire banking industry is in financial trouble, if the Democrats impose further regulation, in the belief that a few good men in Washington can regulate this incredibly complex industry better than millions of consumers, the whole industry may face what the S & L's faced. Only consumers can make this industry, historically one of America's biggest and most prestigious, a jewel on the American economic landscape again, but only if you will let them, exactly the way you let them in the computer industry.

Of course, consumers must be exposed gradually. Most Americans have learned to shut off their common sense, when they walk into a bank, on the assumption that FDR'S ghost, in the form of the FDIC, will completely protect them and their money. Consumers let down their guard more in banking than in any other area, precisely because they have been taught to believe that the Democrats are supposed to be there to protect them. Consumers must be forced to determine if their money will be safe, before they put it in a bank, and pay at least part of the cost if their money is lost

$500 BILLION WASTED BY DEMOCRATS

by a poorly run bank. This is the kind of regulation that ultimately promotes maximum safety and security by keeping everyone (not just a handful of bank examiners and legislators) on guard against the kind of scandal and poor investments authored by the S & L Industry. As always, it is the Democrats who will see more regulation as the answer; the Republicans who will see more regulation as the problem.

ABORTION - PRO-CHOICE FOR THE FETUS

Dear Liberal Democrats,

The debate on abortion has gone on for so long and become so impassioned that most opinion leaders have long since grown tired or frightened of trying to be intellectually persuasive about it. Most articles now focus on the legal or political ramifications of various aspects of the issue. Those who do address the issue directly, do so mostly with the use of emotional appeals that seem to further ensconce people in their positions, but do little to move the nation toward a position of consensus. The issue is perhaps the most fundamentally grave and basic one we face as a nation, since it deals with some of our most important philosophical concepts.

Republicans have no difficulty accepting a gov't ban on abortion in the belief that it is an area, like many, many others, in which the gov't has a legitimate interest. Just as the gov't can reach into private lives and homes to prevent us from committing, say, murder, it can correlatively reach in to prevent abortion. Democrats who argue that Republicans are for limited gov't and should, therefore, be for abortion, are being grossly simplistic.

As usual, the contrariety of Republican and Democratic thinking is easily discernable on this issue. Republicans are generally opposed to abortion, and led primarily by the social conservative wing of the party which strongly disapproves of many of the social changes that have taken place over the last 30 years. This group overlaps the economic conservatives, but is distinguished from them by their primary focus on social issues. Their position inevitably draws support and respectability from the widely acknowledged deterioration in American life in such areas as, drugs, divorce, education, crime, family life, business, race relations and religion. For them the idea is to turn the clock back to a time when things worked the way they were supposed to work.

Democratic support for abortion does not come from the usual sources either. Theorizing about the value of Federal intervention in support of the down trodden, their general theme, seems to play no role in the abortion issue for Democrats. In fact, a normal extension of Democratic thinking

PRO-CHOICE FOR THE FETUS

would lead to the expectation that they would show a natural compassion for the unborn fetus or baby, just the way they show compassion for labor, the poor, or the sick. Support for abortion within the Democratic party focuses primarily on the right of the mother not to have her life unduly constrained by the fetus or baby conceived within her body. It is simply not clear why they choose to feel compassion for the mother, rather than the fetus or baby. Perhaps it is because mothers are organized voters while fetuses obviously are not. This is a problem that Democrats often run into; i.e., one of their special interest groups is in conflict with another group that they normally would feel an equal amount of sympathy for. For example, they have always supported the voters of organized labor, but at the expense of the fragmented voters of disorganized labor. Thus, organized labor gets high wages that drive up the cost of goods that consumers must buy. It is a typical Democratic scheme that gets votes from one group while secretly harming another more helpless or less knowledgeable group whose support they may, hypocritically, also be accepting.

Much of the ardor for abortion or choice within the Democratic Party comes from the feminist movement whose agenda has long been to give women a choice that does not necessarily include motherhood. In the mid 80's, for example, when the Republicans were watching the "Primal Scream" (a film depicting the supposed turpitude of a real abortion), it was the feminists who countered by releasing a film of their own purporting to set the record straight.

When Democratic feminists made the philosophic leap from supporting a women's choice not to be a traditional wife and mother, to supporting a women's choice to achieve those ends by aborting a fetus or baby, they abandoned any rational or moral ground in favor of mere ego-centric or special interest group practicality. Accordingly, they are ultimately on the losing side of the debate because, by virtue of the derivation of their position, they are precluded from employing any serious moral or ethical reasoning in defense of their position. They can say that it's not really murder, but they cannot remove even their own lingering doubts and guilt about whether this is exactly true or not. They prefer to address the very real and important practical aspects of the question that deal with the everyday and lifelong affects of an unwanted pregnancy and birth, but this will not be

ABORTION

enough to sustain them in a country whose foundation is mostly moral and idealistic, rather than just practical.

The history of human development is the history of morality. The more time goes by, the more our sense of morality is sharpened. Today, people care deeply about things that 60 years ago went mostly unnoticed. Today, a homeless man, for example, is given shelter despite being of sound mind and body; if six months later he still has not become self sufficient, even because he prefers not to work, he is given enough relief to rent an apartment so that the homeless syndrome won't set in. Clothing, food stamps, spending money, education and psychological counseling are also given so that no aspect of his life is ignored. Regardless of whether this treatment of the homeless actually causes homelessness or prevents it, it obviously represents a very highly developed sense of empathy and morality that would not have been possible 60 years ago. Still, despite this highly developed sense of morality, there are those among us who recite the problems of America and remind us that in their view, which may well be the correct one, America has a long way to go before the moral journey is complete.

With each passing year our compassion for the rights of the unborn will grow, it is in our nature, just as concern for the homeless is in our nature. We get distracted by other concerns and blinded by our ignorance, but only for the short term. An ever growing respect for all living things would seem to be the natural progression. The route is often strange and circuitous, but the progression down it has been inevitable.

We buy our children pet dogs by the millions in the hope of seeing an affectionate relationship develop, but we turn a deaf ear to the 20-30 million dogs that are put to sleep each year because of over breeding. We eat meat every day without a thought, but would face a serious moral dilemma if we had to see or participate in the daily slaughter this causes. The animal rights movement is new, but it is here and growing; fur coat sales are down 45%. Our sense of responsibility toward all life, even animal life, will continue to grow. When the Bible says, "The wolf will actually reside for a while with the male lamb, and with the kid the leopard itself will lie down, and the calf and the maned young lion and the well fed animal all together; and a mere little boy will be leader over them". Isaiah 11:6-9;

PRO-CHOICE FOR THE FETUS

Hosea 2:18, it is telling us of the direction in which all human sensitivity is inexorably developing.

The abortion movement is following a similar pattern. Today we call it a fetus if we want to abort it, and a baby if we want a child to love. This is a cavalier dichotomy that will not survive our growing sense of morality. Historically, abortion has been prohibited on social and economic grounds, rather than out of concern for the rights of the baby. Early criminal law in America was amazingly precise and intrusive about imposing Puritan standards of behavior. Adultery, incest, living alone without family, were all specifically forbidden, but abortion was not mentioned. By the early 19th century, abortion was becoming a minor issue primarily out of concern for low birth rates among the white middle class and perhaps, to a lesser extent, out of male doctors' interest in capturing the women's health care market from mid-wives and other females who had captured much of the business. Additionally, Catholic\Protestant rivalries caused a competition to develop that emphasized population growth and discouraged abortion, but mostly to gain numerical superiority; not out of concern for the fetus. In the 1860's the Pope issued a formal statement opposing abortion, pointing out that boys gained their souls in half the time as girls, and if they were to be aborted, it must be done sooner for boys than girls. By the late Twentieth Century, human sensitivity has evolved a great deal so that fetus's rights, women's rights, civil rights, gay rights, handicapped rights and even snail darter rights, are regarded with great solemnity by all, something that few would have thought possible just one generation ago.

That abortion advocates have consented to be called pro-choice leaves them in an untenable and amoral position. If choice is all important, why then can't they choose to abort a baby at birth because they don't like the sex or eye color, or a certain deformity. If the answer is that at nine months abortion is murder because the fetus is then human, while at two months abortion is not murder because the fetus is not human, then they are not thinking well. The implication that there is some way to know at what point a fetus becomes a baby is mistaken. The assignment of an exceptable abortion period, the first tri-mester, for example, is purely arbitrary and done for practical purposes. It represents an expedient approach that cannot stand in a country that, thankfully, prefers a moral approach to everything.

ABORTION

The time frame in which an abortion must be performed is most importantly a reflection of the moral standards we aspire to; of the kind of people we wish to become. The less abortion we tolerate the more in harmony we are with the moral standards we wish to achieve; with the moral standards that provide us with the only beacon through life we have. Try as we might, we will never escape the image of a baby's skull being crushed so that it will fit in the abortionist's vacuum cleaner. Demulcent arguments are not proffered on this aspect of abortion.

The "choice" to abort a baby cannot be made to compensate for the choice to get pregnant, anymore than the choice to rob a bank can be made to compensate for the choice to drop out of school. All the choices we make throughout life have consequences; we are better off concentrating on making the right choices rather than on correcting the consequences. To focus on the correction of poor choices inevitably leads to more poor choices; that is why in the period since Roe v. Wade (the Supreme Court decision that made abortion legal) the number of abortions has sky-rocketed.

Another popular pro-choice argument is that if the mother does not want the baby; what kind of life would it have anyway? This puts pro-choice advocates in the morally complex position of determining whether a life may not be worthwhile do to poverty or parental indifference. This is a determination that morality precludes us from making.

Democratic feminism is at the heart of the pro-choice movement, and provides the movement with vocal, passionate support, without which the movement would have very little intensity. Their support for abortion is intimately mixed up with feminist ideology and often is not broad enough to encompass the larger issues associated with abortion. Consider these examples of feminist thought from "The Washington Monthly:"

1) Gloria Steinem seeks to assure us that a fetus is just a hunk of dependant protoplasm and an "abortion is the moral equivalent of a tonsillectomy." That a fetus is or can become a baby does not interest Ms. Steinem. At all cost she wants to avoid this aspect of the debate. That no human being has ever shed one tear at the loss of a tonsil does not stop her from comparing it to a baby or fetus.

PRO-CHOICE FOR THE FETUS

2) Ellen Willis wants us to believe that if we acknowledge the moral status of a fetus we are condemning women to be "things or vessels that are subject to control," control like the kind men have historically exerted over them. To acknowledge that "biology is destiny," at least partially, is not feminist according to this reasoning. A fetus must be meat and nothing more, so that a women can be liberated. She must recognize that "biology is destiny;" that is why a women feels compelled to raise her child after it is born.

3) Katha Pollitt wants us to believe that "children should not be punishment for having sex." A Republican might counter that God or nature intended children as the reward for falling in love and having sex with the person with whom you wish to start a family.

4) Ellen Willis says that "abortion without qualms is part of the exceptance of the female erotic impulse," without abortion, women cannot be as free as men." If the goal of women is to be like men, then they would, seemingly, want to give up the joys of bearing and rearing children, but this would be more of a perversion than a legitimate goal.

5) Barbara Ehrenreich says "the only moral issue has to do with female personhood." This is a very odd statement given that morality has to do with how you treat others; not how you treat yourself. When Napoleon said, "morality is on the side of the mightiest artillery," he was finding an excuse, just like Ms. Ehrenreich, to make himself more important than the people around him; this is what immorality is. Should a women be proud to achieve personhood at the expense of a baby or fetus?

6) Kate Michelman says "The whole debate about abortion is more about the value of women's lives and the respect we have for women." She is clumsily trying to make us feel guilty about not caring for the rights of women, while distracting us from caring about the rights of the fetus and the father, not to mention the rights of the larger society.

7) Linda Gordon says, "When women are able to be self-assertive, that to me is a step toward morality..., that is what my abortion meant to me." Self-

ABORTION

assertiveness, as Hitler demonstrated, has nothing to do with morality. The need to be assertive at the expense of all else would seemingly come from an abusive past during which a normal amount of female assertiveness was crushed by those with whom she should have shared a kind and loving relationship.

All of this feminist rhetoric has one thing in common in that it is so passionately self-centered that it cannot acknowledge the possibility of fetal rights. The day will inevitably come when they mature to the point where they recognize the need to balance their legitimate rights with those of others. For white people, to free black people, it became necessary to not only acknowledge the rights of blacks, but also to recognize that some of their rights, for example, the right to have slaves pick their cotton, would be diminished, but that in the end the process would deposit them on a higher moral ground from which it would be possible to derive a higher level of satisfaction. Similarly, to recognize the rights of the handicapped is to acknowledge that they live among us; and to support that acknowledgement by giving up rights in the form of tax money, for such things as wheel chair ramps and parking spaces.

For Democrats and Feminist to proclaim that a fetus could not possibly be more than mere meat, and that their whole identify is tied to the availability of abortion, is nonsense. Women have their destiny in their hands because they have the choice not to get pregnant; that gives them a big advantage over many other groups in society who have no choice. Old people cannot stop being old, black people cannot stop being black, the handicapped cannot stop being handicapped, cancer patients cannot stop being cancer patients, abused kids cannot stop abuse, but, women can stop getting pregnant, can stop aborting babies, and can still lead reasonably fulfilling, and some could reasonably argue, more responsible lives. To insist that a women is more liberated by the availability of abortion, than by developing the discipline and familial habit of avoiding relationships with men that lead to unwanted pregnancies, is very mistaken. Feminism has evolved a great deal since the late sixties, when women were encouraged to burn their bras, and presumably it will continue to evolve to a point where it gets over its anger at men and biology and seeks to morally balance its rights, with the rights or potential rights of others.

In the mean time, the pro-choice movement (pro-choice for the mother,

PRO-CHOICE FOR THE FETUS

not the baby) remains as another self-centered special interest group that is given cover by the Democrats, rather than a group looking inward, and away from gov't for a Republican solution to its problems.

ABORTION - EMOTIONS AND THE SUPREME COURT

Dear Ms. Ellen Goodman,

I read with interest you recent article about the May 23, 1991 Supreme Court decision (Rust v. Sullivan) in which the court ruled that medical clinics around the country can no longer mention abortion to their patients and still receive Federal monetary support. As a enthusiastic feminist you were so appalled at this restriction on abortion information that you lost track of the central issue, and forgot to express any rationale to explain why the Federal Gov't doesn't have a perfect right to spend its money on only what it chooses.

You got very emotional and said things such as, "if the gov't pays your rent it can now buy your speech, if you take money you must give something back: the party line, a doctor must act like a gov't puppet, a doctor cannot fully discharge his professional responsibility, the court is mixing medical treatment and politics, clinics can take the hush money or cut their services."

You made it exceedingly clear that you want women to have full excess to information about abortion, but you got so carried away that you either, 1) forgot to point out a flaw in the court's reasoning, or 2) were so exasperated that some people actually have the nerve to oppose something you find emotionally obvious, that you couldn't settle down long enough to think up some good reason in support of your position.

To you, the decision was the political work of a court packed with "right to life" Republicans. To the court, the decision had little to do with abortion or politics and a lot to do with the Federal Govt's right to attach strings to all the money it spends on everything from Patriot Missiles to tobacco subsidies. You did not mention one single word about the larger context of the decision, a context that the court has to regard with the highest priority to insure that there is consistency and conformity throughout the legal

EMOTIONS AND THE SUPREME COURT

system. As a knee-jerk, pro-choice feminist, you missed this point entirely. You criticized the court for being political when actually it was you who wished to make the court's decision 100% political by seeing the issue exclusively in terms of the liberal, abortion debate; not in terms of the much larger judicial principles that the court was primarily obligated to consider. You apparently want to politicize the Court 100%; this is certainly not wise for you to propose at a time when the Court, and the President who nominates judges to serve on the Court, is firmly opposed to your politics. Your best hope is to promote the value of non-political judicial precedent so that some of the decisions from past more liberal Courts will be allowed to stand.

For the Court, most of the debate centered around the First and Fifth Amendments. They found in Rust v. Sullivan that there was no free speech violation because there was no imposition of viewpoint discrimination through the use of gov't subsidies. What there was, was a valid and legal decision to support child-birth over abortion, Maher v. Roe, 432 U.S. 464, 474. and a equally valid decision to support that thinking with the use of subsidies. Once gov't had deemed it in the public interest to favor child-birth, which it had done, it no longer had a viewpoint, it had a definite policy that it legitimately chose to subsidize to the exclusion of another.

The court further held that there was no free speech violation because no one was forced to give up abortion related free speech, only to restrict such activity so that it did not interfere with the intent of gov't subsidies. Finally, the Court held that a women's Fifth Amendment right to have an abortion is not violated if the gov't chooses not to subsidize abortion, because the gov't has no obligation to subsidize any constitutional rights, even basic free speech rights. Having the right to free speech or abortion is very different from having the right for your free speech or abortion to be subsidized.

Finally, in your last paragraph, out of a sense of professional responsibility, I guess, you tried to provide some basis for your thinking and fell flat on your face in standard Democratic fashion. You say, "Wasn't it Republicans who told us to worry about the long arm of the gov't." This was your summary and only argument; it purported to show that Republicans,

ABORTION

and in this case, the Republican packed court, had contradicted themselves by allowing the Federal Gov't to have the power to control where and how Federal money is being spent, while often arguing that the central purpose of gov't is to restrict Federal power and control over our lives. This is a very preposterous argument, but it is one that Democrats often make; so, if only for that reason, it is worth addressing.

Firstly, it is important to recognize that there is a world of difference between restricting Federal power and eliminating it. The central problem of gov't is to determine what limited powers it should have. Republicans and Democrats are different, primarily because they disagree about how much power the gov't should have, although both agree that for gov't to be effective, it must have some power. So then, Ms. Goodman, you cannot accuse the Republicans of being inconsistent in this case, unless you demonstrate that the restrictions on Federal spending, as provided for in the May 23, decision, represent a use of gov't power that Republicans normally or traditionally would have opposed. You cannot, and did not attempt to demonstrate this, and therefore your argument did not make any sense at all.

As a general principal, it is safe to say that Republicans do want limited gov't power, but, they are quite prepared to have the gov't wield what power it does rightfully have, with some considerable force, as long as that force is used in defense of individual liberty. Your argument might have made a lot of sense if it had been directed against the Libertarian Party. This is the party that believes humankind can survive and prosper with virtually no federal gov't. Republicans, on the other hand, generally believe in all the gov't power originally mandated by the Constitution, plus some of what was added on later.

So well accepted is the notion of Constitutional power and wisdom, by most political factions, that you often hear debates framed in terms of whether a particular law or point of view is constitutional, rather than whether it is right or wrong. This dependency on the Constitution as a moral and political compass, is at once testimony to how much like sheep we are, and how lucky we are to have encountered our Founding Fathers.

EMOTIONS AND THE SUPREME COURT

The power of history over our lives is something our egos often prevent us from recognizing. We are often inclined to say, "we could have figured that out for ourselves, isn't it obvious to everybody," when in fact it took mankind thousands of years to figure out the tiniest little things. It is not obvious to humans that they are better off if they don't go around randomly killing one another; it is not obvious to humans that they shouldn't make other humans their slaves. People with the finest philosophic and moral minds, from Aristotle to James Madison, were not able see slavery as a evil institution, so great was the genetic tendency to assert superiority, and survival skills, over an environment that had often defeated them. It took thousands of years to figure these things out; they are known today only because they were slowly learned and reinforced over thousands of years. But, this newly acquired wisdom is still something that a Hitler or Stalin can make us forget in a few short years. If not for the fact that all humans die at different times, we would never be more than one generation away from starting human history all over again.

Conservative Republicans have an abiding respect for the long journey mankind has undertaken so far; it is in their nature to put things in a historical context; to be suspicious of ideas that purport to be new; to change things slowly and after much deliberation. In reality, all nations, all groups, and all people evolve slowly at a deliberate pace not easily changed to suit those who imagine themselves as morally superior and faster. This is why Republicans counsel that it is not possible to be purposively critical of those nations, like Saudi Arabia, which recently abolished slavery, just because they are a couple of short decades behind the U.S.

When the Constitution did finally emerge out of history, and then seemed to work to perfection, at least by historical standards, it became the document to define and summarize the religious and political wisdom of the previous 10,000 years. It was the document that created and defined modern man. It is not a stretch to say that the Constitution and the religious values that served as its foundation, gave mankind, and continue to give him, his

ABORTION

heart and soul. Conservative Republicans are very much aware of this, and very much in support of the constitution's encompassing power over our lives.

But this is not to say that Republicans indiscriminately like all gov't power, even that power which is consistent with original intent. In the case of the May 23, Court decision, it was held that gov't could attach strings to the money it spends to insure that it would be used to purchase only those things actually wanted. If the gov't buys missiles, it buys exactly the missiles it wants; not something the defense industry decides is close enough; if it buys health care at a time when the gov't is generally opposed to abortion, then it has an obvious right to insist that its money not be used to promote abortion. To spent gov't money on health does not mean to spent it on what others define as health. For example, to spent gov't money on cancer treatment does not mean it must be spent on treatments the gov't considers phony or not worthwhile. What would be the ultimate result if gov't was content to loosely define the way tax money was spent? As the situation now stands, Congress wrote the Law; the Executive Branch interpreted it; the Court upheld that interpretation, and the Congress failed to pass a new law with more explicit language. With all three branches of gov't solidly against you, Ms. Gooden, it seems that they, not you, should be allowed to specify exactly how the money is to be spent.

For you, Ms. Goodman, to suggest as your entire rationale that Republicans should be opposed to this very sensible use of gov't power-is crazy. Your visceral approach indicates that you are 1) an abortion fanatic, 2) something of a "cheap shot" artist, and 3) possessed of the normal Democratic ignorance of Republican philosophy.

CAPITAL GAINS - THE DEMOCRATS HATE THEM

Dear Mr. Herbert Rowen,

I would like to thank for your editorial which dealt with the capital gains tax, debate. You were fairly accurate in describing some of the Democratic position. Unfortunately you weren't thorough about either parties' positions and you were very inaccurate about the Republican position.

Curiously though, you did not really engage in the debate much yourself; you stated a little of the positions on both sides, cited a couple of studies on each side, and indicated that neither party was soon about to change their position. You closed by expressing skepticism that a commission headed by Alan Greenspan to look into the issue, would do much to resolve matters.

Come on now, President Bush has invested more of his prestige on this issue than any other domestic issue; this was your chance to get him; to make him suffer more than he already has at the hands of Democrats who won't reduce the tax, no matter what. Yet, you avoided the debate and your readers went away knowing little or nothing more than they started with on this issue which seems to be the cornerstone of the President's domestic economic agenda. Further, it seems to be the issue from which the Democrats may derive the most benefit, as they continue to publicly embarrass the President by turning down his constant exhortations to cut the tax.

It is perhaps possible that you didn't get into the debate because in your heart you know the Democratic position is untenable. The Democrats bill themselves as the party of the little guy; the rich guy, the fat cat, the businessman, is their enemy. It is a naturally divisive approach that has won for the Democrats, majority status. They have persuaded voters that programs paid for by the other guy, by the rich guy in this case, can generate enough money to liberate them from the burden of higher taxes.
In truth, there are just not enough rich people to go around, and the programs necessarily get paid for by the very Democrats who mistakenly

CAPITAL GAINS

think they are voting for a free lunch. What appeal would the demotic Democrats have left if voters began to realize that the thousands and thousands of Democratic programs really could not be paid for by some other guy; that to vote for a Democrat was to vote for a tax on themselves. The creation of the illusion that the other guy will pay, has been one of the Democrats' most successful strategies. Total gov't spending now amounts to about $3 Trillion or $30,000 per year per taxpayer. This huge pile of money doesn't just come from the rich, it comes from everybody.

Amazingly, the United States is one of the few developed economies to impose a capital gains tax. The capital gains tax is a tax on assets such as stocks, real estate, factories and equipment. These are the things that form the foundation of an economy. When a new business is formed or an existing one begins to grow, it needs assets first; to put a tax on them is to make them more expensive and therefore more difficult to acquire and pay off. This is something that yields fewer jobs, fewer new products and technologies, a lower return on investment for owners, and, eventually, a economy that can't compete with others around the world.

To start a divisive argument about which group, workers or owners, rich or poor, benefits most from the capital gains tax, is not helpful since a healthy, competitive economy simultaneously requires profitable businesses, numerous and well paid jobs, and, most importantly, the production of goods and services at a quality and price that the maximum number of people want and can afford. To pick out special interest groups within the system, as Democrats do, just to get votes, is counter productive, at least from a Republican point of view, because the system's integration is too tight. The amount of interdependence is such that hurting one group is hurting them all. The capital gains tax is a tax on all Americans; not just the rich.

A recent and very good example of this same phenomena is the 1991 Luxury Tax which Democrats again said would be an excellent way to soak the rich. It turned out that the rich bought fewer yachts and other luxury items; factory production slowed down tremendously; workers lost their jobs

THE DEMOCRATS HATE THEM

and Democrats sheepishly considered repeal of the tax. The capital gains tax and the Luxury tax are identical, except that the causal relationship is more direct and readily apparent in the case of the luxury tax. The Democratic luxury tax is the best recent example of how taxing the rich actually hurts the poor more; yet the principal still remains at the heart of Democratic philosophy regarding taxation, because it has political appeal to uninformed voters.

Sen. Paul Tsongas, the first Democrat to announce for President, now has the distinction of being the first Democrat to consider the revival of the economy, through use of a capital gains tax, as the highest priority, rather than programs to help special interests. This may indicate that finally some Democrats recognize that many of the things Republicans have been saying about economics, are true.

Republicans generally are opposed to business taxation of all kinds, but they don't often say so in public because the Democrats have long since won the emotional debate that it feels good to tax business and the rich, even though it doesn't do a thing to increase gov't revenue or help the little guy. Taxing business allows Democrats to tell the electorate that the fat cat is picking up the tab for gov't programs. In truth, business profits do not represent a separate pool of money from which the gov't can tax with impunity. When taxes go up, the businessman simply passes the tax on to consumers as he does all expenses. If the money weren't taken as taxes, competitive pressures would force business to lower prices, raise wages, or declare higher dividends. In short, 100% of the money would filter down to individuals, where the gov't could tax it in one simple and efficient process. Legions of bookkeepers, accountants, lawyers, tax collectors, stock and bond brokers, and paper manufacturers would have to get real jobs where they produced goods and services that actually contributed to the standard of living, and the health of the economy. Those Democrats who doubt that the money would filter down, have to understand that in a free economy the competition is always to lower price so that a competitor can't undersell you and drive you out of business. The impulse to raise prices and earn more

CAPITAL GAINS

money is always there, but competition inexorably forces prices downward to the lowest possible level that is sustainable.

Another aspect of the Democratic war on business can be seen in the number of lawyers in Japan versus the United States. The Japanese have 100 times fewer lawyers per capita; this is mostly because they tend to be organized toward production, rather than toward a system that encourages divisive bickering about how to divide up the goods and services produced by others.

The major and profound reason to leave business free from Democratic constraints is that money would then be invested where it could be used with the most efficiency and productivity; exactly what is needed to get the United States to perform competitively in the international economy. Investing some or all of the nations resources as dictated by a jumble of conflicting, inconsistent, overlapping, and contradictory, tax laws, passed mostly for short term political advantage, is a formula for disaster, the disaster the U.S. has. Money must be free of gov't control so it can be used where it will yield the highest possible return for the nation.

The current capital gains debate grew out of the 1986 Tax Reform and Simplification Act which increased the capital gains tax by 65%, (the largest capital gain tax increase in history) in return for the decreases that then President Reagan wanted for personal tax rates. When Bush took over, he prayed he could extend the Reagan economic miracle by filling in one more major piece of the economic puzzle. Sadly, the Democrats would not allow him to reduce, or, ideally, eliminate, the tax; accordingly, the U.S. economy took a giant step toward the recession it now has.

Democratic soak the rich demagoguery and the block headed notion that the new, capital gains tax wouldn't somehow hurt the economy, is something not to be believed. On Jan 1, 1987 the tax on capital was to go up dramatically. On December 29, 1986 desperate customers were in commercial realty offices all over the country desperately trying to close transactions because the next day, when the tax took affect, their assets

THE DEMOCRATS HATE THEM

were going to be worth much less. All it took was a simple act of Congress to make real estate, the country's major asset, instantly worth much less, and even depressed. Resources were allocated away from this asset; the banks, including the S & L's, and many other related industries suffered tremendously and the recession began. For a nation to be efficient and productive, scarce capital assets must be continuously allocated on a day by day basis by thousands of businessman experts, rather than on a one time basis by a few Democratic politicians in Washington who pretend, with great cunning, that they can successfully manipulate the economy from Washington. The tremendous dislocations caused by the 1986 Tax Act were devastating to the economy. Huge commercial real estate developments that had been profitable, were overnight made insolvent by incredibly stupid changes in the tax laws that made projected income streams vastly different from what they were, literally, the day before. Projects all over the country collapsed as much of America's resource base was tied up in, what were then, dead real estate projects, and the recession began.

The 1986 Tax Act was what the Republicans wanted. In their zeal to deregulate the real estate business, which had been artificially and very unfairly subsidized with tax revenue from the middle and lower class, Republicans went too far too fast. They changed the rules, literally overnight, so that everything which was put in process under the old rules was virtually wiped out. A huge percentage of the nation's resources were laid waste. Coincidentally, this is virtually the same thing that happened in the Savings and Loan Industry. Republicans instantaneously deregulated. The rules of the game were changed overnight without giving people time to adjust and prepare; the result was disaster. The lesson is clear, gov't should never be in a position to regulate, de-regulate or control the economy, because, very quickly, they will make mistakes for which the whole country will suffer dearly. The free market does not make mistakes because in is in operation 24 hours per day, 7 days per week, 52 weeks per year, making millions of tiny adjustments each minute as millions of consumers vote with their dollars. Trends develop, but slowly and deliberately as real economic changes occur; fast and crippling dislocations like those caused by broad,

CAPITAL GAINS

authoritarian gov't regulation are not possible. Democrats have no appreciation of this whatsoever, preferring instead to believe that the only problem is to learn how to accurately regulate and de-regulate the economy.

Other major areas of the economy were also affected. In January of 1987, stock market turnover (shares quickly bought and sold) and volatility (the range within which stocks trade) shot up as there was much less incentive to hold stock for over six months so as to receive favorable capital gains tax treatment. Speculation was, in effect, encouraged. Junk bond take overs and mergers were encouraged, rather than long term growth. Falsely, the greed of the junk bond era was pinned on the Republicans and not the Democrats' record breaking capital gains tax.

Every corporation must decide how much debt to take on as a percentage of its equity. The more it borrows, the faster it can grow, but the less stable it becomes as earnings are consumed by debt service and not available for operations. A higher tax on equity caused by the capital gains tax, pushed American business down the road toward debt induced instability. This is an affect that no politician should have, or should want to have; it was, however, just one of the unintended affects of Democratic fiddling with a huge and intricate economy that cannot be fine tuned by a few Democrats in Washington.

The amazing Democratic policy of double and triple taxation of corporate profits meant that taxable earnings were worth a lot more if they were, in effect, used to service junk bond debt. This is what made the junk bond, leveraged buyout deals of the 80's so popular and possible. Those deals were really a manifestation of misguided Democratic tax policy. Rather than use heavily taxed earnings to pay stockholders, management could stretch earnings much further by agreeing to sell the whole corporation to a third party who would use what were once earnings, to pay for the new interest expense from the junk bonds that were issued to finance the transaction. Management went along because they often got to keep their jobs, and when they didn't, they were often able to leave on golden parachutes that were really part of the take over deal. Stockholders were encouraged to go along because they were offered a higher than market price for their shares.

THE DEMOCRATS HATE THEM

Leveraged, junk bond, take-overs were a tremendously wasteful and inefficient way to allocate corporate earnings in accordance with Democratic tax laws. An economy should not have to sustain these kinds of dislocations as a consequence of Democratic mis-management.

The Republican approach is to eliminate all artificial restraints on business so that it must survive based on the free market's evaluation of the quality of the goods and services it produces. The Democrats encouraged the junk bond debt of the 1980's with their tax policies, and with great political sophistication outfoxed the Republicans who were made to take the blame. The economy was the real loser as America's corporate resources were channeled to where the tax consequences were greatest, rather than to where the economic consequences were greatest.

Another area in which the capital gains tax is of importance has to do with the so called lock-in affect. It seems that if someone has a capital gain on which he will have to pay a high tax, he is inclined to hold on to the asset rather than sell it and pay the tax. In this way, the Democrats are, unexpectedly, encouraging money to stay in old investments rather than to be allocated to new, possibly more productive investments. Republicans know money must be free to flow where it can yield the highest return for savers and entrepreneurs; not confined in some uneconomic place because of misguided Democratic tax policies.

Standard supply-side theories, which hold that if taxes are reduced or eliminated, economic activity that was constrained by the tax will begin to flourish, apply as regards the capital gains tax. In fact, according to supply-siders, an increase in tax revenue will result from lowering the tax rate because the stimulative affect of the lower tax rate will improve business enough so that more revenue will come in at the new lower rate than at the old higher one. For instance, from 1968 to 1976, Sen. Kennedy pushed the capital gains rate to 49%, and revenue fell by 33%. The Stieger amendment, which lowered the rate to 28%, was then passed at the request of high tech industries who depended heavily on venture capital taxed as capital gains,

CAPITAL GAINS

and revenue rose 42%. After the initial Reagan cut to 20%, revenue from the tax almost doubled. The Democrats know all of this, and should be for the cuts, both to stimulate business and to increase tax revenue, but they are not; they find that they get lots of political milage from telling their constituents how they stuck it to the rich. In truth, Democrats do stick it to the rich, but they also stick it to the gov't, which gets less tax revenue, and to the middle class, which loses jobs and businesses every time the tax goes up.

In fact, the capital gains tax actually has a very broad affect. IRS numbers show that those who benefit from the tax are well distributed across all income levels; not confined to the upper class, as Democrats would have us believe. It turned out that 3,000,000 taxpayers with income below $20,000 per year receive more capital gains than those with income over $200,000. Half of all capital gains go to people with annual incomes of less than $60,000. Many of the poorer people who receive these gains, it turns out, are elderly or children living on a small inheritance from a deceased parent. So in the end, the Democrats, stick it to the poor too. Republicans want to reduce or eliminate the tax so all Americans will be free to stimulate the economy in an ordered logical way as they make their preferences known without Democratic constraints on their behavior.

HEALTH CARE - DEMOCRATS WANT SOCIALISM

Dear Consumer Reports Magazine,

I have just read your rather lengthy article in support of national health insurance which appeared in the September 1990 issue. Of all the Democratic groups that are clamoring for national health Insurance, yours is among the most thorough and most direct. At one point you even went so far as to mention that the universal health insurance you wanted, something very similar to what they have in Canada, was not socialized medicine. This put you light years ahead of virtually all the other Democratic supporters who talk at length and in great detail about health insurance, but never put the issue in an ideological context. With your comment about socialism you at least paid lip service to the idea that political positions have an ideological context, and that arguments presented in a political vacuum are ultimately an abuse of the two party system, since such arguments tend to give the electorate no direction that can be used once they enter the voting booth.

It seems that for most of this Century, the American Medical Association (they represent doctors) in particular, and the Republican Party in general have been successful several times in spearing the idea of national health insurance in mid flight; they have done this by labeling it or attacking it as "socialized medicine." Recognizing that socialism, thanks mostly to its many conspicuous failures all over the world, has a horrendous reputation, Democrats try to promote it here in the United States by disingenuously not labeling it at all. When you at "Consumer Reports" magazine chose to address the issue, it represented a comparatively high level of integrity. On the other hand, your explanation of why the current Canadian system and the Democratic plan derived from it, is not "socialist" was totally fraudulent, and something you should be ashamed of.

Socialism (most closely associated with the Democratic Party concept that gov't is the solution) is an economic\political system that emphasizes

HEALTH CARE

government ownership, planning, control, and income redistribution. Capitalism (most closely associated with the Republican Party concept that gov't is the problem) is a system that emphasizes the autonomy of the individual from government by encouraging voluntary and private economic exchanges between mutually interested parties. The Canadian national health care system is obviously socialistic in that doctors, for all intents and purposes, work for the gov't. A doctor's pay check, in the form of reimbursements for services rendered to patients, comes from the gov't in an amount determined by the gov't. The gov't forces everybody to participate, or sneak off to the United States for faster, higher quality care. Similarly, hospitals are owned outright by the gov't which then determines how long a patient must wait for services, and which of the world's services and technologies are deemed cheap enough and suitable for use in treating Canadian citizens. Whether this system is exactly socialistic or only 90% socialistic is irrelevant. The implementation of such a system was a huge step toward socialism, and necessarily, an equally huge step away from capitalism.

"Consumer Reports" says, "it is not a system of socialized medicine in which doctors and hospitals work for the gov't, and patients are assigned to clinics." This is technically true, but still very, very deceptive. Had "Consumer Reports" been willing to defy public opinion and world history you would have said, "it is a system of socialized medicine in which doctors and hospitals, for all intents and purposes, are controlled by the gov't, and patients are assigned to clinics." Whatever the precise definition of the Canadian system, it is certainly not capitalistic, nor is it an attempt to move toward capitalism. It was clearly a way of increasing gov't involvement to compensate for what was mistakenly viewed as the failures of private capitalistic involvement.

Your support for the Democratic scheme to socialize medicine in the United States comes from your dogged perception that socialism is the best system, for health care and virtually everything else. It is ironic that at the very time when Boris Yeltzin comes to America to openly talk of Milton Friedman and free markets, Democrats want to talk of socialized medicine.

DEMOCRATS WANT SOCIALISM

Democrats seem to believe that the current American health care system is failing because, 1) the U.S. is spending $2400 per year per person, while Canada and other industrial nations spent less, 2) 34-37 million Americans have no health insurance, and 3) in some key areas, most notably, infant mortality, life expectancy, and low birth weight, the U.S. seems to be behind other countries despite overall higher health care spending.

Most Republicans will acknowledge that there are grave problems with the current system, but they believe the problems are caused by the patch work of gov't involvement; so for them it is not possible to pose the issue as a debate between the socialist, Canadian health care system and the capitalistic, American system. For example, Medicaid (gov't health care for the poor) and Medicare (gov't health care for the aged), and The Veterans Administration, comprise 62% of all health care dollars spent in the U.S.; much of the rest is spent by private health insurance companies that are very heavily regulated by the gov't. Given such a high degree of gov't involvement, it is not possible to say that the U.S.' problems are caused by Republican, free market capitalism. Republicans argue that both systems are poor because of the gov't; that the Canadian brand of socialism may be more efficient in some areas, but that neither system is nearly as effective as a pure capitalist system would be.

To start with, the criticism that there is something wrong with spending far more per capita than the rest of the world, is not logical. The U.S. is still, by most measures at least, the richest nation on earth and it stands to reason that it would spend the most. Medical care is a practical luxury that U.S. citizens naturally are compelled to indulge, at least up to the limit of their means. If the U.S. spent less, it would more likely be an indication of a problem; it would mean that the self-preservation instinct of Americans was low or that the system was so bad that it was somehow preventing money from being spent on health care.

That there are 34-37 million people without health insurance is more an administrative problem than a medical\health care problem. Democrats trot out this number to plant the suggestion that thousands die because they are shut out of the health care system. The U.S. is a very civilized and

HEALTH CARE

compassionate country; in fact, last year not one of these uninsured people died or suffered a serious deterioration in a medical condition that was a direct result of a lack of health insurance. People do not get turned away from hospitals in the U.S. The uninsured get old or poor, in which case they get Medicaid or Medicare. Failing that, they go to the Veterans Administration, or they get a job that carries health insurance, or they pay for health care out of their own pocket, or they go into debt to a friend, relative, bank, hospital or other health care provider, or they rely on available hospital, city, county, and state charity. To be sure, this is a sloppy and degrading system in which people get caught between the patchwork of funding sources, but in the end no one is denied; it is certainly nothing like what the Democrats would have us believe.

The third problem, that Democrats and "Consumer Reports" focus on, is spending effectiveness. It seems to them that the U.S. doesn't get value for the $2400 per person, and that's why the high infant mortality, low birth weight, and low life expectancy problems. This argument or these arguments are impossible to follow. Firstly, as regards life expectancies, there is no statistically significant difference between socialized Canada and England (77 and 75 years of age respectively) and the somewhat less socialized U.S. with a 75 year expectancy. Further, even if some scientist could find a meaningful statistical difference in longevity it would probably not be related to health care anyway. Health care is only one factor in longevity. One recalls the Yogurt commercials showing Turks, I think, living to 125 while eating Dannon Yogurt. While the commercials were not too serious they nevertheless did remind us about the tons of very serious research that seeks to find clues to longevity by comparing, cultural, dietetic, environmental, psychological, economic, and god knows what, differences between countries.

The data on infant mortality and low birth weight is fairly conclusive. These are problems that have to do with preventative measures that should be taken by mothers prior to birth, and in many cases prior to conception. These problems certainly need to be addressed, but they are not within the

DEMOCRATS WANT SOCIALISM

scope of what is covered by the Canadian health care system or most of the proposed U.S. derivatives. It is very deceptive for the Democrats and "Consumer Reports" to speak of high infant mortality rates in the U.S. within the context of a debate about health care systems.

As it turns out, the U.S. does get more than Canada for the additional money it spends. It gets private and semi-private rooms, no rationing of hospital beds or services (it is not uncommon for a heart patient to die in Canada while waiting for an operation), slower cost increases (3.93 % vs. 4.28%), rapid introduction of new technology (CAT scans, kidney dialysis, and heart pacemakers which are 3-20 times more common in the United States), no work slowdowns or strikes, five times more specialists as opposed to general practitioners, and, on the negative side, whopping malpractice settlements. In sum, if a person is seriously ill, as we all will be one day, and in need of expensive, highly trained specialists with a lot of expensive high tech equipment, the U.S. is the place to be. A relatively free market like the U.S. market becomes the destination of innovative life saving new products from all over the world because the top end is not closed off to contain costs, as it is in Canada and England. England, for example invented the CAT scanner, but makes comparatively little use of it because the gov't deems it too costly, while the U.S. increasingly regards it as a practical necessity. Without the somewhat freer U.S. market to buy and finance the development of CAT scanners, and other equipment, this equipment would probably not exist, at least not to the extent it does now.

In their battle for socialized medicine, Democrats are now pointing out that at 12% of GNP, or $6000 for every job holder in America, the U.S. is spending at the highest rate in the world, and this rate is just too much. This is an extremely opportunistic approach for them, given that never in their history have they batted an eyelash at exorbitantly rising costs for any of their programs, even those programs which have had the opposite affect as intended. It seems to Republicans that it is not for politicians to know what percent of GNP should be spend to improve peace of mind, prevent illness, and save or prolong life. These are personal decisions that the gov't has no

HEALTH CARE

basis or right on which to render judgement. It would seem that most people would be very willing to spend everything to save or prolong their lives. Allowing them to do so, if they choose, as is not possible in Canada, is a way of telling the market place that new life saving medical knowledge and equipment can profitably be developed and sold to waiting customers. As in the case of the CAT scanner, such equipment that is originally developed for extreme and difficult cases often finds use in a far wider array of circumstances. Besides which, in a manner of speaking, none of this high end equipment is frivolous, since with each passing second, each of us is getting closer to the time when we will need it to save or prolong our lives; at that time we will all thank God that we live in a country where the gov't didn't arbitrarily cut off the high end just to cut costs. Although it is not possible to predict how much and what kind of health care Americans would demand under a free system, it is safe to conclude that the new system would be vastly different and far superior to the largely gov't prescribed system that Americans use now.

With the heavy amount of government interference, the American system is woefully inefficient and far from the Republican free market model. Since it is not in our nature to let anyone go without health care, and since it is often not in our nature to save for our own health care, this would be an ideal situation in which to turn to the gov't to impose upon us a free market solution that would simultaneously improve health care and reduce costs.

If it is know that in 1992 all 250 million Americans are going to spend $600 Billion or $2400 per person on health care; why not simply mandate that everyone open an IRA type savings account and put a weekly percent of their salary into it until they had, say, the equivalent of 5 or 10 years, of paid up insurance for themselves and their dependents in the account? When children grew up and were no longer dependant, the money could be transferred to the children's health account or spent. Much like an IRA, the money could only be invested in safe places and withdrawn for specified purposes. As long as the insurance was paid up in rough actuarial accordance with age and health, a person could stop contributing and spend any interest

DEMOCRATS WANT SOCIALISM

as it accumulated. Any money left over at death would simply become part of the estate. Catastrophic illness not covered by the self-insurance would be paid for out of general revenue. Those not working, not dependant, and with insufficient money in their accounts to cover the cost of illness, would also have to be covered out of general revenue until such time as their self-insurance account was paid up. Theoretically, this system would cause no initial hardship as the $600 Billion currently spent ultimately comes from only those who work anyway.

This system would have enormous benefits over the current socialized systems of the U.S., Canada, and Britain. Firstly, all Americans would be insured and spending their own money, money that they would have to replace; this would discourage them from spending one cent unnecessarily, and it would finally put the health care industry in a competitive environment, and on notice that unnecessary costs due to waste and inefficiency would be instantly exposed by the competitive free market, just as in, say, the automobile industry. Eventually their jobs would be threatened if consumers did not judge their performance to be sufficiently competitive. It would be as if everybody had a 100% deductible, but didn't have to pay one cent more than they are paying now. Medicaid, Medicare, The Veterans Administration, and private health insurance companies would all be gone. The massive waste in the current, gov't regulated system is highlighted nicely by Blue Cross/Blue Shield of Massachusetts. It employs 6700 workers to cover 2.7 million subscribers, which is more workers than used by the socialist system of Canada to cover the whole country of only 27 million people. Under a capitalist system, this kind of abuse would not be possible. Huge, wasteful, and inefficient bureaucracies are only possible when the gov't is in control or nearby.

In the first year, without gov't intervention, $600 Billion would theoretically be spent by 250 million Americans who would have every incentive to care about how every cent was spent. Currently, the consumer's money is mostly spent by gov't, health care or insurance company bureaucrats, all of whom have little or no incentive to be careful with the $600 Billion. It is very possible that by the second year, health care costs could be cut in half and health care improved. Without a free market

HEALTH CARE

standard, there is virtually no basis on which to judge how over priced the current system is. Recent examples from East Germany can help to clarify this point. Without free market competition, they had no incentive to improve their domestically manufactured cars, which required a manually operated dip stick from outside the vehicle to determine fuel level. A capitalist market constantly creates pressure to drive costs down and quality up, while a socialist market drives costs up and quality down.

Without the less socialistic Western countries to compare themselves to, countries like the USSR and China would have no basis on which to determine how wasteful and inefficient their systems are. During the very period when the Democrats have heavily socialized medicine in the U.S., there has been a general explosion in knowledge and technology in all fields that might have been translated to phenomenal gains in health care, but the U.S. won't ever find out what the upper limits are, and what reasonable costs are, until the socialistic constraints are removed. Health care is too important to be managed by the same Democratic philosophy and the same people who manage the Post Office. Sadly, President Bush and the Republicans feel unable to do much about the problem, but their proposals to employ the free market as a major part of the solution are an important but small step in the correct direction.

FREE TRADE-DEMOCRATS DON'T LIKE FREEDOM

Dear Mr. Herbert Rowan,

Your recent editorial regarding President Bush's proposal for a free trade zone with Mexico highlights the internal conflicts among Democrats which make many Americans question what future viability the party has. You spend virtually all of your column going over the case for and against the free trade zone, but in the end you don't take a position yourself. When a Democrat doesn't take a position on a issue that would have normally provoked a knee-jerk reaction, it must be a sign that something is amiss. You start out by saying that a bitter fight is shaping up, with organized labor and Democratic liberals leading the way against free trade, but you show no passion yourself.

Interestingly, Michael Kinsley editor of the "NEW REPUBLIC," probably the best known scholarly journal for Democrats, has written that he favors free trade. Richard Gephart one of the obvious choices for the Democratic presidential nomination has recently said that he was 99% of the way there toward supporting free trade with Mexico. It seems many Democrats, even the most liberal ones, are moving toward free trade because the intellectual battle against it has long been lost. The last and final movement toward free trade is being held up by some lingering loyalty to Democratic special interest groups and to mistaken arguments which have never had any intellectual support in the U.S.

In fairness, it should be noted that free trade has often been opposed by big business Republicans; this continues even today as, for example, we watch the sad spectacle of Lee Iacocca marching off to the White House to ask for import quotas every time his business turns down. The primary source of modern protectionism, though, lies within organized labor and the liberal wing of the Democratic Party. Supporters of protectionism have been fighting a losing battle since 1930 when the Hawley-Smoot Act was passed by Congress as a desperation measure to combat the Great Depression by imposing the highest tariffs since 1828. Virtually 100% of economists, at the time, opposed Hawley-Smoot and virtually 100% of the profession still does.

FREE TRADE

With the weight of virtually unanimous support from most of the economics profession, tariffs have gone down steadily and dramatically ever since, although it is clear from the very real opposition that the Mexican Free Trade Agreement is generating, that support is still strong in some quarters.

The major source of support for protectionism is organized labor, which comes off as an intellectually unprincipled special interest group that is rapidly becoming an embarrassment to Democrats. If it were up to labor, American borders would be sealed to foreign imports so that everything consumed in America would be made in America, no matter how high the price, how low the quality, and how limited the selection. To organized labor, it means nothing that Americans select a lot of foreign merchandise because they are attracted to the price, quality, and variety. Labor would happily deny all Americans this choice so that they can go on producing and selling what are, sometimes, inferior goods at inflated prices. According to the "Institute for International Economics" trade barriers already in place cost each American family $1200 per year in higher prices. The IRS tells us that there are 35,000,000 businesses in America, with 90% having fewer than 100 employees. Each one of these businesses would like to have trade protection so that their products didn't have to compete with foreign competition; so they could relax a little about quality, and raise prices a bit. Each one of these 35,000,000 businesses and their employees are just as deserving as organized labor, but because they are spread out across the country and can't be easily organized into coherent voting blocks, they are ignored by Democrats, who favor large, identifiable, special interest voting blocks. This shameless pandering between organized labor and the Democrats is now finally becoming too much of an intellectual embarrassment for many Democrats, and presumably will hasten the final death of anti-free trade sentiment.

A less easily understood, but equally important aspect of the debate between Democrats and Republicans has to do with the affect of foreign trade on the number of jobs in America. When organized labor talks about jobs, they are talking only about their own; when Republicans talk about jobs they are forthrightly talking about the total number for all Americans. When an American buys a foreign product because it saves him money, either because it costs less initially, or because it is of higher quality and lasts longer, the money that is saved can then be spent elsewhere so that it then

DEMOCRATS DON'T LIKE FREEDOM

stimulates employment. This new employment is often not in industries that labor has organized, because those industries tend to be smaller, more spread out, and difficult to reach, but they are generally more competitive than big unionized companies because of, in part, the lower wages they pay their employees. Overall, unemployment is not reduced when Americans buy imports, it is often just shifted from union to non-union jobs. This is why unemployment throughout the 80's stayed very low, 4-6%, while over one half million union jobs, mostly in the automobile industry, were lost to foreign competition. Free trade will often eliminate high paying jobs in inefficient industries, and create competitive wage jobs in truly competitive industries. A good way to impoverish a nation is to shield it from world competition so that its goods and services don't have to be of he same high quality and low price as those produced by other countries. The Communists in East Germany, for example, produced automobiles, in a fully protected environment that were expensive and of such low quality that it was necessary to use a manually operated dip-stick from outside the vehicle to determine the gasoline level. In short, they produced a car in a protected environment that embarrassed and impoverished East Germans, while their cultural and genetic counterparts in West Germany produced the Mercedes and BMW. Republicans love free trade because it forces American business to compete against much broader and tougher competition than is available nationally, and thus produce higher quality goods and services which more quickly raise the standard of living.

Further, the dollars with which Americans buy foreign goods are ultimately of no value to foreigners unless they can be used by someone to buy valuable things from the United States, where the dollars ultimately must be spent. This ultimate repatriation of the dollar stimulates employment in those American industries where it is spent. If Americans made only cheap junk, foreigners would have to raise their prices in America so that they would get enough dollars to buy enough merchandise in America to make trading worthwhile, but the higher they raised prices, the fewer units they would sell and the fewer dollars they would have. That foreigners can still sell at low prices in America is testimony to their productivity, and just as certainly, our own.

Many Democrats, most notably Richard Gephart, thought they had found a wedge to keep the free trade door closed. They often argue that if, for

FREE TRADE

example, Japan wants to prevent all foreign products from entering their country, the U.S. should do the same in the interest of fairness. This is not at all sensible because it would lower our standard of living by cutting us off from low priced, high quality Japanese goods. If Japan does not spend the American dollars it earns on obvious American products that the Democrats notice, it must nevertheless do so in a less obvious way, for example, by trading the dollars to other countries that produce the natural raw materials that Japan needs so desperately, but, for which they have no indigenous supply. The Japanese have to do something with the U.S. dollars they have. In this case, they might buy raw material from Brazil. The U.S. trade deficit with Japan, that Democrats are so frightened of, might become a trade surplus with Brazil. Whoever gets the U.S. dollars takes them only with the expectation that they can be used to buy valuable things in the U.S. This is something the Democrats would ignore because trade deficits with Japan can elicit votes, while routine trading with less important countries cannot. That organized labor has a home within the Democratic Party from which to conduct what it describes as its most important legislative battle in 1991, the defeat of free trade with Mexico, should be a warning to all Americans to vote Republican.

These are the essential issues of free trade; they apply equally to Japan and Mexico. According to your article, Mr. Rowan, Democrats who remonstrate against free trade, like those at "The Economic Policy Institute," argue that free trade will threaten industrial competitiveness and undermine the wages of American workers. It is not possible to explain how free trade would threaten industrial competition when, in fact, it would secure and intensify industrial competition; yet this is the lie many Democrats would have us believe. When they say that free trade undermines wages, what they really mean is that it undermines artificially high union wages, and supports non-union wages in areas where American industry is competitive, but where workers are not politically organized.

You imply, Mr. Rowan, that the scholarly work done by Walter Russell, also of the Democratic, "Economic Policy Institute" indicates that America is doubly threatened by foreign countries that pay low wages and have high tech, efficient production that matches or exceeds that of the U.S.' The

DEMOCRATS DON'T LIKE FREEDOM

argument being that, a low paid foreigner with a hammer can't outproduce a high paid American with a computer. But, when the low paid foreign workers have computers too, like in the Pacific rim, and Mexico, they can outproduce Americans. To a free trade Republican, this is silly for several reasons. Firstly, since the days of the Triangular Trade between the Colonies, England, Africa, and the Caribbean, the U.S. has always maintained relatively high wage jobs while trading with its much poorer neighbors around the world; there is no reason to get cold feet now. Secondly, low wages and high efficiency abroad, make for low cost, high quality imports, the very thing all consumers want in order to improve their standard of living. Thirdly, if these imports were really costing Americans their jobs, they wouldn't have the money to buy them in the first place, and in that way the imports and trade deficits would disappear. The huge American market is only valuable to foreigners if they can use the American currency they earn to buy what they regard as quality American made goods and services.

Lastly, we need to recognize that Americans may never be able to build relatively mundane products, like automobiles, as well as people like the Japanese. The Japanese and most of the Pacific rim cultures, generally speaking, have produced comparatively docile citizenries who are comfortable doing morning calisthenics and then dutifully and diligently working all day on automobile assembly lines or in management. Americans come from pioneer stock; this makes them more inclined toward independence and entrepreneurship. American entrepreneurs have always been the envy of the world because they developed the businesses and technologies that sustained the world. Socialists in Russia only knew what to produce and plan for by looking to the West for a frame of reference. American business began to decline during the 60's and 70's, precisely as Democrats began to score points with their general thesis that business was the enemy which needed to be taxed, controlled, regulated and socialized. MBA students in the 70's took courses that alerted them to the competitive immorality of huge multi-national conglomerates that were "govt's onto themselves." Harold Geneen and ITT were at the center of the storm. Today America prays for the revival of such successful entrepreneurial companies.

President Bush has been desperate for a capital gains tax cut that would, among other things, make it far easier for venture capital to flow into new business, but the Democrats are firmly opposed because business is their

FREE TRADE

enemy, and rich people who have money to invest in entrepreneurial activities are also their enemy. It is no wonder that with this Democratic policy and attitude, and many others, that the American entrepreneurial advantage is being killed off. Republicans, as always, want to free American entrepreneurs to do what they always have done.

You then go on to point out that not only are wages lower in Mexico, but working conditions, fringe benefits, workers' rights, and environmental concerns, all favor cheaper production in Mexico, at the expense of American jobs. The standard of living in Mexico is a tiny fraction of what it is in America, and while our religious values make us feel sorry that the lack of capitalism within Mexico has impoverished the country, it should in no way prevent us from helping them, by buying their products. It is not exploitation to help someone by buying from them that which they have freely determined is in their best interest to sell. The one tiny conclusion you do make, Mr. Rowan, that the U.S. should get assurances that working conditions will improve in Mexico before it will buy their goods, represents very silly and misplaced compassion. It is not for us to add to the expense of Mexican imports by imposing costly conditions on manufacturers that will raise prices to Americans, cause them to buy less, and in turn cause the loss of desperately needed jobs in Mexico. It is amazing that in one instant you grudgingly acquiesce to the superior Republican free trade arguments, only to have your gut Democratic instincts compel you to take one last little and impotent lunge at the free market by suggesting that the U.S. arrogantly proclaim, to impoverished Mexicans, that a little pollution in their air is more important than food in their mouths.

In trade regulation, as in all areas of gov't tinkering there are unanticipated consequences. One sad example is the 63% import tax on the flat-screens which may become dominant in the television and computer industry. To avoid the tax and keep prices competitive, Apple Computer has had to move production and jobs off shore where there is no tax. Who would argue that this tinkering produced a net benefit.

Some Democrats, realizing that their historical position is threatened on the free trade issue, and many other issues, are trying hard to quickly evolve a new position that will be more attractive than either the standard

DEMOCRATS DON'T LIKE FREEDOM

Republican or Democratic position. In "THE AMERICAN PROSPECT" a new and very scholarly journal that is trying to reincarnate the Democrats before they wither past the point of help, Robert B. Reich claims to have discovered a new facet to the standard debate. He calls his new discovery, "outward looking economic nationalism." According to Mr. Reich, protectionism involves promoting your own business interests at the expense of others; i.e., if we protect our auto industry we will being doing so at the expense of the Japanese. Free trade, according to Mr. Reich, primarily involves the belief that ultimately both countries will be improved with the free flow of goods, as they specialize in the things they do best. Outward looking economic nationalism is the new and superior position, he claims, because, "each nation takes responsibility for improving the wealth-creating capacity of its citizens, but works with other nations to ensure that these improvements do not come at their expense."

In short, Mr. Reich, doesn't like protectionism because it benefits one nation at the expense of another, and he doesn't like free trade because businesses need more help than they can get from one another (as when G.M. and Toyota built a very successful plant together in Freemont, Ca.); so what he advocates is a domestic industrial policy (socialism) in which gov't, with its infinite wisdom, identifies and gives money to the most important industries and technologies. He then couples this with an international industrial policy (super socialism) whereby countries get together to predict and agree which industries in which countries should be subsidized and by how much, so that zero-sum, wasteful competition between nations doesn't develop. It is hard to pick a place to begin arguing against such incredibly misguided statements.

Consider that between 1950 and 1985 IBM was perhaps the premier company in the world, it had become the most profitable company in the world, and the world was still just beginning to develop an appetite for computerization; the future seemed unlimited. A couple of short years later, the situation is dramatically reversed, the future for IBM is bleak, the Company is losing money and downsizing even though computer use is still spreading. This is the nature of all business. IBM had all the money, and many of the most ingenious people in the world; yet their own industry, the

FREE TRADE

very industry they grew up in and knew better than anyone in the world, was changing at a rate faster than they could understand. If Mr. Reich and a handful of Ivy League, intellectual academicians, or even the incredibly more knowledgeable executives at IBM, really thought they could direct the world economy, we would all be well advised to run for cover. The solution to IBM's problem can only be found by 1000's of risk taking entrepreneurs at IBM, or by the other 1000's of entrepreneurs who were spawned by IBM's massive failure; not by Mr. Reich and his Democratic friends who presume to tax and denigrate entrepreneurs and businessmen alike, while somehow picking the ones to develop new products and industries. It should never be forgotten that less than 10 years ago, IBM was the enemy of the Democratically controlled gov't which sought to destroy the company that was the jewel of American business with the most massive anti-trust lawsuit in history. Fortunately, the saintly Reagan administration came to power and put an end to the Democratic treachery. Business is in trouble precisely because the Democrats have always tried to control, socialize and even destroy it.

In just a few pages Mr. Reich feels he has buried traditional free trade and protectionist arguments and replaced them with domestic and international, socialist planning; oops, I mean, industrial policy, or maybe "outward looking economic nationalism." In case Mr. Reich and his Democratic friends do not succeed at this attempt to geometrically enlarge the Federal gov't, it is certain that they will maintain their comfortable home within the Democratic Party, a party they have never voted against.

CRIME - REPUBLICANS REDUCE CRIME

Dear Tom Wicker,

Your recent editorial in "The New York Times" about crime in America was typical of the new approach many Democrats are taking now that statistics about what looks to be a shockingly deteriorated situation are in hand, and the 1991 Crime Bills are slowly making their way through Congress.

Not once in your article did you use the term Democrat or Republican, as if to imply that anti-crime legislation and criminology was really a gentleman's concern far above the seamy reach of partisan politics. Once again, nothing could be further from the truth. Democrats and Republicans will shape the future of criminal justice, and they have diametrically opposed ways of thinking about it which are based on their respective ideologies.

Republicans believe in individual liberty, and concomitantly, individual responsibility. They reason that government is empowered to protect liberty so that people are free to shape and create themselves as they see fit. To a Republican, good behavior is the natural order; to a Democrat good behavior is adventitious. If an individual becomes a criminal, it is because he elects to do so having been forewarned that only he will be held directly accountable. This is not to say that family, neighbors, friends, and society should not feel that they have failed the criminal, but rather that a free society emphasizing individual liberty can only be sustained and strengthened when each individual is given the maximum incentive to be fully responsible for his own actions. Accordingly, Republicans are, to use the common term, "law and order types" who support punishing criminals. Rehabilitation is seen as the result of swift and appropriately harsh punishment.

CRIME

Democrats believe that an individual has no free will; that he is a mere creation of the larger society around him. Wherefore-it is society that is responsible for the criminal acts of individuals. Incarceration becomes societal self-flagellation. The criminal becomes the victim of a faulty society; jailed only with great shame; just long enough to give society the time to perfect itself. Democrats buy this basic concept and have always been labeled by Republicans as softer on crime.

The modern manifestation of this concept was created by Karl Marx, the father of socialism, in the mid 19th Century, when he said, "It is not the consciousness of men that determines their being, but, on the contrary, their social being that determines there consciousness." The Democrats have always subscribed to a variety of diluted versions of this thinking. Huey Long, a populist with no intellectual pretensions, thought society could make every man a king. Franklin Roosevelt, who had much intellectual support, eventually came to believe that, gov't, as the organ of society, could offer everyman a "New Deal." Lyndon Johnson tried to create a "Great Society" from Washington. Always, the emphasis was on what society could do for and to the individual; not on what the individual could do for and to society.

When it came to the crime issue, in the last Presidential election, George Bush, with great concision, simplified the whole matter into two words; namely-Willie Horton. Willie Horton, in case you have forgotten, was a Massachusetts rapist\murder who, when let out of jail on a temporary furlough, committed a similar crime. Democrats going into the 1992 elections are still complaining bitterly about the use of Willie Horton in what turned out to be an accurate and brilliant Republican political maneuver. Sam Donaldson the Democrat from ABC NEWS even went so far as to ask the murderer, Horton, whether he could forgive Bush and the Republicans for exploiting him. But the Democrats still don't have a defense because they still cannot escape their philosophic commitment to blaming society for an individual's crime. A person who fears becoming a crime victim, hasn't got time to wait for the Democrats to perfect society, he wants the criminal removed today; this is something Republicans have always done with somewhat more alacrity than Democrats, and the electorate knows it. This perspective was 100% lacking from your article, Mr. Wicker.

REPUBLICANS REDUCE CRIME

Democrats, out of political desperation, are now making a half hearted effort to promote a more astringent crime package. The 1991 Bush Administration Crime package includes, most importantly: more liberalized use of the death penalty, restrictions on appeals from death-row inmates, and higher penalties for a range of crimes from selling weapons to terrorists, to selling drugs to pregnant women. The Bush bill, sadly enough, contains virtually nothing substantive to cause a general reduction in crime. The Democratic bill is very similar. In true Democratic fashion, they want to spend $1 billion more (a 2% increase) on crime prevention, and ban assault weapons. The Democratic bill, may actually be slightly tougher than the Republican bill, but neither purports to have any chance to seriously reduce crime. The bills show both parties, for the time being, have run out of both political and intellectual capital on this issue. Politically, the issue is always at or near the top of voters' concerns; so neither party is willing to risk a move from the status quo and the attendant potential consequences from a misstep. Intellectually, the Republicans have mostly gotten their way, while Democrats have had to follow along because they lack the politically necessary, short term solution to what they see as a long term societal problem.

In one sense the Republicans have done everything they always wanted to do, they threw the book at everybody, and then threw everybody in jail. In 1970, there were 196,000 prisoners in Federal and State prisons; in 1980 there were 315,000; in 1990 their were 900,000. It is by no means clear whether the crime rate went up or more criminals went to jail. The FBI, which collects statistics from police departments, concluded that violent crime went up dramatically during the entire period, but they have been roundly criticized for releasing bad data that was not adjusted after they encouraged local police to report more extensively and more accurately during the 80's. Bureau of Justice statistics apparently have been reported from more stable sources and are somewhat more reliable. Both agree, though, that violent crime about tripled from 161 incidents per 100,000 population in 1970 to 540 incidents per 100,000 population in 1980. FBI statistics, probably due to reporting methods, show violent crime continued to rise during the 80's while Bureau of Justice statistics show that it declined somewhat during the 80's.

CRIME

The Bureau of Justice statistics, if you believe them, and you probably should, are even more impressive when you consider, 1) that there was a bulge in the very criminal 15-24 year old population during the 80's, 2) in 1986 an unprecedented crime producing drug epidemic (crack) engulfed much of the country, 3) an increase in poverty in the period due to Reaganomics, at least according to Democrats, 4) the emergence of a new and more materialistic ghetto population that valued such things, as $120 sneakers and leather jackets, enough to kill for them.

With a little luck, the Republican approach might continue to work, and at an accelerated rate as the 15-24 age group declines, and the crack problem runs its course. But this is a dangerous chance to take given that the Republican approach, 1) in its current form may not be working despite tentative suggestions from the data, 2) one million behind bars (the highest rate in the world) is a tragedy for the victims, the criminals, and the nation, that must be diminished and 3) new problems may arise pertaining to poverty, drugs, and morality that will exacerbate the current situation, whether it is improving or not.

Unconstrained by politics and Willie Horton, Mr. Wicker, you support the traditional, purist Democratic approach to fighting crime, which ultimately will be pulling the Democrats off the Republican ground that they currently are attempting to occupying. In typical Democratic fashion you recommend the following: 1) programs of community correction, 2) work release, 3) restitution to victims, 4) community service; intensive supervision, 5) repeal of mandatory sentencing, 5) shifting of emphasis from law enforcement to prevention, 6) shortening of prison sentences, 7) prisoner education, drug treatment, and vocational services, and 8) preventative community policing. In all of your so called reforms you did not mention one word about how to more effectively punish criminals to rehabilitate them against returning to a life of crime, after their release. Your only real prayer is that the above listed more "sensitive" approach will save a little money and not significantly endanger public safety. You don't even pretend that it represents meaningful criminal justice reform, or a significant change from current practices.

REPUBLICANS REDUCE CRIME

It would seem that the most obvious purpose of the criminal justice system is to apprehend and punish criminals. Any meaningful reform of the process would have to address this issue head on. Pretending that the criminal justice system is really part of the social welfare system, as Democrats have traditionally done, compromises the effectiveness and integrity of both. If the emphasis is on rehabilitation without punishment, as Mr. Wicker seems to propose, the deterrent affect is near zero. A would-be criminal now has a 3% chance of getting caught and doing time. If on top of this, the emphasis is shifted even more toward rehabilitation, a potential criminal will have nothing whatsoever to fear.

A primary moral obligation of society is to protect future victims through deterrence of present and future criminals. To accomplish this, little needs to be done as regards the police. They seem to be more than capable of bringing in as many criminals as the system can handle. It is a fairly straight forward system whose results are easily measured. If an officer or department doesn't make enough arrests, he or they can be easily identified and replaced. In many towns, for example, the police are often on a first name basis with many of the drug dealers, having arrested them, and worked with, and around them so often. The problem is not finding criminals, it is what to do with them after they are found or arrested.

By now, everybody has heard that prison tends to make criminals worse rather than better; that the U.S. can't afford to build jails fast enough to house the new convicts; that shorter periods of hard time and creative community service alternatives seem to work as well or better than traditional prison sentences. A focus on these ideas is nothing but a backhanded way for the Democrats to promote their idea that society rather than the criminal is to blame. In your article, Mr. Wicker, you talk a great deal about the exorbitant cost of the current system. It is very strange for a Democrat to worry about the cost of anything, particularly criminal justice, which only costs about $64 Billion per year, as compared to $600 Billion for health care, $300 Billion for defense, and $168 Billion for debt service. If you are worried about cost, why not worry that it costs more to keep a man in jail for a year than to send a student to Harvard for a year. Why worry

CRIME

about the $64 Billion spent to address what, according to survey research, is often the most important issue to Americans. In short, you really wouldn't do it unless you were unctuously trying to use the cost issue to promote your real objective; rehabilitation without punishment.

This is not to say that old fashioned Republican punishment has worked particularly well either. It is based on the fundamental and mistaken concept that there is an important relationship between a crime and the jail time it generates. For any particular crime, it is believed, according to traditional criminology, a convict gets a proportionate amount of time in jail. The more severe the crime, the longer time spent in jail. But it is by no means clear that giving a murderer 15 years, and an armed robber 5, does anything at all other than describe how non-criminals view the relative severity of murder and armed robbery. After 15 years in jail a murderer may come out, 1) grossly unskilled at surviving on the outside, 2) determined to show he has not been broken by the system; that his only asset, his pride, has not been destroyed, 3) very dependant on prison as a psychological reference system and as a provider of food, clothing and shelter, and 4) without family, friends, and neighbors. For whatever the combination of reasons, the longer someone goes to jail the more, it seems, he needs to go back after he gets out. A longer punishment for a more serious crime may cause, rather than prevent, another serious crime.

What is needed, is a not a meaningless punishment that is chronologically related to the crime, but one that can realistically be expected to reduce the probability of the crime, or a crime, being committed again. Alternative sentencing, bootcamps and community service, for example, are now being used on 200-500 thousand people who would otherwise be swelling the prison population by 20 to 50%. But for now these sentences are largely intended for nice criminals like, Michael Dever, and Za Za Gabor and they tend to be so easy and so meaningless as not to be punishment. To be fully effective these programs must be harsher and used against a wider array of prisoners to, 1) instill a social conscience, 2) provide work that is harder than any a convict is likely to encounter on the outside, and 3) provide

REPUBLICANS REDUCE CRIME

convicts with personal habits and skills that will equip them to find and keep employment and personal relationships on the outside. Modern penology accomplishes none of these. According to Mark Corrigan of Brandeis University, "If you go to jail today, you'll see that most offenders are sitting idle, lifting weights or playing basketball." It is no wonder that simply warehousing prisoners makes them and society worse off than before.

Suppose offenders had to work 6.5 days a week, 12 hours per day, collecting garbage, or harvesting crops, or laying asphalt, or stuffing envelopes, or collecting tolls. Suppose they had to attend church every Sunday. They would pay for themselves and then some, to satisfy your concern about money, Mr. Wicker; plus, they would have every incentive not to return to prison. Those who were deemed too violent or who failed at outside work, could be incarcerated in traditional prisons until they earned the right, through work, for a condign, alternative sentence outside the prison walls. If they were forced to run or walk laps to earn their food, and to earn a new opportunity for an alternative sentence, which would eventually lead to release, it would be far more humanitarian to both criminals and victims than a sentence of forced idleness, basketball, and weight lifting.

If creative alternative punishment worked for those in prison, it would also have a tremendous deterrent and humanitarian effect on potential criminals and their victims. It is estimated that only 3% of felonies lead to prison time today. The whole system is greatly overcrowded, and run mostly by Democrats who have great sympathy for criminals. Every possibility to keep criminals out of the system is considered and explored. If the creative alternative punishment system worked well enough so that there was new room in the existing jails for new offenders, and the will to punish was real, the deterrent effect would be enormous.

The humanitarian notion of certain, swift punishment that also rehabilitates is very Republican, but Republicans are not proposing it. Republicans are sticking with the tiny amount of punishment that money and the Democrats will allow; Democrats are sticking with the tiny bit of

CRIME

rehabilitation that the Republicans and Willie Horton will allow. A meaningful combination of both punishment and rehabilitation is not likely to be proposed by a divided gov't. By default and ignorance, voters are closely divided on this and many issues; politicians understandably won't risk an aggressive initiative that could alienate a divided, but hair trigger, electoral constituency.

If intelligent criminal justice reform does emerge, it will come from the Republicans, but only after they have a larger and more stable majority behind them. The Democrats will always migrate toward rehabilitation as a means to coddle criminals who they see as the victims of society. The current system is a harsh tragedy for those millions who are needlessly drawn into it.

MEDIA - BIAS AT ABC NEWS

Dear Peter Jennings and Barry Sarafin,

ABC News likes to advertise that more people get the news from them than "from any other source." If this is true, and there is no reason to doubt it, you, Mr. Jennings, as the nightly news anchor, and, you, Mr. Sarafin, as an ABC correspondent, are perhaps two of the most important political figures in the country. Although you may not like to think of yourselves as politicians and your viewers as constituents, you should consider it. It would be more honest and show more integrity than pretending to do the impossible; namely-to be non-partisan newscasters. If ABC were to start the news each night with a caption titled "The ABC Evening News featuring the Democratically inclined Peter Jennings and his similarly inclined staff," the constant charge of Democratic bias in the media, at least in your media, would be eliminated, and you could rest comfortably knowing that you weren't exploiting and abusing the intended privileges of a free press.

Surveys show that only 5% of Americans can identify the President, Vice President, and their two Senators, and only 30% can identify differences between Democrats and Republicans. Given that the media, and other institutions, have so dramatically failed to educate the electorate, and that viewers have only the vaguest grasp of political ideas, the potential for manipulation is enormous. The insidious way you often inject your Democratic sympathies into news broadcasts is designed to take advantage of this sad situation, with self-centered manipulation, rather than to try to correct it by informing and educating your viewers. Strictly speaking, you are subtly abusing your First Amendment privileges when you promote your political agenda without labeling it as either Democratic or Republican.

MEDIA BIAS

For example, on June 13, 1991, you and Mr. Sarafin did a piece on energy conservation. Mr. Sarafin dug out about 3-4 examples of how Federal money had been spent to develop new technologies that save energy. In each case you pictured the supposedly new technology (one was a window that kept out heat in summer and let heat in during winter) and gave estimates of how much money could be saved in energy consumption relative to the cost of developing the technology. Mr. Sarafin closed his piece, apparently with your consent, by saying that, "the smart investment of tax dollars will keep the energy saving technology coming." At no time did you mention where in the Federal Gov't the money was coming from, who was actually developing the technology, and who was coming up with the estimates about energy savings. The implication was that viewers were to trust you completely, and that gov't merely had to speed up the process 100 fold so that it could solve the U.S.' energy problems once and for all.

At no time during the report did you even use the term Democrat or Republican. Neither of you vaguely alluded to the salient fact that Democrats always believe gov't can solve problems, while Republicans always believe that gov't, generally speaking, either causes problems or makes them worse by trying to solve them. Had you been interested in balance and integrity, you would have closed your report by saying, "and by the way gentle viewer, the report you have just seen is entirely mistaken when viewed by Republicans who have always believed that only a business subject to free market restraints on designing, manufacturing, and selling goods and services, is likely to come up with an effective product that will find a profitable and sustainable market niche." It would have been possible to do a balanced piece on this subject, and most other subjects, by simply making reference to the Republican and Democratic point of view.

None of the three major networks has elected to pursue this approach because, 1) reporters are about 85% Democratic and prefer to push their idealogy even though they feel somewhat compelled, by their modest sense of integrity, to do so without the specifics of labels, 2) many in the media believe they are in hot pursuit of the truth, and if it turns out to be

BIAS AT ABC NEWS

Democratic, which, they feel sure, it mostly does, they should be free to present it as truth, rather than as mere Democratic perspective, 3) the presentation of balanced news would be somewhat more complicated, and more difficult for viewers to follow, and possibly result in lower ratings, 4) reporters are possessed with a condescending sense of gentility which makes them feel that civil war or something similar would erupt if they were to subject Americans to a real dose of the combative nature of democratic, two party politics, 6) news reporters are often intellectually shallow and cling to the belief that history is unfolding according to a set of socialist mathematical truths (thesis, synthesis, and antithesis, etc.) that they can reveal; not along a random pattern that, so far, has defied the limits of mere human perspective, and lastly 7) reporters may be intrinsically fearful that, if they do present balanced news in a way that focuses attention on the real differences between Democrats and Republicans, they will come off making the Democrats look bad. None of these reasons should evoke any sympathy or respect for ABC and its staff.

The difficulty of viewing the news, or any subject from just one perspective, as ABC does, is intellectually insurmountable. This problem is highlighted on college campuses today by those who believe in what is variously called multi-culturalism, or deconstructionism, or poststructurism. Adherents to this thinking, those who run the English Dept. at Duke University, for example, believe that there is no truth or objectivity; that the history, law, and literature of Western Civilization is the personal and biased perspective of dead European racists and sexists, and, as such, should be dismissed by today's more virtuous scholars. If these deconstructionists should be able to build on the already impressive inroads they have made, we can all say goodbye to Western Civilization. Oh well, who really needed it anyway.

In the field of philosophy, existentialism has become dominant and changed the traditional religious view of the meaning of life. And, in economics, monetarism has replaced Keynesianism as the best explanation for the way the economy works. In The USSR, Republican free markets and Boris Yeltzin have gained dominance over Communism and Lennin.

MEDIA

The world has always been, and remains, in ferment. Indeed, Western Civilization, to which all of us owe so much, is the product of such ferment. Certainly an American institution, which ABC is, should not feel compelled to provide the anti-American and anti-Western deconstructionist perspective, but it should recognize that the ferment between Democrats and Republicans is well within acceptable cultural limits and essential to the growth and well being of the country.

The ABC, Peter Jennings, Barry Sarafin, report, on how gov't financed research on energy saving windows has saved tons of energy dollars, could have been followed by or intermingled with a Republican capitalist report describing that, 1) the millions of dollars in savings was really fictitious, 2) the windows in question were too costly to justify the purchase price; so nobody buys them, 3) all major replacement window companies including, Pella, Anderson, and Acorn have developed and enhanced the energy efficiency of their windows, without gov't money, and in harmony with what the market will absorb and, 4) the gov't is not in the window business; knows nothing about it, or how to invest in it, and 5) this is one of many examples of how Republican capitalism can yield a better result than Democratic socialism.

Such a balanced view of the issue would have put it in a meaningful perspective or context. Viewers would have learned a little about, windows and energy, gov't and industry spending on windows, Socialism and Capitalism, Democrats and Republicans, and how to vote. And most importantly, they would have been empowered to develop an understanding of the context in which issues exist. Viewers would have become a part of the dynamic history they are living in. The possibility of a fast paced and meaningful Democracy cannot be realized if the media shuts out and dulls its audience with one unlabeled, but Democratic perspectives on each issue. The result of what the media is giving the U.S., is a kind of slow motion confusion that leaves voters alienated, disinterested, and confused; a divided gov't, like the one currently in Washington, is the result.

Two nights after the energy report, Mr. Jennings, you hosted an hour long show on WNET (Public Television) about health care in America. It

BIAS AT ABC NEWS

was the kind of show that was so blatantly in favor of Democratic socialism that even ABC\Capital Cities Inc. did not let you broadcast it on their airwaves. I have to assume that you tried to air it, or would have wanted to air it, before the relatively huge ABC audience, but were prevented by your sense or ABC's sense of decency. Again, you handled the socialized medicine report in much the same way as the socialized windows report, but this time you spent a whole hour making your biases much more apparent. And you did it about an important subject, health care, that currently consumes $2500 per year for each person in America.

Your show had one purpose and one purpose only; it was to promote socialized medicine in America, just like the kind you have in your native Canada. Throughout the entire show, though, although you went through the entire history of the attempt to bring socialized medicine to the U.S., you did not mention that Republicans always opposed it, while Democrats have always favored it. Somehow you and many of the others in the major media, have established some bizarre set of principals which enables you to feel free to support any piece of Democratic legislation, while masquerading as objective newsmen, so long as you don't precisely label it as Democratic. Such labeling would cross the bounds of democratic propriety and create a new obligation to present both labels and both points of view; Democrats seem to sense that if this were to happen, it would spell the beginning of the end for them.

At one point in your show about socialized medicine you got to a place where it became impossible to go much further without explaining why it is that America lacked something that you were presenting as the most obvious thing since sliced bread. You didn't want to tell the truth by saying, American doesn't have national health care because Republicans know that gov't will foul health care up the same way or worse than it fouls up the Post Office, or the current health care system which, between Medicare, Medicare, the Veterans Administration, heavily regulated private insurers, and absurd malpractice laws, is virtually socialized, anyway. Instead, after you detailed all the problems with the current, virtually socialized system,

MEDIA

you said, "when problems get this serious, people inevitably turn to the gov't for help." To a Republican, with National health care you would get the warmth of the IRS; the efficiency of the Post Office, and the cost containment of the Pentagon. You seem to be a socialist true believer right down to your socks, Mr. Jennings, and as such it didn't even occur to you to present the position of the Republican Party which, by the way, is, in some ways, the majority party in the U.S. If you had said, "when problems get this serious Republicans look to get the gov't out of the way so they can be solved," the show would have had, theoretically, a neutral but very, very democratic impact.

Of course, Mr Jennings, this would not have been remotely acceptable to you, as you have little interest in promoting the democratic process at the expense of the Democratic Party.

EDUCATION - FREEDOM OR CONTINUED DECLINE

Dear Liberal Democrats,

As you know well, when President Bush campaigned for the office he now holds, he declared that he would be the "Education President;" now that he has finally unveiled his plan, many of you have written about it in a very critical way. The plan was politically masterful in that some aspects of it actually appeared to embody Democratic principals about the importance of big gov't and, accordingly, much of the criticism was substantially dulled. Even so, the same old divisions between Democrats and Republicans were readily apparent as regards Bush's education initiative, which is currently stalled in the Democratic Congress.

Coretta Scott-King, a women for whom all Americans have a great deal of sympathy and respect, but whose politics is extremely liberal and deeply rooted in the 1960's, was perhaps the most definitive in her distaste for the plan. Her primary objection was to the voucher like system whereby parents would choose, among competing schools, each of which had a somewhat different orientation and emphasis, the school they wanted their children to attend. Her rationale was that parents are often poorly educated themselves and therefore not able to make a good choice. Her rationale, which is common throughout the Democratic Party, cleanly and neatly revealed the basis for most Democratic thinking, which is, to be quick and accurate, as follows: people in gov't are smart, and the rest of us are stupid and in need of gov't supervision.

Thinking about the implications of her noisome attitudes is truly not a pleasing job. Suppose the Pilgrims of Plymouth Rock and the John Smiths of Jamestown had decided they wanted to find a country where smart people could make the right decisions for them. Suppose that John Adams and Thomas Jefferson had decided that England was a very wise old country

EDUCATION

with the wisdom to best manage the Colonies. Suppose Abraham Lincoln had decided that blacks were better off living under better educated, white owners. Supposed 19th and 20th Century immigrants had elected to stay in the lands of their birth, believing that their mismanaged and totalitarian governments would serve them better than the uncertainty of freedom in America. Suppose Woodrow Wilson and FDR had felt that the freedom of Europeans was not important during the world wars. Suppose Gorbachev had felt that his people were too stupid for freedom, and the responsibility that comes with it. Suppose that President Bush thought that the people of Kuwait weren't smart enough to be free them from Saddam Hussein.

Democrats don't understand that freedom was never a guarantee that good things would happen to those who received it, although good things always seemed to happen to free people, but instead it was a passport to wherever a person's courage, and hopefully his religious values, would take him.

America's cultural ancestors, the Pilgrims, Puritans and Calvinists, to name three, undertook grave risks to found this country because freedom meant more to them than life itself; had they sought a guarantee, they never would have set foot on or near a 17th Century sailboat. That freedom has worked out so well for all those who have suffered to achieve it, is testimony to the wisdom contained within each human being that can find personal and societal expression only when finally free from the domination of gov't. This is the noble sentiment, that brought the Pilgrims to America; that Patrick Henry echoed when he said, "give me liberty or give me death," and that modern New Englander's rejoice in when they adopt a state slogan that says, "live free or die." Indeed, this thinking is at the heart of the Republican Party; it explains why patriotism comes so naturally to them, and why they rail so much against big gov't. In this very critical sense, Democrats care little for freedom; instead they want guarantees from the state on everything from education to health care to social security. To them, freedom is that which is given by the state; they care not at all for the lessons of history which indicate that once a state is empowered, it can take, as well as give freedom, and its tendency has always been to take far more than it gives.

FREEDOM OR CONTINUED DECLINE

Moreover, Democrats care not that what the state gives an individual, he cannot then give himself; this is why modern, Democratically controlled ghettos grow, while previous ghettos shrunk and disappeared in short order.

The United States is a country, unique in history, that has singularly defined itself with an unprecedented belief in the dignity, goodness, and wisdom of the individual. With this belief the 13 Colonies reversed 10,000 years of history and in less than 200 years surpassed all that had become before. The U.S. became the moral and economic savior of the world based on its belief in the sanctity, wisdom, and self-sufficiency of the individual. This is precisely the thing that separates the U.S. from China and Russia, countries that live generations behind the U.S., countries whose gov't planners would have even less idea of where they were going or what they were doing, and be still further behind, if they could not copy basic ideas from Western free markets and cultures.

Blacks are a unique immigrant group in the U.S. in that they started out as slaves; this meant that they never had the responsibility to manage all aspects of their lives as other immigrant groups before them had done. This is the feature of their history that has made freedom even more problematic for them than most other immigrant groups, but it is by no means an excuse to deny them their freedom. Sadly, the road to freedom and independence for all Americans, particularly Black Americans, is being obstructed by Scott-King and other Democrats who have a basic distrust of freedom and a patronizing contempt for their own constituencies. Scott-King ought to decide exactly when and if today's parents get to be "free at last, free at last" as her husband so passionately wanted. Scary though it may be, freedom is what propelled the U.S. to a rate of development that was unequaled anywhere in the world. Constantly looking to gov't, in this case to parent the parents, is not a solution for someone who believes in basic American values.

According to a September 1991 poll done by the Gallup organization, it is poor blacks who want "choice" the most. Their children are the ones who attend the worst ghetto schools, and understandably, they want a choice that

EDUCATION

will get their kids moving in a positive direction. According to the survey, 70% of blacks favor choice, but only 62% of whites. Further, in Oregon, after a recent referendum, a higher percentage of people with income under $25,000 were in favor of "choice" than in the over $45,000 income group.

Scott-King goes on to worry that competing schools would waste valuable educational dollars on marketing and advertising. She does not realize that all products need marketing and advertising as a matter of course so that prospective buyers will know that they are available and of high quality. Without advertising and marketing, whether word of mouth or TV, no good product would exist because few people would know about it; the smaller quantity then consumed would be more costly for the manufacturer to produce and thereby affordable to fewer consumers. King may believe that people, being incapable of functioning in a free environment, would just be tricked by the advertising.

Then she worries that schools which didn't perform well in the new competitive world would victimize their students by somehow keeping students against their will. This seems silly given that the basic purpose of "choice" is to provide parents with the choice to take their children out of poor schools and put them in what they think are better schools. "Choice" is far better than being stuck in the same poor school forever, which is what happens now throughout America, precisely because there is no "choice" and no competition between schools to make them better schools.

Next, King goes on to deride the Bush plan because it doesn't provide for enough new education money. She pays no attention to already overburdened and beleaguered taxpayers, and a huge Federal deficit that makes new spending a political and practical impossibility. In typical Democratic fashion, she feels deeply that more spending is necessary, if only as a manifestation of gov't caring, but she says not one word about exactly how, in the case of education, it would help things, and why increased spending has never worked in the past. She doesn't mention that education is just one of many areas where Democrats would love to keep taxing and spending.

Next, King goes on to worry that because most education money comes

FREEDOM OR CONTINUED DECLINE

from local and state tax collectors, there would be a great disparity between per capita spending in rich and poor regions. Republicans do not dispute this, neither do they feel that the Federal Gov't was formed to redistribute income and thus destroy incentive as happens(ed) in China and Russia. There is a silver lining as regards money, though, which indicates that money may very well not be the answer anyway; that the lack of it doesn't hold people back today anymore than it held back all the impoverished millions who arrived as immigrants over the last 150 years.

Everyone recalls the stories about how Abraham Lincoln learned to read and write by walking miles to get books; by reading late into the night without adequate lighting; by using the back of a shovel or the dirt floor as a tablet. Even today, education is much more about attitude than money. The Democrats will always scream for more, even when none exists; they will always point out the disparity between rich and poor, but they will never point out that in Utah where per capita education spending is $2,571, students test better than in New Jersey where per capita spending is 300% higher at $7,571. Neither will they point out that in Chicago, private parochial school spending ($2300 per student) is less than half of what it is in the public schools, and the results are better. Those die-hard Democrats who then argue that the public schools get worse students should note that the drop out rate in public schools is many times higher. More over, Catholic school, which are often located in ghetto's, simple do not regard ghetto life as an excuse for general disorder and poor results. And, public school spending has gone up in recent years, despite Republican efforts to prevent it, and results have gone down. In New York State, which is typical, spending went up 51% between 1982 and 1987, while the percentage of students graduating, to pick one important index, went down.

The disparity in education spending among the states is something that constantly alerts us to the problem the gov't has in establishing an exact causal relationship between money and results. With one national policy, the data to establish a relationship between spending and education , or the lack of one, would be very scarce; bureaucrats would merely be guessing at

EDUCATION

what the correct spending levels were. With competition among the states, and then hopefully among the schools within the states, the market price for a certain quality and quantity of education would constantly be evaluated and set by the free market, rather than fixed at the wrong level by gov't bureaucrats.

Jesse Jackson argues along the same lines as Coretta Scott-King, only he is perhaps even more expansive. For him it is a systems issue, not just an educational one. He wants more money for prenatal care, infant care, Head Start, school breakfast and lunch, food programs for women, infants and children (WIC), Native American Education, and child-care block grant programs. Jesse Jackson never saw a Federal program he didn't like. He fought so long and so hard and so admirably for these programs that he cannot be expected to have the capacity to re-evaluate them after watching them fail for 25 years. Still, being such a passionate and decent man, he is very hard to resist.

As a tentative concession to reality, Jackson now will frequently tag on a few lines to his speeches and writings to the effect that people are responsible for their own fate; that they can't count on the Federal Gov't to bail them out all the time. In this case he says, "We need parents who will turn off the television each night, teachers who will teach with passion, and students with a revived sense of personal responsibility, who may be behind, but will run faster to catch up."

This all sounds very good and very Republican, but because Jackson, like most Democrats, is not really committed to the American notion of individual responsibility, he won't let us see the plan, mostly because such a plan doesn't exist, and can't exist alongside his perpetual calls for total gov't responsibility. His bizarre courting of socialist dictators, all around the world, reveals more of his true sentiments, than a few gratuitous lines about individual responsibility which are now tossed into his speeches.

Republicans believe that individual responsibility from students, teachers, and parents will come from the competition and choice which Jackson and Scott-King reject. Teachers will compete with one another to get results, just

FREEDOM OR CONTINUED DECLINE

the way business managers do. Those who succeeded would gain more power, influence, and money, in order to identify and expand their success. Teachers, like businessmen, athletes, musicians, doctors, dancers, and Japanese, would get to know the pressure and pleasure of always having to do better. Some schools might copy the Japanese model, others might focus a short four hour school day on just Math and English so that students who needed to, could work in the afternoon. Some might stress religious values, others might stress vocational skills. Nobody knows what schools and what curriculums would emerge, anymore than they know what music styles or personal computer operating systems will emerge. Where choice has been implemented, it has been done in gradual stages and to varying degrees in accordance with results as they became apparent. What is known, is that ultimately the new system will be a dynamic, competitive one that will naturally explore new, higher and different boundaries, rather than drift aimlessly downward like the current socialist system which is liked so much by Jackson, Scott-King, and the Democrats.

Under "choice" parents might get their tax money handed back to them, perhaps in the form of a tuition voucher, and consequently be very encouraged and enthusiastic to spend it wisely on behalf of their children. They would carefully monitor progress in preparation for the next spending decision. Parents would have to think about which school, curriculum, and teachers were best for their children. Currently, parents have no choice and little involvement; they don't educate their children, the state does it for them. Who would trust the state to select for them, their automobile? Yet, as regards something much more expensive and critical, the cultural and academic education of our children, we somehow have let control slip away to the Democrats and the state.

When parents and teachers have a better attitude, due to the "choice" environment, students will naturally follow along as their world is shaped largely by well meaning parents and teachers. A student will always be favorably inclined toward a situation where he can perform well, both intellectually and psychologically. Choice in the marketplace will create more alternatives for teachers and students so that the likelihood of a child and teacher finding the situation in which they can be the most effective, will go up markedly.

EDUCATION

Competition among teachers and merit pay, a basic Republican capitalist concept, similar to what is used in most areas outside of the Democratically controlled education system, would certainly attract and produce better, more inspiring teachers, who would in turn produce more educated students. In the state of New Jersey, a class of 30 students represents a revenue stream of $227,000. If this money was largely paid to the teachers as salary, teaching would instantly be among the most respected and popular professions in the country, attracting many of the most talented people in the country, from a pool that would literally be thousands of times larger than it is now. Effective teaching not only requires a well educated teacher, but a teacher who can motivate, attract, lead, and appeal to students. John F. Kennedy had an enormous capacity to attract and lead people; it is that capacity to one degree or another that allows a truly superior teacher, to teach or govern her students. All of us can look back on our school days and recall one particular teacher who may have meant more than all the others combined. To consistently get these kinds of teachers in the school system, in large numbers, we need a competitive pro-choice system that is designed to attract them. The current, system makes no provisions for this.

Those who doubt that spending $7500 per student in public schools is mostly waste that otherwise could go to teachers, should consider that in NYC the number of school administrators in the public system out numbers those in the private system by a ratio of one thousand (1000) to one (1) on a per capita basis, and the private, largely Catholic schools get much better results. Of course, it might be expected that NYC would have the worst numbers in the country since it is virtually at the geographic heart of liberalism. A look at another city might provide more representative numbers. Take Chicago for example, its public school system has 390 administrators per 100,000 students while its private parochial schools have 26 per 100,000 students, and guess which schools get better results? The Republican idea of "choice" in the nation's schools is a very concrete and very actionable one that will lead to improvement without increasing the already exorbitant cost of education. The Democrats have only vague gov't plans to spent even more money in support of the badly failing status quo.

ENERGY CRISIS - SOLVED BY THE REPUBLICANS

Dear Coretta Scott King & Herbert Rowen,

I have just finished the articles that you both wrote to criticize George Bush's energy proposals. Both of you came to exactly the same conclusion, that now is the time to adopt firm measures that will reduce U.S. dependance on foreign oil. The Reagan years, and now the Bush years, have not been satisfactory to you as regards energy policy because little or nothing has been done by Washington to promote energy conservation.

Republicans and Democrats divide fairly predictably on this issue, although both of you fail to present the debate in a context that will enable your readers to make an informed choice between the two. Democrats believe that most things of importance must be handled by the Federal Gov't because people, when left on their own, simply won't do the right thing. The best, brightest and most moral people, they believe, often work in Washington where their wisdom can be used to instruct and direct the remaining citizenry. Further, they feel it is in the nature of things that certain economies of scale and efficiencies are achieved through centralized management from Washington.

Conversely, Republicans feel that the basic religious foundation of American society; the firm political restraints imposed by the Constitution, and the discipline imposed by an essentially capitalist economic system, is sufficient regulation to achieve the best possible energy policy.

It would seem that environmentalism has become a major cause among Democrats mostly by default. Without a war to oppose; without other domestic problems with obvious Democratic solutions, many Democrats have no outlet for their exuberance; for their need to see collective gov't

ENERGY CRISIS

action which can score quick and decisive blows against the forces of evil. As if to stress the importance of your subject, Ms. Scott-King, you start by saying, "oil dependency is the leading cause of the global environmental crisis that threatens the very survival of this and future generations." Meanwhile, Democratic Sen. Gore claims in his new book that global warming is "the most serious threat we have ever faced" even though there is no scientific consensus that it even exists. Republicans shutter to think about what would happen if Democrats were set free to attack environmental problems in the 90's the way they were set free to attack poverty in the 60's.

To stress how good the timing is for gov't to mysteriously end U.S. dependence on foreign oil, you cite Ms. Scott-King, a survey conducted by the "Union of Concerned Scientists." You don't say what the scientists are concerned about; you leave it to your readers to conclude that they are concerned about the same thing you are; namely, building a case that environmental disaster may strike tomorrow, and that now the timing is right to do something about it. Without much pretense that the USC is impartial, you cite their study which shows that 75% of respondents supported a reduction in demand for fossil fuels and 80% wanted to increase auto fuel economy to 40 mpg by the year 2000. It must be assumed that the questions were very misleading and designed to evoke the desired response. If the question were phrased in a more complete way to include whether respondents would support a reduction in fossil fuel use if it would cost them $1200 per year, the number in favor would probably drop from 75% to about 20% Further, the number that did favor a reduction would then have to be reduced still lower because it is far easier and politically correct to tell a researcher that you will spent $1200 than to actually do it.

Next, you indicate that U.S. dependence on foreign oil is a threat to world peace. Your reasoning apparently was that if the U.S. did not need foreign oil, it wouldn't have needed Kuwait or Saudi Arabia, and could have turned a deaf ear on the rape and plunder. This is a queer attitude from a person who is generally regarded as a champion of the necessitous. A quick look through history will show that it is very difficult to predict where or when war will come. As a general principal, though, it is safe to say that economic dependency on other nations and other people, encourages harmony by minimizing the inclination to act on mere ideological differences.

SOLVED BY THE REPUBLICANS

If it was just dependency on Arab oil that provoked the U.S. to rescue Kuwait, we needn't feel bad about it. If it was our primal addiction to rock and roll music that provoked the largest charity concert ever to help feed starving children in Africa, we needn't feel bad. If our dependency on a buffer between the U.S. and totalitarianism provoked us to rescue Western Europe during World Wars I & II, we needn't feel bad. It is important that charity happen; not that we belittle it by identifying what are often partially self-serving motives.

If a worker is dependant on his boss, and a boss dependant on his worker, then they both are forced to get along. The world of work, forces civilized coping skills on people that they would not learn without dependency. If it is true that people who need people are the luckiest, then it is also true that nations that need nations are the luckiest. The complex array of dependencies between Arabs, Jews, and the rest of the world is, by and large, a peaceful force. Before technology encouraged the regular and intimate dependencies that exist today between nations, there was certainly no shortage of war.

Next, you say that the Gulf War will go down in history as the Oil War; the implication being that if the U.S. cuts its dependance on oil, the possibility of future wars would go away. For a host of reasons, almost none of which are connected to avoiding future wars, Europe and Japan have already done this by imposing enormous taxes on the use of fossil fuels, to the point where gas is more than double the cost of what it is in the States.

Not surprisingly though, despite far lower per capita consumption levels, both Europe and Japan are more dependant on foreign oil than the U.S. European taxes marginally reduce consumption and marginally improve air quality, but perhaps the major affect is to reduce demand in Europe and Japan, and thereby increase supply and lower prices in the U.S. So then, the high cost of oil in Europe and Japan may actually reduce the incentive for American entrepreneurs to bear the cost of finding alternatives to the relatively inexpensive U.S. gasoline. As always, it is very difficult to predict the ramifications of governmental actions that tamper with incredibly complex free markets.

ENERGY CRISIS

The Arabs are businessmen; like all businessmen they survive by keeping their customers dependant on their product; they will always lower the price enough to prevent customers from switching to alternative fuels. If the U.S. were to go ahead anyway and pay the premium cost of alternative fuels, the premium would probably be 100% wasted. Imagine if the U.S. had imposed a European style, $1.00 per gallon tax on gasoline back in the early 1970's, when the first oil crises hit. At that point Democrats completely abandoned the little faith they had in the free market and urged massive gov't intervention to make the nasty problem go away. At 500 gallons per car per year, the tax in the United States on gasoline between 1972 and 1991 would have been well over $20 Trillion, and it would have all been wasted since the market drove the price back down to pre-crisis levels anyway. The cost of the Gulf War ($50 Billion) was trivial by comparison to that of a gas tax. Besides, the cost of the war was mostly picked up by U.S. allies, and inflated to include the costs that would have been incurred anyway by personnel and equipment employed by the military prior to the war. Now that the war has been fought, the U.S. is closer than ever before to Kuwait and Saudi Arabia, and it is very likely that the supply of oil is more secure and plentiful than ever before. This may be the costliest time ever to cut dependance on foreign oil by dreaming up new gov't schemes.

You go on to say that there is little in the President's bill to discourage imports. In standard Democratic fashion, you would have us believe this is due to Republican ignorance or oversight, rather than their policy of using the free market pricing mechanism to regulate supply and demand. Republicans understand that the price of any commodity is a reflection of all the factors affecting that commodity. In the case of oil, for example, the price is a largely a function of how much oil is known to be in the ground, how much is left to be discovered, and the stability of the delivery system as determined primarily by politics. If, in the extreme case, the supply was noticeably diminished, something that is not happening as Democratic experts told us it would, and political instability rose in the oil producing nations, we would expect gasoline prices to go up. Assuming the situation persisted, alternative fuels like ethanol, perhaps, would soon become

SOLVED BY THE REPUBLICANS

cheaper than gasoline and a new ethanol industry would begin to grow. This is how the U.S. switched from wood to coal to oil to natural gas. To force the change sooner than the free market dictates is to throw money away. The free market takes into account all the variables that affect supply and demand, at each daily price fixing, with far greater precision than would be possible by a few arbitrary pricing decisions made by Democratic bureaucrats in Washington. Democrats refuse to recognize the greater wisdom of the marketplace because it conflicts with their own pretentious vision of themselves being in control.

While your article, Mr Rowen, is decidedly more academic in nature than Scott-King's, it mirrors the same sentiments exactly. You want conservation now, and you want a whopping gas tax to get it, even though money is especially scarce due to the recession, particularly among those in your natural constituency. Beyond the gas tax, you want the average milage per gallon on cars sold in the United States raised from the current 27.5 mpg to 40 mpg, even though the American auto industry is more recessed than the economy as a whole.

In the case of the gas tax and the mpg standard, it is striking and particularly Democratic of you not to present a rationale to explain why or how the benefit of the proposed action is sufficient to justify the cost. It is always up to Republicans to say, "these are the full set of ramifications from the action you propose, and it seems that the cost is greater than the value of the solution." If you were to sit down with a group of economists to gain a thorough understanding of the actions you propose, you would quickly find out that it is virtually impossible to determine with any accuracy what the actual affects would be. Nevertheless, Democrats persist with their simplistic schemes to beat the Republican free market because it's the easiest way to think and often the easiest way to appeal to action oriented voters. The mpg standard sounds nice during a four day war in the Middle East, but it will mean smaller, more dangerous cars. Moreover, it will further strain the already depressed domestic auto industry in favor of the Japanese who have always been better at making small cars. How does a Democrat know that his standard is better than the free market standard.

ENERGY CRISIS

When bureaucratic gov't does get involved, as in agriculture, mail, or health care, the result is often disaster.

You close your article in an emotional flurry by saying, "But how many times does George Bush think the American people will be willing to replicate Desert Storm, with its cost in lives and physical resources, merely to assure that Americans can drive their gas guzzlers on cheap gasoline? That's the issue Bush needed to address and didn't."

God knows what point you think you are making here. As mentioned earlier, if Americans give up their gas guzzlers for little cars like the ones Europeans and Japanese drive, this does not mean that the U.S will be less dependant on foreign oil, anymore than Europe and Japan are less dependant. And, it would seem obvious that the Gulf War made the supply of oil safer and more plentiful than ever, not to mention that it may bring peace, with all the attendant global benefits, to the age old conflict in the region between Arabs and Jews.

Moreover, Americans can reasonably plan never to replicate Dessert Storm again. There is simply no reason for you to worry that it will become a regular affair. Both of you, without saying so directly, are asking for trillions of dollars for energy independence, even though your primary constituencies, poor black people, care about these issues very little, as compared to the more basic issues they worry about on a daily basis. Unbelievably, it is for your primary constituencies that you reserve your really big gov't programs. All of which goes to show that Democrats regard politics, the way a child regards a toy store. When they leave the store (after the war is over and the Democrats have calmed down) they quickly forget the thing for which, just a moment ago, they were willing to move heaven and earth.

JUDGE THOMAS-A MAN WHO SCARES THE DEMOCRATS

Dear Anthony Lewis,

Your recent article about the Supreme Court, distributed by The N.Y. Times News Service, was deplorable in the way it confused the difference between Democrats and Republicans. It is hard to believe that such a distinguished editorial columnist and Court reporter, could be so misleading and mistaken about the most basic aspects of the American political system. The impending confirmation of Judge Thomas, which will create an even more solid and long lasting Republican Court, must be giving you and your Democratic friends such a heartache that it is blurring your normal inclinations to be generally decent and forthright about your advocacy of Democratic causes.

Your first conclusion is that the Bush administration is being deceitful by saying it wants a conservative Court, while it applauds the current court, largely of their own making, which is "statist" or non-conservative. According to you, the court is statist because it has build up the centralized power of the President.

You must certainly understand that the Republican Bush administration practices a conservative political philosophy which means, practically speaking, that they want to limit the power of the gov't and thereby enhance the power of the individual. This concept makes Republicans the primary guardian of basic American values such as freedom and individual liberty. When Bush appoints a Republican like Judge Thomas, he is doing so in the belief that Thomas will use his tenure on the Court to generally limit the power of the gov't; this is something that may be facilitated by an in increase in the power of the Presidency. However, an increase in the power of the Presidency, has nothing to do with the overall power of gov't, something Republicans always and consistently seek to diminish .

CLARENCE THOMAS

If the Administration supports Court decisions that build the influence of the President and the Executive branch of gov't, it is not being deceitful, statist or inconsistent, as you claim. Any increased influence in the executive branch, as long as it comes at the expense of another branch of gov't, leaves the power of the entire gov't, over the individual, at precisely the same level. Conservatives don't really have a philosophy about the relative power of the three branches of gov't; they are preoccupied with reducing the power of the entire gov't.

In the case of President Bush, there has been a decided attempt to wrest influence from the Democratically controlled Congress with the help of a increasingly Republican Supreme Court. With the Federal Gov't evenly divided between Democrats and Republicans, it's not surprising that the separate branches of gov't are fighting with one another to achieve the majority power base that a divided electorate will not give them.

Having based your article on a grossly mistaken notion, each argument you make thereafter becomes increasingly more strained. In the second and third paragraph you say, "it is an increasingly statist court for use to make end runs around Congress, the opposite of what the conservatives who wrote the Constitution had in mind; the opposite of what conservatives wanted through most of history."

Firstly, it was very nice to hear you admit that it was conservatives who wrote the Constitution. This should help you to understand why it is that conservative Republicans are the ones who feel the greater connection to American values and, accordingly, are able to portray themselves as more patriotic. Secondly, a Court cannot be statist because it is only one branch of the state. A Court does not make the gov't more statist by increasing the power of one branch at the expense of another. You acknowledge this, without realizing it, when you note that the Court is making "end runs around Congress" and redistributing influence or power to the Executive Branch.

Next, seeming genuinely impressed with yourself, you note that the Court being created by the Bush conservatives, being statist, is not

A MAN WHO SCARES THE DEMOCRATS

really conservative according to historical definitions. This is by no means true. During the Democratic Roosevelt Administration in the 1930's, to pick an arbitrary but distant starting point, the conservative Court was very much opposed to the New Deal which sought to vastly increase the power of the state in a misguided effort to combat the Great Depression. Today, the definition of conservative remains the same, as Judge Thomas made very clear when he spoke with great skepticism about the ability of the state to improve the lives of people in general and black people in particular. If the current Court is willing to enhance the Executive Branch, it is important to remember that it is done with the expectation that the power will be used to diminish the power of all branches of gov't while maintaining, with consummate political skill, the relative ascendancy of the Republican, Executive Branch, over the Democratic, Legislative Branch.

Indeed, the Republican Bush administration has opposed virtually every legislative bill the Democrats have proposed or thought of proposing, from civil-rights to health insurance, because these bills rely on the power of the state, rather than the individual, to solve problems. Statism, the enhancement of gov't authority at the expense of individual liberty, is the philosophical heart of the Democratic Party, and is something that real Democrats have always supported. That you are against statism, Mr. Lewis, shows what a confused Democrat you are, or how willing you are to confuse your readers.

In what seems to be an unrelated argument, you note that the much revered constitutional concept, separation of powers, has been "tilted out of recognition" now that so much power is concentrated in the Executive branch. Firstly, why should you care, given that the Constitution, as you admit, was written by conservatives with whom you have little sympathy. I guess you are trying to frighten your readers by suggesting that one of the most critical foundations behind the Constitution has been shaken by recent Republican actions. When James Madison wrote in FEDERALIST NO.47, "No political truth is certainly of greater intrinsic value, or is stamped with the authority of more enlightened patrons of liberty, than that...the accumulation of all powers, legislative, executive and judicial, in the same hands....may justly be pronounced the very definition of tyranny," he was thinking of a very different situation than the one faced today. Today's situation is a fully anticipated and very constitutional one, in that it is the obvious result of successive Republican Presidents who have constitutionally exercised their authority by nominating successive Republican justices.

The separation of powers doctrine would be threatened if one branch of gov't lost a basic and intrinsic function; not because two branches become populated by people with similar philosophies, as is the case with the current Judicial and Executive Branches. You are trying very hard to find a major constitutional problem where there is none, rather than face the fact that your party has an increasingly limited following and, therefore, less and less control over gov't. Please keep in mind that there is nothing in the Constitution to prevent the whole electorate and the whole gov't from becoming Republican. If this were to happen, it would have no affect on the gov't being able to still operate in harmony with the separation of powers doctrine.

The separation of powers doctrine would be threatened, for example, if the famous Marbury v. Madison case were overturned so the Judiciary no longer had the power of judicial review; i.e., the authority to examine laws for basic constitutional consistency. If the Senate was no longer empowered to override a Presidential veto, this would also represent a diminution of Congressional power that would markedly change the separation of powers doctrine.

In Rust v. Sullivan, a very recent case that you use as your best example, the Bush administration was given new authority to interpret a 1970 law, which previously had been interpreted to authorize the use of federal funds to instruct women about the availability of abortions, so that now, information about abortion could no longer be proffered at Federal expense. The basic balance which enables the Congress to write bills and provide funding for them, while the Executive branch interprets and then administers the bills, was not altered. It should be noted that if bills are subject to interpretation by either the Judicial or Executive branch it

A MAN WHO SCARES THE DEMOCRATS

is mostly because Congress did not write them precisely enough. This is something the Democratic Congress often does rather than face their constituencies, who are often less liberal than they are, having left a precise paper trail that details their exact positions. When Democratic Congressional language is finally interpreted by another branch of gov't, which is controlled by Republicans, the Democrats scream like petulant children, rather than admit that their language was unclear or cowardly, or that they didn't have enough control, even in the Congress, to get the language they wanted.

About Rust v. Sullivan, you go on to say, "it was a novel executive interpretation of the law, not easy to justify in the words of the statute, but the Supreme Court upheld the regulation." Forgive me Mr. Lewis, but when you write that, it can only be concluded that you were writing without having read the statute or the Court's decision. Section 1008 of the statute says, "none of the funds appropriated under this subchapter shall be used in programs where abortion is a method of family planning." It seems very obvious that when a doctor at Planned Parenthood Inc., who is being paid with Title X funds, advises a client with an unwanted pregnancy that he can arrange an abortion, as a method of family planning, he is clearly in violation of the statute. You could not possibly present a basis on which it might be concluded that the Supreme Court interpreted the statute in a "novel" way.

You go on to say that the court, in Rust v. Sullivan, established the "remarkable doctrine that whenever the gov't aids an institution it can dictate what anyone there can say." It is really not so remarkable when you think about it, and then realize that the Court often has to balance contradictions, in this case, Freedom of Speech (established by the Bill of Rights) against the govt's right to make a value judgement favoring childbirth over abortion, and the implementation of that judgement by allocation of public funds (established by Maher v. Roe). The Court balanced the two positions by pointing out that a person can preserve his free speech right to talk about abortion by merely talking about it when he is not on the payroll of a gov't that represents people who generally oppose abortion. This is similar to saying you can yell "fire" any time you want, so long as it's not in a crowded movie theater; i.e., an unreasonable time or place.

CLARENCE THOMAS

When a Democrat on the Judiciary committee asked Clarence Thomas whether Rust v. Sullivan meant that the gov't could dictate what books were on the shelves at libraries that received Federal funds, he probably should have said, "It all depends. If a public library elects to stock one book favorable to Hitler, it would seemingly be well tolerated under the First Amendment, but if the library chooses to stock thousands of such books in order to become a Hitler advocate, then a natural law would exist to enable us to make a value judgement that transcends the First Amendment." Rust v. Sullivan follows precedent nicely and does not open up any remarkable new doors as you would have us believe, Mr. Lewis.

The 1971 Griggs case was very similar to Rust v. Sullivan in that the Executive Branch, in its capacity as administrator, again re-interpreted a vague statute, to the chagrin of Democrats, and was supported by the Court. To imply that this shift of authority to the Executive Branch represents a great constitutional crisis, is to cower from the real truth, which is that the Democrats in Congress no longer have the clout or courage to write and enact laws to their liking. The real solution for the Democrats is to go out and elect a few more Democrats; not to pretend that the increasingly Republican majority, is fostering a constitutional crisis by rolling back some of the failed programs that are left over from the old glory days of the Democratic Party.

You inexplicably go on to mention how embarrassed the Republicans should be by their predecessors's behavior in the 1930's, at which time they resisted executive interpretation of general legislative mandates by the then Democratic Executive Branch. There is really no poignant historical irony here, just an example of the Republicans legitimately trying to maximize their influence in accordance within constitutional provisions. The difference between then and now is that now the Democrats are being deeply disingenuous by pretending that their current problems have to do more with a Republican created, constitutional crises than with their lack of popularity with the electorate.

A MAN WHO SCARES THE DEMOCRATS

What is very ironic, though, is that you would dare mention the Supreme Court of the 1930's, during an article in which you are trying so hard to present the Democrats as reverent constitutional servants who wouldn't ever think of challenging the Framer's intent. Of course, nothing could be further from the truth, in the 30's, FDR, the Democratic President, didn't like the Republican Court so he proposed that every Republican judge over 70 was too old and should have a younger Democratic judge to "assist" him. It was a totally outrageous and unprecedented attempt to subvert and intimidate the court. The FDR plan failed to pack the court with Democrats, but it was sufficiently intimidating to force the Court to propitiate. To this day the incident serves as a potent reminder of the lengths to which the Democrats will go to promote their heartfelt, self-righteous and very mistaken idealogy. In your case Mr. Lewis, you are willing to invent a constitutional crisis where none exists; in the case of FDR, he was willing to subvert the court merely because there were too many Republicans on it to suit him.

Of course, when FDR was critical of the court in 1936, and when Sen. Joseph Biden, chairman of the Senate Judiciary Committee, was critical of Clarence Thomas in 1991, the words Democrat and Republican were never spoken. This is because, as always, America is deathly afraid that its sense of community will be destroyed if it acknowledges that partisan politics, rather than a higher make believe truth, is at the heart of our interest in the Court and the CIA and all of our other institutions. The high point of the Thomas hearings came at the end, when Sen. Howell Heflin, a Democrat, faced down a panel of distinguished Thomas supporters. Outnumbered five to one, the situation looked hopeless for Heflin, he summoned up all his courage and bravely asked each panelist to state his or her party affiliation. Each panelist gulped, hesitated; then answered, "Republican, Republican, Republican, Republican, Independent." Heflin had pulled off a upset, but only because in a moment of desperation he had forgotten the pretense and asked the first honest and relevant question about what lies at the heart of our interest in the Court.

RAPE - A SPECIAL DILEMMA FOR THE DEMOCRATS

Ms. Joan Beck,

As a Democrat, it must have been very difficult for you to write your editorial about rape. On one hand, as a female, you certainly appreciate the horror of rape; but on the other hand, as a Democrat, you are opposed to really punishing individuals who commit crimes. Instead of punishment, Democrats prefer to perfect society, the real culprit that produces criminals, so they won't have to deal with the nasty business of punishment. The Democratic approach to which you subscribe is to go on and on, scheming to perfect society, while men rape women at the highest per capita rate in the world. The Republican approach is to hold individuals responsible for their actions by punishing them severely enough to bring about a change in their behavior, and in the behavior of those who would follow in their footsteps.

The split between Democrats and Republicans on this issue is standard. One party focuses on the individual, while the other focuses on society. To a Democrat, all the good things that can happen must be initialized from Washington; all the bad things, even if they were caused by Washington in the first place, must be corrected from Washington. The subtle but pervasive message that the Democrats have sent to individuals is that they are less and less expected to act responsibly, because, unbeknownst to them, there is a universe of influences out there which are playing havoc with their free will. Most of these supposed influences, were discovered by Karl Marx, the father of Socialism, and are the basic influence behind much of the Democratic Party's thinking that criminals are the victims of society.

Sadly, the nature of man has always been a delicate mixture of good and evil. The Twentieth Century has been no different, even though it has been punctuated by moments of great civility. Many historians are willing to bet that the Twentieth Century, given all that has happened, will be known

A SPECIAL DILEMMA FOR THE DEMOCRATS

to history as only the second century to be distinguished by continuous war, the first being from 1337 to 1453. It is against this violent history, which features mankind's very tenuous hold on civilized behavior, that Democrats have seen fit to free mankind from the notion that taking responsibility for his actions is of paramount importance.

When Democrats talk about rape, there is an immediate sense of the quagmire in which they have placed themselves, and America. Because their philosophy leaves them without a clue about how to deal with rape, they have a boring tendency to intellectualize about the crime with endless books and articles that carefully examine rape from a sociological, psychological and political point of view. Democrats think, that if they can just understand the intricate dynamics of the human mind, and the complexity of sociological interrelationships, then and only then, will they find the magic to prevent rape.

For example, Ms. Beck, you close your article by saying,"but Americans are growing more aware and less tolerant of crimes and abuses involving discrimination. Maybe, just maybe, labeling rape as a hate crime, as illegal bias against women, could make it easier to fight." First you note that 2,000,000 women get raped each year in this country; then you say that,"maybe, just maybe." Perhaps when the number gets to 4,000,000 you will stop intellectualizing about how to label and think about rape, and suggest a new plan that would obviously have a marked affect on rape, or at least on our knowledge of what works to control it and what doesn't.

As a Democratic writing about rape, you were compelled to join in the trendy debate about whether rape is a crime of sexual passion or a crime of violence against women. You stated, without rationale, that it was obviously a crime of violence, a position that is the current fashion within the women's movement, although recently some scholars are seeking, with modest success, to carve a niche for themselves by reversing this fashion. Gloria Steinam recently sought to bolster the feminist position that violence

RAPE

toward women, by men, is almost natural when she lubricously noted that American pilots were shown pornographic movies before missions in the Persian Gulf. There is no reason to doubt that this is true after seeing the movie "TOP GUN" in which an F-14 Tomcat pilot said, as he sensed the presence of an enemy plane, "I'm getting a hard on, he must be close." In reality, though, those were the words of a brave pilot saying he was looking forward to a death defying encounter with a Mig-31 at 20,000 feet, with the same eager anticipation and fear with which he would look forward to a sexual encounter with a desirable women. Further, it is not possible to understand how rape could be purely a crime of violence given that a man must be sexually aroused to commit the crime. No matter, these are just small squabbles among kindred spirits within the Democratic Party.

At another point you go on to explain that American women are several times more likely to be raped than Europeans, and 26 times more likely to be raped than Japanese. These are truly sickening and embarrassing numbers that make even Republicans wonder, if only for a short time, why they are so patriotic.

Instead of being fighting mad in the next paragraph, you speak of the Biden proposal, which your column is designed to support, by saying, "what Biden proposes isn't likely to make America much safer for women." In other words, it's just designed as more Democratic bombast to show how intellectual and thoughtful you all are. The 2,000,000 yearly rapes can be dealt with at some other time.

Susan Brownmiller, the heavyweight feminist intellectual and karate student, wrote perhaps the definitive Democratic book on Rape, "AGAINST OUR WILL," and she too accomplished little more than you, Ms. Beck. Brownmiller sees rape as the defining event in male-female relations. It is, she claims, "the conscious process by which all men keep all women in a state of fear. The human family was formed, she discovered, because the female feared an open season of rape; for protection she became the male's property and had to bear his children." Well, this is certainly a dreary view of family life. Fortunately, more than rape is involved in human history; anthropologists, zoologist and biologists

A SPECIAL DILEMMA FOR THE DEMOCRATS

most often tell us that the human family was a mutually beneficial formation. The human female would offer a continuous and stable sex life to the male; in return the male would protect the female, something she needed since her body was designed more for pregnancy than defense or hunting, and help raise the children, something that was also needed since two adults had a far better chance of getting some of the offspring through childhood than one. The family was formed so that both male and female could fulfil their most important evolutionary directive; to successfully reproduce and propagate the species. Rape probably had nothing to do with the development of the human family. Still, it is easy to see how an obsessive and sadly arrogant, Democratic feminist, might pervert things just enough to make human history conform to her views. It is odd that we don't hear of Democrats coming forward to suggest that these people are too embarrassing to be in their party; that their revisionist theories should not look for a home within the Democratic Party.

For all her macho bluster, Brownmiller, like you Ms. Beck, ends on a whimper. After a very long and very bitter account of history, Brownmiller closes by saying that her purpose was to give rape a history; "now, she says, our purpose must be to deny it a future." That's all well and good, but you would think she would present a plan; right now, after all, 2,000,000 women got raped last year, and they were the daughters, wives, and mothers of men, something Brownmiller probably would overlook.

She does offer up some clues about the plan that may someday emerge. She says, "the approach must be long range and cooperative, and must have the cooperation of many men as well as women. Fighting back-on a multiplicity of levels, that is the activity we must engage in."

To be really specific and solution oriented, Brownmiller wants a "gender free, and non-activity specific law governing all manner of sexual assaults, plus the law must rid itself of other out dated masculine concepts. The law about rape within marriage must take a great philosophical leap forward; the law must erase the difference between rape and incest; the battle for full equality will be won in the enforcement area if and when

RAPE

women receive full equality; elimination of pornography and prostitution are also central; curtailment of scenes of violence in movies and TV that promote the masculine ideology of rape must be eliminated; and lastly women must no longer let rape be a crime of shame, a crime about which they are afraid to speak."

So far it is quite possible to count on one hand the number of rapes less than 2,000,000, that Brownmiller will eliminate with her proposals. While each of her proposals are probably worth working toward, to wait for them is to wait for the millennium. What is needed is a practical place to start.

Brownmiller says, "Since,"Castrate Rapist," has become a slogan in certain circles I guess I should say for the record I am against it as I am against cutting off the ear of an informer or the hand of a thief." Her reasoning seems very flawed, on what is the only practical subject in her book, that is, if you buy the concept that the crime must fit the punishment. To cut off a persons hand would be a disfiguring, crippling, permanent, and psychological cruel punishment in retribution for the relatively harmless crime of thievery. Permanent or temporary castration for someone who subjects a women to the long term horror of rape is vaguely appropriate. All women would infinitely prefer to have their TV stolen, while they were away, rather than to be raped. The psychological affect of castration on male egos might be so chilling as to seriously reduce the number of rapes from the 2,000,000 level. All rapists, for example, could be sent to a special prison designed for the treatment and incarceration of rapists. Perhaps on a first offense they would come out with a temporary treatment that might dissuade them from ever going back. Perhaps being segregated with other rapists would have a good affect. A five year experiment in one state, the time it took Ms. Brownmiller to write her book, would tell America if rape can be significantly controlled in this manner. If constitutional and psychological prohibitions make this a cruel and unusual punishment, then those prohibitions should be removed so that this cruel and unusual crime can be stopped; so that next year's 2,000,000 victims can be spared; so that each of us won't have to live knowing that there is a 100% chance that one of the five closest women to us will be raped at some time during her life.

A SPECIAL DILEMMA FOR THE DEMOCRATS

Democrats should stop trying to perfect society, and instead punish those who commit rape, or they should just get out of the way and turn the matter over to Republicans who are less scared of taking action to prevent crime.

WOMEN AND FREEDOM-BREAD LINE OR FREE MARKET

Dear Ms. Goodman,

Your recent article on "sexism and suckerism," must have left your readers wondering why a person who probably has a degree in English, and definitely no specific expertise beyond, would be writing political columns that inevitably deal with economics.

In this case, you wrote about a study which showed that white men can negotiate a better price for a car than either a white women, black man, or black women. As a Democrat you were undoubtedly attracted to this study because it gave you an opportunity to corroborate your party's philosophy that America is a sexist and discriminatory country that is in urgent need of your Democratic prescriptions.

Firstly, it must be assumed that the study wasn't scientifically accurate; which is to say that the results probably couldn't be replicated by other researchers. It was learned long ago that research of this type must be double or triple blind so that no participant, designer, or analyst can consciously or unconsciously let their bias, perspective or interest in seeing a particular result, influence the outcome. In this case, you say, "the researchers' instinct was to question whether the civil-rights laws go far enough to protect the victim." To a scientist this would be equivalent to saying the researchers' instinct was to design an experiment to corroborate his own bias. With this approach, even cold fusion can be temporarily discovered. The phrase, "there are lies, damn lies, and statistics", may indeed have been coined right after this study, which you find so meaningful.

Secondly, the number of people sent to car dealerships was not large enough to yield a statistically significant result. For example, if you

BREAD LINE OR FREE MARKET

were to flip a coin twice, and it came up heads each time, you could not reasonably conclude that it would always come up heads. You would need to do the experiment, in this case, 50 times, before you could be certain that the coin would come up heads half of the time. In the case of the auto dealership study, the number of people from each of the four groups tested was not sufficient to tell us more about discrimination in the auto industry than flipping a coin twice would be sufficient to tell us about the probability of a coin coming up heads.

Let's say that despite researcher bias and incorrect research design, we accepted the results anyway. Are they really incriminating? The results show that if the average price of a new car is $12,000, the maximum range between the price given to a white male and black female is $900 or 7.5%. More importantly then, the average premium paid by a black women is - 3.5%; black man - 2.9%; white women - 1.9%. Even these inflated results, obtained from a poorly designed experiment, aren't much to worry about when you consider that all of us pay different prices all the time, anyway. White men are probably better negotiators than black women, and accordingly may save a few dollars when they buy a car, just the way a white person who was a good negotiator would save a few dollars over a white person who was a poor negotiator. But what are you proposing the U.S. do, invoke the Civil-Rights statutes, as the researchers want, so that everyone pays the same price even though we have no way of knowing whether that price would be higher or lower than the one paid after free market negotiation.

In most towns a black women can walk into a dentist's office in a poor neighborhood and get work done at about half what it would cost a white man in a wealthy neighborhood, in large part because the dentist to the poor knows his customers have less to spend, and he had better charge them less if he wants their business. Is this discrimination against white or rich people? Jews pay more for kosher food at Passover, is this religious discrimination? Busy people don't have time to clip food coupons, is this discrimination against busy people. People who negotiate often get a better price than those who don't. Is this discrimination against bold people? In all of these cases, the free market that Republicans worship is not ideal, but it is certainly the best, since it provides a lower average price for everybody than would be possible if the Democrats were allowed to set an arbitrary price that would destroy competition and cause far higher, average prices.

Ironically, if black women do end up paying a tiny premium, either because salespeople discriminate or because black women are 3% or less, worse negotiators, or because they aren't bold enough to negotiate at all; the free market is the ideal mechanism to correct the problem. If the free market has not yet corrected the possible discrimination found in this study, it is only because the premium is so tiny or non-existent that neither car dealers nor black women have noticed it. If the premium were noticeable, say, 10%, then some enterprising auto dealer would be compelled to corner the market by targeting an advertising campaign at black women; informing them that they could save 10% on the price of a new car by buying it at his dealership. Of course, not to out done, the competition would soon follow along, and the free market, which only Republicans love so much, would have made the premium disappear.

As you delight, Ms. Goodman, in this silly research that points out what a sexist and discriminatory country the U.S. is, you close by saying, "For once, let the seller beware." Let the buyer beware, as you know, is the frequent pejorative epithet that Democratic minded thinkers hurl at free market capitalism to detail how vicious and cutthroat the American market place is to consumers. In this instance, you are attempting to reverse the phrase so that businessmen, who tend to be disproportionately Republican, will "for once, beware." In truth, the market place is much harsher on businessmen than consumers, although it is not possible to know how to quantify the degree of harshness.

Consider that there are 30 million businesses in the U.S., 90% of them small, and that around 1 million declare bankruptcy or merely go out of business each year. In most cases this spells personal tragedy for the owners, families, and employees involved; tragedy far worse than losing 3% or less on a new car purchase. Consumers show no remorse at driving a business into bankruptcy just because its products are marginally more costly or of slightly lower quality; even if this occurs for reasons that can

BREAD LINE OR FREE MARKET

not be controlled. Consumers show no remorse at bankrupting hundreds of thousands of businesses each year because those businesses had locations which may have been one block out of the way, the color combinations chosen for business logos or product packaging were slightly out of fashion, they failed to produce the best quality, they named their products in a less endearing way than other competitors, or their advertising didn't have the right pretty girl or the right handsome jock. Businessmen spent thousands of hours on the tiniest and most trivial details to satisfy their customers every whim, because they know that the consumer holds the power of life and death. Indeed, "let the seller beware" has always been the operative phrase in a capitalist economy, you just didn't know it, Ms. Goodman.

It would be wonderful to hear you commiserate with business people who live and die each day depending on whether they please alternately wise and fickle consumers. For you to say, "for once, let the seller beware" is to totally misunderstand the nature of free enterprise. Oh well, this is something Democrats do regularly, anyway. A Democrat inherently distrusts business, even as America's businesses falter in the face of international competition. They will always look for an excuse to criticize, regulate, tax, control, or socialize business so that the decline will be hastened along. To move toward their goal, a Democrat will pretend that the consumer is the victim of business. In Russia and other socialized countries, a gov't controlled business will make a person wait in line for hours to purchase a tiny supply of food; this is a very good example of what normally happens when business can operate without capitalistic restraints.

CIVIL-RIGHTS - THE SELF-RIGHTEOUS DEMOCRATS

Dear Mr. Clarence Page,

I have recently read your article about the 1991 Civil Rights Act, and found that it does more to politicize and confuse matters than to make them sensible and actionable. You closed your article by advising Democrats to counter the Republican claim that the 1991 Civil-Rights bill is a "quota" bill, by saying that the Republican counter proposal is a "discrimination" bill. Fortunately, for the quality of the debate on this issue, and this issue already has the lowest quality debate of any in the U.S. today, Democrats are too polite, too politic, too socially conscious, and too sophisticated in their understanding of Republican philosophy to go around falsely labeling Republicans as racist discriminators, or at least they ought to be.

As usual, the debate about civil-rights forms very clearly along party lines. Democrats, as always, believe in gov't action, while Republicans do not. Being much less conceptual, Democrats usually confine their criticism of Republicans to charges about discrimination and racism, while ignoring the larger issues. Republicans have been so battered and bullied by the charges that they generally support the Democrats on civil- rights, rather than resist what Democrats have made de rigueur. In 1992 the Republicans are still hypocritically, sheepishly, and sensibly following the Democrats, but they have managed an absolutely brilliant political maneuver with the creation of the "quota" issue, and have actually managed to turn the issue into a vote getter. This approach may eventually encourage Republicans to actively promote their own ideas on civil-rights, rather than foot drag Democratic approaches.

The idea of civil rights is embodied in the Bill of Rights, a separate but integral part of the Constitution. The idea was to protect the majority against the possible tyranny of a minority vested with political power. To America's Founders, the only relevant rights were those that protected citizens from a threatening gov't; the idea of re-distributive rights did

THE SELF-RIGHTEOUS DEMOCRATS

not even occur to them despite their exhaustive and ingenious study of history. The Russian Constitution (pre Glastnost) also concerns itself with rights; it supposedly empowers or entitles Russians to have the right to: vote, work, rest, leisure, support during times of (sickness, old age, and disability), complete sexual equality, and complete voting freedom.

The Russian Fundamental Law or Constitution, something, by the way that most Democrats would feel extremely comfortable with, promises the equivalent of the American Bill of Rights, and a whole lot more. To a Democrat, the idea of promising many nice things, and empowering the gov't to provide them, is just fine. But, they fail to understand that to promise more, and give more, a gov't must take more. In the course of taking from its citizenry, a gov't diminishes individual liberty. For those who get more from the state than is taken away, it appears to be a bargain, at least in the short term. In the long term it becomes less of a bargain because the gov't will inevitably and naturally turn out to be corrupt and\or inefficient so that few get more than they give. And, most importantly, even those who potentially have the most to gain from trading with the gov't will lose more and more with the passage of time as their talent, ambition and spirit is crushed under the weight of a contradictory relationship with their gov't which involves more receiving than giving. Those who initially give more than they receive by trading with the gov't are similarly crushed as they sense their loss and the purposelessness of the trading. Class, and special interest group conflicts then break out as each tries to get more than it gives. Although the Democratic Party in the United States and the Communist Party in Russia and China, work on different scales, they nevertheless employ the same concept regarding rights.

George Bush opposed the Civil-Rights Act of 1964, the foundation of the current civil-rights movement, apparently believing that it was a case of the gov't promising a right it could not delivery at an acceptable cost, or in a way that would that ultimately be of benifit. Today he looks wiser than he did then, but nevertheless he was both correct and incorrect. The 1964 Act was good for White America in that it made them feel somewhat less guilty about slavery and its aftermath. It made it impossible for Blacks to claim that they had no power. It also gave them a certain feeling that they

CIVIL-RIGHTS

were finally doing the right thing by taking affirmative action. Democrats and blacks, under the leadership of Martin Luther King, badly wanted the 1964 Act to assure themselves that America was indeed a good and religious country, and in the belief that gov't could magically and quickly confer rights on blacks in a meaningful way. In a practical sense it didn't turn out to be a good trade for blacks. The day after the new legislation, blacks were not one bit more talented, educated, ambitious, family oriented, or less affected by a background that included the poverty, the non-western development of Africa, and the slavery of America, but they were in possession of a grossly inflated and self-destructive sense of what their rights and entitlements were. After the long and hard won civil-rights battle, blacks focused on receiving what was now rightfully theirs; not on developing Western social and productivity skills, as minority groups, including Japanese, Chinese, and Jewish, had done before them. Their ability to give in proportion to what they wanted to receive was severely compromised. It was as if they wanted to receive everything that had been denied them since emancipation and before. For blacks as well as whites, it was one of those sad cases where the most cherished dream turns out to be a nightmare when realized.

According to Republican philosophy, this is the way things that so heavily involve gov't generally turn out. But, the need in the country and in the Congress to get something done, to show that at least a problem was recognized, and hearts were in the right place, was so great as to cause most Republicans (82% in the Senate) to vote for the 1964 law. To this day, even though it is apparent that in many key areas blacks are worse off than they would have been had the progress they were making before 1964 been allowed to continue uninterrupted, many still think it was the best thing, if only as a psychological reaffirmation of the country's commitment to the concepts embodied by the Bill Of Rights.

In the early 1980's The Griggs decision reinforced the 1964 Civil-Rights Act by expanding the definition of discrimination and forcing an employer to prove that his hiring practices were non-discriminatory, rather than placing the burden of proof on a would-be employee. Republicans were

THE SELF-RIGHTEOUS DEMOCRATS

opposed as a matter of long standing principal, but for the same political and psychological reasons as in 1964, went along with the Democrats, but now more grudgingly than acquiescently. The civil-rights mentality by then had a history, and the evidence from that history was becoming hard to ignore. Many prominent and intellectual blacks, most notably Roy Ennis, William Raspberry, Clarence Thomas, and Thomas Sowell, were beginning to speak up about the failures and limits of civil-rights. But still the Zeitgeist demanded that Republicans follow along.

By 1989, there were more Republicans on the Supreme Court, and several decisions were made, most notably, Wards Cove, that had the affect of shifting the burden of proof, regarding discrimination, back to the employee, thus making discrimination suits, and the mentality they produced, less of a realistic option for those inclined to adopt the posture of a victim fighting for his rights. Republicans quietly applauded the decision; Democrats, not willing to let the now Republican Court, in effect, become a legislative body, began to formulate a bill that would reverse the Wards Cove decision, and, this time, make their intent so obvious as not to be subject to judicial interpretation.

During the summer of 1991, Republicans realized that Congress heavily favored the 1982 Griggs case, which put the burden of proof on the employer; so they reluctantly conceded the issue to the Democrats. But, the Nixon Southern Strategy, refined by Lee Atwater and perfected by Jesse Helms, provided a way for Republicans to get back in the civil-rights arena.

It seems that Americans are overwhelmingly in favor of affirmative action and opposed to quotas and reverse discrimination, just as they were in favor of sending troops to the Gulf War (according to the polls) but only so long as none of them got killed, and just as they favor an improved infrastructure so long as it doesn't mean more taxes. For Jesse Helms, the operative word became "quota;" it capitalized very effectively on the reverse discrimination side of the equation, and was in harmony with the Republican position that gov't can't freely and meaningfully dispense rights.

CIVIL-RIGHTS

By 1991 it was clear that the Democrats had the muscle to force a Civil-Rights bill on the nation, but not enough muscle to get President Bush to sign their bill, which he would have vetoed as a "quota" bill. Under pressure from the censorious Democratic Congress, Republicans will probably have to introduce and pass their own Civil-Rights bill or sign the Democratic bill. The Republican bill too, will have to use the language of the Griggs Decision, because most of Congress insists, and it will therefore be very similar to the Democratic bill, which Bush would have vetoed as a "quota" bill, but different enough to marginally move civil-rights back toward the Republican direction, but still nowhere near Wards Cove.

Most importantly, Republicans have learned that they can use civil-rights to get votes just as well as the Democrats always have, and, they can push the issue in their direction, the direction that will ultimately help blacks the most. Sadly, many old fashioned civil-rights advocates like you Mr. Page, can see nothing more than simple racial discrimination, or racism, in the Republican position.

The one possible pratfall for the Republicans is David Duke, the gubernatorial\presidential candidate in Louisiana. He is now talking just like a Republican, despite his racist, anti-semitic past. Whether Duke's conversion is genuine, is something that is not known and not relevant from a practical point of view. Above all else, he is an embarrassment to Republicans who just do not want him saying the same things they are saying. He has become a heaven sent, but purely emotional weapon for the Democrats to use against the Republicans; as a result, Republicans may again have to tone down their rhetoric in order not to lose the entire racial vote to the Democrats. If voters were encouraged to understand idealogy and vote accordingly, the pretty, charismatic face of David Duke would not be important to the voters of Louisiana; instead, they would substitute a Republican with a clean history. As it now stands, the voters of Louisiana gave themselves a choice between an ex-crook and a ex-racist, making a serious ideological contest even more remote than ever. The popularity of Duke, for the time being, will virtually wipe out the hard-won Republican recrudescence in the civil-rights area.

THE SELF RIGHTEOUS DEMOCRATS

Like many Republicans, President Bush doesn't believe in gov't imposed "quotas" but does believe in personally imposed "quotas." While gov't is not often in a position to help people, even those people who proclaim, "I know my rights," individuals are free to help one another; this is something that Bush's 1000 points of light is designed to symbolize. Democrats who scoff at individual liberty cannot appreciate President Bush's idea. Stated simply, the gov't can not help your sick brother better than you can. Just as the lord helps those who help themselves, the gov't can best help those who help themselves. The Founding Fathers put in place a gov't whose purpose was to preserve a system whereby citizens were free to help one another. When Winston Churchill said that a nation is know stronger than the sum of its people, he was recognizing that each bit of gov't help serves to make a nation a little weaker. The concept of long term re-distributive rights represents a perversion of freedom and the individual responsibility that comes with it. Perhaps modern Democrats think that our Founding Fathers lived in a country where the citizenry had no problems and no need of gov't assistance; that it is up to them to now teach Americans how harsh life has always been.

In the recent book, THE COMMANDERS by Bob Woodward, John Sununu is quoted as saying to Dick Cheney, the Secretary of Defense, that he wanted 30% of the 42 open jobs at the Pentagon to be filled by women or minorities. Additionally, The Washington Post reports it has found a letter written by Bush to the Senate minority leader asking that Senators make a special effort to find female, black, and hispanic candidates for Federal judgeships. In both cases, Bush was directing his staff in a clear and very obvious way to use "quotas;" this shows his decency, compassion, and interest in doing the right thing, but this is certainly not to say he supports gov't imposed "quotas." Unfortunately, this is a point that most Democrats are intellectually not able to understand. To them, the good, caring Democrats support Federal civil-rights legislation, and the bad, uncaring Republicans don't.

THE GULF WAR - REPUBLICAN IMMORALITY

Dear Mr. Lars-Erik Nelson,

Please let this serve as a response to your article on what you describe as the immorality of American Foreign Policy in the Persian Gulf. What was most striking about your article was that you did not once mention the word Democrat or Republican. It would seem that if you are going to make such a blanket and self-assured condemnation of American foreign policy, you would want to put your tirade in a meaningful context so your readers could take some specific action; i.e., vote Democrat or Republican. By avoiding this, you have become part of the sad myth in America which says that it is only appropriate to specifically express sentiment for or against a political party in the privacy of the voting booth. It is difficult to realize that everything ever written about politics ultimately has no value until it has been reduced to a point where it can be used to help make the one simple little choice that each American faces each time he enters a voting booth: the choice between Democrats and a Republicans.

Had your intention been to make your column actionable, you might have said, "President Bush and the Republicans are immoral; they naturally have a immoral foreign policy; if you are a moral person, like me, you should vote for the Democrats who have thoroughly opposed the immoral Gulf War." Of course, those who found your reasoning to be without persuasive merit might infer a obligation to vote Republican.

Let's look at how you and the Democrats reason about foreign policy. Your claim, which sounds very similar to that of Mario Cuomo, is that Republicans are very immoral because they singled out Kuwait for assistance while ignoring several other nations and peoples who were truly innocent, or at least as innocent as the prosperous people of Kuwait.

REPUBLICAN IMMORALITY

You say with great certainty that Bush singled out Kuwait for assistance because he wanted the money and oil contained there; that all the talk of moral imperatives was really a fraudulent cover for President Bush's immoral and materialistic interest in Kuwait.

The implication was, that to stop being immoral, America would have to take action in some or all of the other places in the world where significant human rights abuses occur, and where nothing would be gained, except the approval of God. You did not imply anything about what America's moral status would be if it did nothing as regards foreign policy. Your sentiments were echoed by many Democrats, and by many all over the world who believe the concept that American foreign policy is imperialistic as a consequence of the intrinsically immoral, capitalist economic system that drives it.

You must be congratulating yourself that you saw through the morality stuff and found-oil. Your sentiments are very reminiscent of the comments made by an elementary school student, interviewed on the news, who similarly indicted Republicans by saying, "all we really wanted was the oil." Like yours, the analysis was accurate as far as it went, but it didn't go far enough to be really accurate or complete. Bush very clearly stated, on many occasions, including a long cover story in "Newsweek" magazine, that the oil was of central importance. Secretary of State Baker said, in a now famous speech, that it could all be summed up in one word; "jobs." It would seem, then, that money as well as morality was the clearly stated goal of the Republican, Persian Gulf policy. The Republicans were not shy, nor should they have been, about saying that money and jobs was a part of the foreign policy equation.

Morality is a good thing, in fact, the very thing that America is based on, although a Democrat would never concede this. But it doesn't burn our lights or fuel our cars-oil does. For you to condemn Republicans as immoral because they sought to simultaneously secure our supply of life giving oil, and rescue the people of Kuwait, is an indication of how deeply Democrats mistrust their own basic survival instincts and those of their country. It is not immoral to want to survive. It is only immoral when you choose to do so at someone else's expense; this is something America did not do.

THE GULF WAR

Democrats are generally critical of basic American ideals, and are therefore foot draggers on foreign policy, which is ultimately a projection of those ideals. They don't like America enough to confer on it the right to be assertive or aggressive about promoting and defending its way of life around the world. A Democrat's focus, as he thinks of America, is on the still enormous problems faced by many of its people, particularly blacks, poor, elderly, children, women, and homeless.

Given this preoccupation with what they see as America's failures; its half empty glass, it is easy to see why they are deeply suspicious about the morality of projecting and imposing those failures internationally. Until now, virtually all foreign policy was anti-communist. Democrats had very little sympathy for this since they shared some basic beliefs with socialists, most notably, that gov't had to get involved to solve people's problems. When Oleg Klugin, the KGB spy chief in Washington during the 70's, wanted a recruit on Capital Hill, he has now indicated, he looked successfully among liberal Democrats. W. Averill Harriman, a close friend to FDR (perhaps the most popular Democrat ever, even though he presided over 10 years of economic depression and four years of World War) once remarked on nationwide TV, that FDR was jealous of Joseph Stalin because he had the governmental power to do anything he wanted in an effort to help his people. As the evidence piled up that communism didn't work, Democrats were still sympathetic, because eventually, they thought, it might be made to work in some modified version, and they knew they still didn't like the Republican approach. A weak foreign policy fit well with their basic sympathy for left wing governments all around the world.

Beyond an abiding sympathy for gov't "good works" which makes Democrats distrust America's historic preoccupation with private "good works," Democrats are reticent about foreign policy because they are, in a very real way, cowardly. For a child or child like adult to grow, he must be allowed his own growth process, he must be allowed to try and fail and suffer and learn and grow. A Democrat is emotionally inclined to be squeamish at watching the process and will need to intervene; to

REPUBLICAN IMMORALITY

put the child on top of the stairs to spare him the difficulty of getting there on his own. The concomitant loss of skill and self-esteem becomes secondary to the immediate pain that both he and the child will seek to avoid, if given the chance. Similarly, Democrats are psychologically inclined to develop gov't programs that will spare people the painful process they often must endure to become self-sufficient. When it comes to foreign policy, which often means military involvement, the Democrats, again, are more emotionally inclined than Republicans, to focus on the possible short term pain and suffering, rather than the eventual good that might result.

The concepts of bravery and cowardice have always been central to the development of history, and immorality has often been the charge cowards used to defend their inability to take action. Can Americans really claim to be the rightful inheritors of their forefather's legacy, if they don't feel that they too have the bravery to have to sailed with the Pilgrims to Plymouth Rock and the courage to have fought with Eisenhower against the Nazis. This is, by no means, to say that the exercise of bravery, without morality, is an acceptable explanation for a vigorous foreign policy, but rather to say that when action is finally required, as it surely will be, incredible bravery will also be required. If bravery is to be there tomorrow, it must be valued today. Democrats pretend to worry that by making bravery a cultural virtue they will be doing something that can lead to an aggressive foreign policy. Similarly, Democrats are reluctant to be tough on crime because it might promote the death penalty. In both cases they are hiding from their own pusillanimous nature.

Republicans tend to be very proud and patriotic, seeing the glass as half or more full. Milton Friedman, perhaps the leading Republican economist, will look at a recent immigrant toiling away under very harsh conditions and probably say, "relax, allow her the process, she is working very hard, saving money, learning the language, developing a skill, plotting her next move, and soon she will be up and out to bigger and better things." To a Republican, getting squeamish, and short circuiting this natural process, from which all habits of self-discipline, and self-sufficiency ultimately derive, for the mirage of instant progress, is a mistake of the immature.

THE GULF WAR

The more a Democrat interferes with a persons opportunity to develop the skills and attitudes he needs, the longer he is condemned to reside in a static position on or near the ladder's bottom rung. A Republican will argue that if the Democrats had been around in their current form, to take care of all immigrant groups, the way they take care of modern immigrant groups, America would be a third world country. The shift in modern policy toward allowing the gov't to help, rightly or wrongly, is in large part derived from the increased wealth which enables America to extend a helping hand, today, that yesterday, was too poor to be extended. Such behavior is at once an act of Judeo\Christian compassion, and cowardice. The American ambivalence about extending a helping hand is not a sign of immorality, as Democrats like to think, but rather a sign of intelligent morality.

Democrats tend to misunderstand the journey which all immigrant groups are on; they find in poverty, a rationale to explain their skepticism about basic American principals. To Republicans, the process of extending freedom, and little more, to immigrants, was the historic marvel that propelled America to the highest and best standard of living in the world. The results conferred upon America a position of moral leadership that the world implicitly acknowledged through World Wars I & II, the Korean War, Vietnam, and now the Persian Gulf.

I would not claim that your blanket denunciation of the immorality in American foreign policy makes you a mainstream Democrat. This would not be really fair since your article was written just days before virtually the whole world, with the exception of American Democrats, got behind the American commitment to use force in the Gulf. You must have toned down your rhetoric a little, but nevertheless you do represent the essential spirit of the Democratic Party, and can thereby be very instructive to those who wish to see an obvious example of Democratic thinking which is not obscured by subtlety. Perhaps you are the real conscience of the party that would be much more evident if Democratic rhetoric didn't always have to be toned down in the face of an emerging Republican majority.

DEREGULATION - THE DEMOCRATS HATE IT

Dear Mr. Rowen,

I found your column on U.S. airline deregulation badly biased toward the Democratic point of view, although the facts you were compelled to present made the case that your arguments were actually very mistaken.

You took the standard Democratic view that business needs to be controlled from Washington, presumably by very wise regulators, whose management skill, you must have great confidence, is better than that of those who regulated, say, the Savings & Loan Industry. Your perspective might accurately be called socialistic, but this is a label you probably don't like since the Russians (pre-Gorbachev) and much of the world use it in a more extreme fashion than you are probably comfortable with. It has always been disquieting to Republicans that even though so many countries have tried socialism in so many forms, and have never achieved nearly what America has achieved, that most Democrats still find excuses to support it, over and over again. Exactly how much misery and failure does it take before you give up, and consider the Republican free market alternative.

You and your party have apparently learned something though, in that for the 1992 elections you will give the same old stuff a new name; i.e., industrial policy, a name that perhaps the electorate will find palatable, particularly if it can be positioned as similar to the policy that drives the soaring Japanese economy. Since you chose to write exclusively about industrial policy as it relates to the airline industry, perhaps this industry is your best example of how brilliant and efficient Democratic management of industry can be.

You start your argument by noting that the number of major carriers has been cut in half since the onset of deregulation; you close your argument by noting that four more companies (PAN AM, TWA, Continental, Eastern, Midway) are about to disappear or downsize.

DEREGULATION

You further note, in your last sentence, that in foreign countries, all of which regulate their airline industries, there has not been a single bankruptcy.

Republicans, conversely, even those with Nobel Prizes in economics, have never thought to have a position on how many competitors there should be in any given industry, particularly a complex one like the airline industry. They recognize that the correct number is not one that is discernable to a committee in Washington. Your implicit assumption is that there is a correct number of competitors and that you know of a way to figure out what that number is. Why then didn't you tell us? Perhaps you would appoint a board of governors to debate about the exact number. But you provide no rationale, whatsoever, that would lead us or your board to even approach the problem of determining the correct number of carriers. You seem to be saying that since there is a lot of carnage out there in the industry, you would like to step in to help those poor business people. This is a contradictory attitude from a Democrat who is generally opposed to business interests and in favor of the worker and consumer.

Republicans, often criticized by Democrats for being too sympathetic toward business, are indeed sorry for the carnage that the free market is causing in the Airline Industry, and for the carnage it causes in all industries, but view it as an essential price to be paid for the constant experimentation that leads to constant growth in our standard of living. In pre-Gorbachev Russia, for example, there was no experimentation because the gov't pretended to know how many companies there should be, and what they should produce, as well as everything else about how companies should operate. As a result, their socialist economy was not responsible for one single consumer product innovation from 1917 to 1989. They even failed at producing basic staples, whose existence, in some cases, they would not even have known about had they not seen them in the West. During the same period in the West, civilization was rocketed toward prosperity by the constant experimentation and bankruptcy caused by free market capitalism. The H. J. HEINZ CO. (Heinz 57 Varieties) actually went bankrupt eight times before it finally hit on the right formula to

THE DEMOCRATS HATE IT

satisfy the American public. The Hershey Chocolate Company had six failures before it came up with a successful way to make and sell chocolate. The public, as they voted with their dollars everyday, was the final arbiter of what got made and sold, of what really constituted an improvement in their standard of living; not gov't regulators. The Ford Motor Company, Model A, emerged only after years of competitive experimentation. This kind of experimentation can not occur under regulation; particularly when a company's existence is guaranteed by the gov't, as you propose doing for the airline industry.

The airline industry has been deregulated for only about ten years, and they were the years of the Reagan economic boom when the Dow Jones Index, to pick one indicator, went from 1000 to 3000. Now that the first post deregulation recession has arrived, it is no surprise that another round of pruning is upon us. However, it is not for gov't regulators to know what length of time it will take for an industry weaned on 50 years of gov't protection, to stabilize and stand easily on its own two feet.

Your closing argument, that foreign countries have no airline bankruptcies, is very irrelevant since almost all of those countries heavily subsidize their carriers as a matter of national prestige and socialist principal. This is something that should, theoretically, be abhorrent to you as a Democratic, a self appointed defender of the little guy, since it necessarily involves collecting money from the little guy who often doesn't fly much, to subsidize the big, rich guy who flies frequently. Democrats normally prefer that scarce tax revenue be used on gov't programs to aid the needy. Would you really want it to support an industry used mostly by comparatively rich people?

Most importantly, you devote only one tiny paragraph to what certainly is the only important way to measure the specific gains or losses from deregulation; namely, ticket prices. Not surprisingly, even with deregulation, airline food is still airline food, and you still can fly to virtually the same destinations as before deregulation. Commercial aviation technology is relatively static and is likely to remain so for at least another

DEREGULATION

decade. Accordingly, the most that could have been hoped for with deregulation was lower prices, the very thing that is most important to air travelers who often want to fly as much as ticket prices will allow. According to you, Mr. Rowen, the U.S. did, in fact, get lower prices, although you seem very reluctant and saddened to admit it. You quickly mention several studies done by Alfred Kahn, (The world's foremost expert on free markets as they apply to the airline industry, and, obviously a Republican) the Department of Transportation, (probably Republican oriented after 10 years of stewardship under Elizabeth Dole and Ronald Reagan) and The Brooking Institution, (the most respected Democratic think tank in the world) all of whom concluded that prices had gone down substantially during the period of deregulation. This is excellent evidence that the free market accomplished exactly what Republicans said it would.

Bizarrely, you countered these elaborate and scholarly studies from both sides of the political spectrum by saying that it couldn't possibly be true, since your airline ticket had gone up 60%, to $280, in the last two years, for a round trip shuttle ticket between Washington and New York. According to my own quick investigation, the American Airlines Eagle Shuttle, on 4\18\91, was quoting a price of only $180 Dollars for the same ticket; this leads to the obvious conclusion that you were mistaken about your own experience which, whatever it was, was not sufficiently representative, and therefore inadequate to confute the three major, scholarly studies you cited.

You did mention one other study by Paul Steven Dempsy, a Democrat opposed to deregulation, which showed that fares had gone up 2.6 cents per mile over what they would have been if the downward price spiral of pre-deregulation fares had been allowed to continue. God knows what this means, 2.6 cents per seat mile translates to $13 (4 to 7%) for the New York-Washington shuttle. In the late 70's (pre-deregulation) the major carriers, most notably Pan Am and TWA, were always on the verge of bankruptcy; fares were constantly very erratic as desperate executives alternately lowered fares to increase volume and then raised them to boost profits per seat mile. There were $99 fares to Europe, that many college kids took advantage of, as well as many other special fares. Anyway, to decipher a price trend out of this period; project it fourteen years into the

THE DEMOCRATS HATE IT

future, allowing for inflation, changes in the cost of labor and capital, temporary fuel and pollution surcharges, terrorism, competition from satellite phone conferences, overnight delivery services, changing tax laws, fax machines, subsidized foreign competition, general economic conditions and the myriad of other factors that directly relate to the cost of an airline ticket, is virtually impossible. To be bold enough to attempt it and then to discover a mere 4 to 7% increase, after a fourteen year period, when you are predisposed, as Mr. Dempsy was, to find an big increase, is simply to indicate that the task is too daunting. Who is to say that the particular array of factors affecting the cost of airline travel should not have caused a 10% increase in fares over the fourteen year period. Or, who is to say that the modest price declines prior to deregulation should be used as a base to which all future prices should be compared? Why not compare to a period prior to deregulation when prices went up? Who can say that the modest price decline prior to deregulation would not have been dramatically reversed if regulation had been continued? The point is: only the free market can accurately and meaningfully determine what the price ought to be.

The free market price is the desired price because it is the lowest price that can be achieved. The socialist price, or the price dictated by a Democratically managed gov't, will always be higher and therefore affordable to a smaller number of people. Under a free market system, any business that unreasonably raises prices will be undercut by a competitor who is efficient enough to still make a profit at a lower price. The process is brutal to businesses, four out of five of which go out of business within the first five years, but it is necessary to provide consumers with the lowest possible prices and the highest possible quality. A gov't price will be either too high, in which case consumers will be impoverished by having to pay too much, or the price will be too low, in which case business can not cover its costs, and will go out of business or lower its quality. Those who can't survive in an existing market, either because their price is too high, their quality too low, or their entrance too late, after customers have become loyal to existing competitors, are forced to abandon the business or offer creative and innovative new products to establish their place in the market. In this way a society's standard of living is increased at the fastest possible rate.

DEREGULATION

So why are you for airline industrial policy/regulation? It seems that as a Democrat, you feel you must find an excuse for gov't regulation no matter what situation comes up; even if you can't find any reasons. In this case, you were forced to cite several major scholarly studies, from both sides of the political spectrum, which concluded that deregulation had actually worked to lower prices. You refuted these studies with one mistaken little story, from your own personal experience, about the cost of an airline ticket between NY and Washington, D.C., and another done by a Democrat which showed little or no significant change in ticket price. If Democrats would just get as far away from business as possible, the free market would put all the pressure in the world on business to keep lowering prices and raising quality. Democratic regulation, taxation, and control has the opposite affect, and is largely what is responsible for the current recession.

EDUCATION-REPUBLICANS WANT FREEDOM OF CHOICE

Dear Mr. Richard Cohen,

I have just finished your article about "choice" in the American educational system. While many Democrats are now willing to try "choice", if only because there is not a more widely accepted alternative to the badly failing system now in use, you, according to your article, are one of those who is still very negative on "choice", although, interestingly, you do not mention the alternative you prefer. The modest and limited rational you provide for being opposed to the concept seems to have no basis in logic at all.

Most of the remaining Democratic opposition to "choice" has to do with a concern that poor or disadvantaged students will be even less well off under the new system. The Democratic way of viewing this situation is, as always, socialist in nature. Their idea is to somehow distribute the achievements of the successful, to the less successful, so as make a more just society. The Republicans want freedom for the schools, teachers, and parents so they will be forced into a competitive environment that encourages them to constantly do a better job.

In education, Mr. Cohen, your concern is that "choice" will mean the "abandonment of the progress class" (the educationally resistent class). You say, "the plan could create nothing more than academic holding pens for the educationally resistant; it is not clear how the plan will help the poorly motivated children; even the vaunted market system does not work for those who cannot afford to consume; choice may become another chance for tracking or dumping the educationally resistant."

Your plan, apparently, is to maintain the status quo, which virtually all acknowledge is a failure, so that those at the bottom can remain as integrated as possible with those in the middle or on the top. Whether the issue is education, health care, social security, or the environment, the

EDUCATION

Democratic approach is always knee-jerk and emotional, rather than calm and rational.

You begin your article by mentioning that in your school, as a child, those who were very poor students, were dumped in the progress class, "but whatever they did in that class it wasn't progress." You first admit the public schools failure with these kids; then you spend the rest of your article worrying that Republican "choice" is the same horrible thing. Why not give "choice" a chance. According to all the most recent studies, all American kids are dumped in the equivalent of progress schools where they learn very little. Your whole article is devoted to saying that "choice" will create a horrible situation, even though you and most of the world admit that the current situation is already horrible. To so desperately and emotionally avoid the Republican free market solution, when you have absolutely nothing better to offer than the failing status quo, is a sad commentary on the intellectual rut you and your Democratic colleagues must be in.

You did make one very quick allusion to a statement by the Republican Education Department which has said that "choice" will provide "new hope" for these educationally resistent kids. You dismissed the possibility out of hand, saying, "any changes in the way schools are administered and staffed would be a political and bureaucratic hurdle of Himalayan proportions. "Good, Mr. Cohen, lets forget it then, it's only our children's education, anyway, we'll just stay with the current system and try to manage it better. It is frustrating to see how a Democrat will resist a Republican solution even after his own have failed.

Kids with special needs are generally more expensive to educate; they may require anything from school buses equipped to handle wheelchairs, to teachers with highly specialized skills. It is a financial burden that many states require their schools to bear. Under the "choice" plan, the money that is already being spent on these kids would, in effect, be given to their parents so that they could spend it on behalf of their children at the school they chose, rather than on the school the state chose for them. With the

REPUBLICANS WANT FREEDOM

exact same amount of money being spent, there is no reason to believe that the quality of education would go down, and much reason to believe it would go up; possibly way up.

Special needs kids present a variety of challenges to parents and teachers. Firstly, they often start out by getting batteries of tests, administered by experts, to determine, if it is possible, what all the physical, emotional and intellectual problems are, and what the likely educational alternatives are. From there, the kids get tracked into a classroom with other kids of, hopefully, similar needs. A problem arises in that special needs kids have a much wider range of problems and capabilities than other kids, and the likelihood that they will be in a class with their peers is much less. The more dissimilar the kids in a class, the less likely it is that any one child will get the specific attention needed for his specific situation.

Gov't schools, even the ones that make an effort to handle these kids, are simply not well equipped to handle the variety and complexity. As large bureaucratic organizations they are best suited to handle large numbers of average students. While they seem to do a poor job with average kids, they do a far worse job with special needs kids, if they even offer particularized programs for them. Just as the free market can create supermarkets that offer 20,000 items to satisfy any possible taste or need at very low, competitively induced prices, a free market in education would create many new opportunities in education for special needs kids that don't exist now. With "choice," parents often would have tuition money in their pockets with which to shop around for that one special teacher or situation or school that could reach their child; that could make the difference between a wasted life and a productive, self-sufficient life. If they chose to supplement the amount given to them by the state, another whole range of choices might open up for their children. No one can predict how a fully implemented "choice" system would work, anymore than they could have predicted that modern supermarkets would have grown to carry 20,000 items, but it is certain that especially in the area of

EDUCATION

special needs kids, it would indeed open up a new world of possibilities just as the Republican Education Department believes.

While your thinking on this subject is by no means complete, Mr. Cohen, it is certainly not the worst the Democratic Party has to offer. So enamored of socialist principals are many Democrats that not only do they want all kids in the same non-choice gov't school, but they want all the kids in the school, in the same classroom, so that the poorer students won't get left behind.

Tracking is often the word chosen to describe the segregation of students into groups or tracks distinguished by academic ability. Republicans generally favor it as a way to improve the quality and efficiency of education. They believe that if a teacher can explain something once, or in one way, to a group of students all on the same academic level, it is infinitely more efficient and effective than having to explain something several times, or in several ways, to accommodate students on varying academic levels.

To take action against poor performance on the national math test, Connecticut's Education Commissioner, Gerald Tirozzi, urged schools to end the widespread practice that separates students based on perceived ability. He claims that ability grouping or tracking causes some students to get shut out of courses that are needed as the foundation for higher level or college prep courses. He further says, "tracking and ability grouping really has to cease...I hope it comes as soon as possible. Once you fall off the conveyor belt in education, it's so hard to get back on." Tirozzi further notes that regardless of economic status or race, those students who took higher track courses did better on the national math test.

With people like Mr. Tirozzi running the educational establishment, it is no wonder that education keeps getting worse and worse. He is so steeped in Democratic tradition that he cannot consider a new idea no matter how compelling the evidence. For him the heartfelt idea is to try to take from the good students, as if they were rich taxpayers, and to try to

REPUBLICANS WANT FREEDOM

give to the poorer students, as if they were economically disadvantaged adults. The Democratic approach doesn't work in either the education system or the work place, no matter how well intentioned and heartfelt.

Tirozzi implies that tracking groups students according to perceived ability rather than actual ability, or, that being tracked low, becomes a self-fulfilling prophecy. This is probably true, but it is also true, as many studies have shown, that even among kids in the same classroom and with the same ability, that a teacher will identify or track students as slower or faster than average, and that their performance will adjust in accordance with this informal tracking process. It seems that teachers naturally track students even if they are in the same classroom and have been tested to have very similar ability levels.

It is true that self-esteem is hurt when a student is put in a lower track, but it is also true that a student is hurt more when he is forced to compete with students on a higher track. The greater the disparity in a classroom the greater the chance for harm. The brainy kid in the chair next to you is far more unnerving than the one in the next classroom. Similarly, the kids who get tracked out of academic schools into vocational ones, spend very little time worrying about the superior academic students across town or in another building. It is often said that a student drops out when the disparity in his classroom becomes so embarrassing that dropping out is emotionally easier than staying in. Being tracked with students of the same ability, as much as possible, is an obvious way to keep kids in a comfortable, educational environment.

Tracking occurs everywhere, whether it is preferred or not. Assigning students to grades K-12 according to age is a form of broadly tracking students according to ability; yet nobody is complaining about it, yet. Teachers naturally express preferences for grades that are deemed easier or more fun to teach. Will Democrats complain that this kind of natural, teacher self-tracking must stop so that certain grades won't receive less teacher talent and interest.

Democrats tend to have a myopic view of most problems, this case is

EDUCATION

certainly no exception. They want to move the poorer students onto one higher track so that, in effect, the best students have less chance to work to their capacity. Working against the top tier is something Democrats always do. When the best students have no opportunity to move up in accordance with their ability and ambition they are, in effect, tracked down to accommodate the slower kids now in their class; there is no net benefit. The kids on the bottom of the track lose valuable time as the teacher takes time to accommodate those on the top of the track; the kids on top lose valuable time as the teacher takes time out to accommodate those on the bottom. It becomes a zero-sum game. With extensive tracking, in contrast, everybody, including the top students, assuming good administration, has an opportunity to work toward higher standards or tracks, rather than being pushed toward the middle. The emphasis must be placed on all students moving toward a higher track; not force feeding the lower track into an arbitrarily defined "top" track. A competitive, choice system that promotes an evolving higher standard, is something that is essential in American schools as they combat the woefully low educational standards that the media so often trumpets.

To be sure, there are problems with schools that use tracking, but they are problems more with administration; not tracking. Tracking students downward, will often lower achievement and I.Q., not improve even vocational job opportunities, promote lower self-esteem, increase classroom misbehavior, reduce homework, and generally label kids as dumb. This can all be avoided by, 1) standardizing curriculums so that all students study the same subjects wherever possible, 2) not labeling kids as, for example, bluebirds (smart) and cardinals (dumb), 3) giving the slower kids more rather than less homework, 4) keeping all the kids mixed in homerooms and other classes where practicable, 5) by paying teachers based on how much they actually teach, and 6) paying teachers for not allowing the lower tracks to become an excuse for laziness.

Out of desperation, it has become very popular of late for Democrats in education to say that students should all be tracked together because they teach each other. In your article, Mr. Cohen, you describe this as

REPUBLICANS WANT FREEDOM

"educations dirty little secret." You provide no explanation about why it is a dirty little secret. In truth, it is not a secret that kids don't teach each other as well as teachers teach kids. Kids are not sent to school to be teachers are they? If some students become part time teachers, isn't this evidence of a severe tracking system, indeed, a tracking system that encourages some students to be tracked right out of the student body onto the faculty.

The difference between, say, Harvard University and Slippery Rock University (if there is such a place) is one of tracking. Top students are tracked to Harvard while bottom students are tracked to Slippery Rock. Students are encouraged all their lives to work toward the Harvard track. If all students got in regardless of ability, there would be no Harvard track, and therefore no Harvard.

When Intel Corp. hires engineers to design and manufacture new computer chips, it seeks out students who have been on the highest track all their lives, not students from a track diluted by misguided efforts to help those on the lower tracks. Would anybody argue that America's top engineers would be better off if they had spent their school days tracked with America's worst engineers?

When Americans buy automobiles they look to countries where workers are strictly tracked toward the highest possible standards. They don't buy a lower quality car out of sympathy for lower track workers, or in the belief that eventually the low track workers will begin to produce a high quality car.

It is positively frustrating that you, Mr. Cohen, and your ideological colleague, Mr. Tirozzi, are so locked into pitiful and failed Democratic thinking that you can't consider a new Republican idea which can reverse the disastrous trend in American education. Why not consider free market "choice," so that parents, students, and teachers will have a new incentive regarding quality in education. Why not lengthen the school year from 180

EDUCATION

to 240 days so that it is as long as those in the countries that produce better students. Why not lengthen the school day to Japanese length? Why not cut out some of the Mickey Mouse courses and double up on Math and English? Why not propose a higher base pay for those who teach the lower tracks, or a lower base pay coupled with bonuses for the teachers who teach enough to qualify students for a higher track? Why not stop resisting national educational tests and the national standards that would evolve from them?

This whole debate, like many others, almost always takes place without reference to Democratic or Republican labels, but the labels exist; unfortunately they often only appear in the voting booth. In this case, the Democrats are for gov't schools; the only concession they make is that perhaps they should be managed better. The Republicans believe that the gov't schools have failed miserably and should be privatized so that competition will force on them the higher standards that can not be achieved any other way.

IDENTITY CRISIS - A HUGE DEMOCRATIC PROBLEM

Dear Democrats,

I have just read several articles about why the Democrats always lose presidential elections despite being the majority party on all lower levels. It seems that most, if not all, Democrats misunderstand the rationale behind this trend that is so adversely affecting their party at the national level. The rest of America can therefore happily anticipate that the Democrats will not soon win a Presidential election. To explain what is happening to the Democrats is an interesting exercise that reveals the deep problems within the party that cannot be solved by mere strategy.

To begin with, national politics is vastly different from state and local politics, primarily in that the intensity of media coverage is so great as to often give candidates a new image or persona that they didn't have the day before their national candidacy was announced. The two most recent and obvious examples of the power of the national press are Sen. Dan Quayle and Sen. Edward Kennedy.

Before national politics, Dan Quayle was a very successful and well liked Senator from Indiana. He was young, handsome, ideologically committed, and very popular with women voters. These were all attributes that presumably would have been very valuable to the somewhat stodgy Republican image. During Quayle's very first appearance with Bush, in New Orleans at the nominating convention, the day after Bush selected him as his running mate, Quayle introduced Bush with the go get'em chief, rah-rah, pep rally style that had served him so well in high spirited Indiana. Bush, being an older more dignified, Yalie, preppie, Easterner,

IDENTITY CRISIS

just couldn't follow Quayle's exuberant lead, although he may have wanted to. In retrospect, he did his party, his Presidency, and Quayle, a huge disservice by not dissembling in accord with Quayle's unfortunate lead.

At first, Bush was embarrassed because he couldn't or didn't want to follow Quayle's lead, even though the stage had been well set for him to do so. Bush recovered quickly but acted like, well, like Bush, but from then on, Quayle's callow and youthful exuberance was seen as something that left him without sufficient stature to be taken seriously as the Vice-President of the United States. If Bush had tried to act like Quayle, just for that minute, the joint performance would have been interpreted as suitable for that very joyous occasion; instead Bush stayed in character and the difference between the two men was just too much. Anyway, in literally the first 15 seconds of his national life, Quayle had let the media destroy him by dramatically exposing his most obvious vulnerabilities - youth, exuberance, and inexperience; Quayle has never recovered.

Sen. Kennedy had a similar experience. In 1980, the polls indicated he was ahead of all contenders, including Jimmy Carter, who were seeking the Democratic nomination. The pressure from his party to openly seek the nomination was tremendous; so eventually, despite apprehensions, he threw his hat into the ring. Kennedy and the Democrats knew that Chappaquiddick would be a liability, but still, they thought, he was way ahead in the polls; perhaps because the electorate desperately wanted to believe that he could bring a little of Camelot back. Anyway, immediately after Kennedy announced, he sat down for his first interview; with Roger Mudd, then of CBS. Mudd surprised Kennedy by quickly asking him about Chappaquiddick. Kennedy portrayed himself very poorly as he talked about himself in the third person, saying, "the behavior was inexplicable," as if it was someone else's behavior. In an instant, Camelot was gone, and Chappaquiddick was back. Such is the power of the press, at least on the presidential level, to instantly clarify or change something deep within the audience's psyche so that it will have an entirely new meaning. Mario Cuomo may now be in a similar position. He has many assets that give him the lead as Democrats view him from a distance, but when the

A HUGE DEMOCRATIC PROBLEM

national press brings him up close and personal, his candidacy, if there is one, might vanish overnight due to his extreme liberalism, his eccentricities, or the grave problems in N.Y. State which include the lowest bond rating and the highest per capita level of services.

Democratic candidates for president have usually lost because of this dramatically intense media exposure. Even if Democrats can get by the skeletons that may be in their closet, they are very weak on foreign policy, as they so strongly demonstrated in the Persian Gulf. Their tax and spend domestic policy makes them vulnerable there too, because, 1) there is no money left to spent now that the deficit is $350,000,000,000, and 2) even if Democrats could print all the money they wanted, and spend it on more programs like those from their past, it would do them little good as the public perception is now that the desired results from gov't programs would not be forthcoming.

Media scrutiny on the national level, is too intense for it to miss the obvious failings which lie at the heart and soul of the Democratic Party. On the state level, media scrutiny is much less; the Kennedys and Quayles can often do well. Media attention is comparatively so slight that the electorate often has no idea what a candidate stands for, and if they do know, it is often considered less important than the perception about the likelihood of a candidate being able to beg, borrow, or steal for his constituency. It is often felt by voters that it is the state candidates who bring home the entitlements; social security for the old; welfare for the poor, and a little something for everybody else. Voters are inclined to vote for the nation when they vote for President, and vote for themselves when they vote for lower candidates. The media covers candidates as if this is a legitimate perception. The lack of electorial and media diligence is so great that it is not uncommon for an electorate to simultaneously elect a liberal and a conservative.

The Democrats know their basic ideas are bankrupt and cannot withstand the scrutiny of a national election, but out of pride, blind loyalty, and the need for a political home, they are compelled to salvage the same old ideas and pray that there is still some milage left in them.

The Democratic Leadership Counsel (DLC) is a salvage effort. Its

IDENTITY CRISIS

stated goal is to wrest control of the party from liberals and give it back to mainstream, or less liberal, Democrats, on the theory that mainstreamers can win the Presidency just like they win state and local elections. Even if this were a reasonable theory, which it is not, the problem then arises about whether a moderate will be made to appear by the media as simply a wimpy liberal. The DLC manifests a sickening realization, at least to Democrats, that in either case, now that the tax and spend cupboard is finally bare, they face an identity crisis that mere repositioning may not help.

Gary Hart, an political opportunist down to his socks, was perhaps the first modern Democrat to confront this issue head on, by presenting himself as non-partisan and, non-ideological, but somehow still a Democrat. He apparently didn't feel too bad about this obvious deception, even though it was brightly illuminated by his absolutely standard and liberal Democratic voting record in the Senate. He prefaced his book on military reform by saying, "one of the reform movements greatest traditions: "Republicans and Democrats, Liberals and Conservatives working together for reform." Hart wanted us to believe that defense wasn't a partisan issue; that all good Americans, and Presidential candidates should support non-ideological reform or, in other words, good management of the military. It was a good ploy as long as no one asked him to point out who the bad guys were, the guys who, apparently, were in favor of bad management. When Hart was pressed to specifically identify his ideological sympathies he protested, like the cat who swallowed the canary, by saying; "I am not ideological; I am not going to label myself; the American people aren't ideological." When opponents began to ask, "where's the beef",(derived from a then popular Wendy's Hamburger commercial) the Hart campaign began to fade, although it was adultery that finally killed it. Hart knew full well that if he gave himself an accurate label, he would be promptly rejected, rejected because the media knew, and even those who stood to profit most directly from the next new Democratic programs, knew, that the Federal deficit was huge; the cupboard was finally bare, and the goodies would not really be forthcoming.

The DLC, out of desperation, may ultimately be the Democrats way

A HUGE DEMOCRATIC PROBLEM

of institutionalizing the pragmatic dishonesty of Hart and, later, Dukakis, who claimed to stand for competence rather than ideology despite his perfectly liberal record. Rep. Barbara B. Kennelly, a top official in the DLC, is distraught at having to embrace positions once held only by Southern Democrats, even though see knows her party cannot win a presidential election unless it breaks the Republican strangle hold on the South. She is extremely liberal, to the point of supporting national health care as a citizenship right, and yet she is eager to be a part of the more conservative DLC. She badly wants her very liberal ideas to be popular even though they are not, so she has joined the DLC where she can front as a moderate in order to get re-elected and vote as an extreme liberal. When pressed about her positions and her vote at the DLC, she prevaricates badly, "The DLC convention is not where I cast my ballots; The DLC balloting is not worth the paper it is printed on. I don't like litmus tests and I don't like labels." She and Gary Hart both don't like labels, especially when they are accurate.

Paul Tsongas hoped at the DLC convention that his party would be, "not too liberal and not a Republican wannabe, but a party that remembers its heritage as a fighter for civil-rights and women's rights." God knows that the Senate voting record of Tsongas did not make him look like a Republican wannabe, it made him look like the liberal Democrat he is. The Senate voting record of Gary Hart and Paul Tsongas, and the House voting record of Barbara Kennelly, represent a paper trail that these Democrats have often been able to hide, from state and local media, but it is something that the national media will inevitably focus on as these Democrats attempt to ingeniously squirm away from the accurate labels, that they so proudly earned in years past, but which are now out of favor with national, and many state voters.

Governors Rockefeller and Wilder said at the DLC, "the most progressive action the gov't can undertake, is to root out and prevent unnecessary spending of hard earned taxpayer dollars." It is sad when two of the most important Democratic Governors can find no other purpose for gov't than this. If the founding fathers could hear these Governors, they would surely wonder why they had spent so much time on philosophy before writing the Constitution, or they might just conclude that any

IDENTITY CRISIS

democracy which produces such mundane rhetoric from its highest officials must have certainly failed. Actually, both of these men are very committed liberals who know they have lost the philosophical war, and if they are to continue the fight for liberalism, they must change the subject away from the all important liberal/conservative debate which they lost as their programs failed. They, it would seem, want to form the "against unnecessary spending" wing of their party. Perhaps if they can panic the Republicans to form a adversary and counterpart wing called the "for unnecessary spending" wing, they will have successfully changed the subject, and for the first time be well positioned to win a debate.

If Governor Wilder could root out some unnecessary spending, presumably he would support using it according to the DLC plan which called for new Democratic programs to break dependance on old Democratic programs (welfare was noted in particular). An accurate label for this new Democratic approach might be "Conservative Republican" or "oops we were wrong."

Governor Bill Clinton, a certain Presidential candidate and head of the DLC has a very bright future in his party. As an experienced campaigner for Democratic principals and an Ivy League graduate, he knows better than to be too honest about his political heritage. In his DLC speech, Clinton went even a little further than Hart by announcing that ideological solutions on the left and right were no longer relevant and a "new choice" was necessary and forthcoming; from him. The so called "new choice" involved keeping the Democrats' traditional commitment to the poor, but this time around, selling themselves as advocates of the middle class too. First Clinton denied idealogy; then he described his "new choice" in standard ideological terms. The Democrats have always wanted to use the gov't as a tool with which to extend kindness and charity to everybody; that is why they are widely derided as the party of special interest groups. This time around Governor Clinton is covering all his bets by including the entire middle class, a group his party quietly raped and lost over the last 25 years to pay for the lower class programs. If he could see fit to include the upper class too, then the whole country could be declared a Democratic special interest group and the Democrats would never have to worry about losing another election. Of course, the money to pay for middle and upper class programs would have to come from another planet.

A HUGE IDENTITY CRISIS

This huge and very public identity crisis that the Democrats are having is something that cannot be hidden from the national media. It is now a glaringly apparent aspect of all that goes on in the Democratic Party. Sen. Kennedy could not hide from Chappaquiddick; Vice-President Quayle could not hide from his youth, and the national Democratic candidates certainly cannot hide from their sudden realization that without traditional, big spending liberalism, they are unable to say one word about the meaning of their party that makes sense. This is why the leading Democratic candidates, Tsongas and Clinton, are following the lead of Hart and Dukakis in trying to persuade the electorate that idealogy, after thousands of years, no longer matters. What they really mean is that even though their big gov't tax and spend programs have failed miserably over the last 25 years they still want to get elected.

MEDIA BIAS - DEMOCRATS AT NBC NEWS

Dear Mr. Chancellor,

I caught your commentary the other night, during which you spoke of an alleged incident in which President Truman offered to step down as President of the United States and run as Vice-President under General Eisenhower in 1948. You went on to talk of past American Presidents who had been Generals, most notably, Washington, Jackson, Grant, Roosevelt, and Eisenhower. You spoke with delight and glee about all this, apparently hoping to arouse interest in your commentary, and closed by saying, "a general for President in 1996, after the Bush phenomenon has past, - why not."

As hard as I tried, I could not figure out why you or anybody else should care if the next president is a General or not. After all, we have had an actor, peanut farmer, and haberdasher who did extremely well, or poorly, depending on whether you view them from a Democratic or Republican perspective. While military experience is perhaps more relevant to a president than, say, peanut farming, it is also a potentially huge liability to a historically minded nation that may generally prefer the peaceful aura of a civilian Commander in Chief, except, it would seem, when flushed with the self-righteous exhilaration that comes from a recent military victory. In any case, you gave no explanation for your enthusiasm, which was apparently reserved for either Colin Powell or Norman Schwarzkopf.

You might have pointed out, as you spoke of Eisenhower, that he refused to run as a Democrat, as he indicated in his auto-biography, for an extremely good reason; namely, he did not believe in their philosophy which holds that more and better gov't regulation of our lives is the solution to our problems. Instead, The General believed in traditional

DEMOCRATS AT NBC NEWS

Republican thinking which holds that freedom from gov't, even if the governors are stronger, wiser, and kinder than their subjects, is the answer to our problems. Moreover, Eisenhower was philosophically very opposed to the isolationist, Taft-wing of the Republican Party. It has to be regarded as a major positive that he recognized that political behavior, if it is to have meaning, must be labeled, identified, and evaluated in a historical and philosophic context.

Eisenhower's popularity was such that he probably could have won on either ticket, and perhaps on a third of his own design if he had so chosen. Thankfully he recognized that there have been no new political ideas under the sun for the last 2000 years, and that Democrats and Republicans embody the history of political philosophy very nicely.

Political reality doesn't ask of us that we forgive Eisenhower for running a politically neutral campaign and presidency after modestly paying what was apparently just lip service to Republican philosophy. Sadly, his actual approach to the presidency rested more on his personal popularity than anything else. That Eisenhower turned out to be so neutral as regards domestic policy, and got away with it, is largely the fault of folks in the media, like you Mr. Chancellor, who shield the public from the Democratic\Republican debate, as you did by advocating, of all things, a General for president, without even mentioning that ideology might be more important than military experience. The media is often accused of being biased to the left; in this case you were biased to nowhere.

Perhaps you intended that the general represent a new party: The Generals' Party. With men like you in charge of the nation's major media it is not likely that Americans will ever learn the difference between Democrats and Republicans. Do you really think America can survive forever with an impotent and divided gov't? Why is the media so resistent to helping the electorate understand the difference between Democrats and Republicans?

MEDIA BIAS - NBC WANTS YOU TO RECYCLE

Dear Tom Brokaw,

While watching "The NBC Nightly News" today, I was very interested in the way you and Fred Francis handled the segment on Earth Day. The segment closed with Mr. Francis saying, "recycling will only work when the Federal Gov't forces everybody to do it."

Had you wanted to be impartial you might have said, "Democrats believe that most programs, including recycling, won't work unless gov't, especially the Federal Gov't, forces people to participate, while Republicans believe that throughout history people fought for and earned their freedom from gov't, and are generally responsible and inclined to do the right thing in the absence of the govt's maternal and guiding hand.

In this case, apparently you and Mr. Francis were motivated by a common Democratic technique that, oddly enough, is what accounts for much of the Democrats' status as the majority political party in the United States. It seems that the philosophy of the Democratic Party is far easier to understand than that of the Republicans. For example, if it is agreed that recycling of some things is good, then the only remaining problem is to get people to participate. To a Democrat, the obvious source of power, and authority with which to get this job done is the gov't. The gov't merely needs to flex its muscle a little bit, and in an instant all Americans are recyclers. People are forced to separate their garbage into a couple of recycling categories, the garbage is collected by gov't or by gov't subsidized collectors, and eventually sold to business for recycling so that the use of landfills, incinerators, and original natural resources is minimized. This is a simple solution that is easy for viewers of the "NBC Nightly News" to understand. The Republican solution, conversely, is much

NBC WANTS YOU TO RECYCLE

more complex because it involves an understanding of the way free markets work. The Republican position is generally not explained by the media because, 1) 85% of those who present the news are registered Democrats who got into the business to affect change toward the Democratic philosophy, and 2) the complexity of the Republican position is such that ratings might go down if viewers were subjected to the kind of comparatively complex arguments that are often a part of Republican philosophy.

The recycling segment on your show lasted about 2-3 minutes, during which time you outlined the scope of the entire waste management problem and presented the Democratic solution. If your goals were to partially inform the public, maintain or improve ratings, and promote the Democratic position, it was probably a very successful piece. If your goal had instead been to inform the public so that they could make a reasoned choice between Democrats and Republicans, then the piece was an terrible failure, a failure that after years as a participant in, you are probably no longer capable of seeing, much less correcting. As someone who surely likes to think of himself as a man of integrity, you may have even convinced yourself that your reports are balanced or non-ideological.

If you had tried to present the Republican position on recycling, you would have had to mention that while Democrats believe America is running out of landfill space, the space where it dumps 76% of its garbage, Republicans are not at all sure that this is the case. Redoubtable economists like Malthus and lately computer scientists (The Club of Rome), have long predicted that with resources being finite and populations growing, we would all soon be impoverished as fewer and fewer resources would be available for each individual. Their predictions have always turned out to be wrong. The most famous example is probably, oil. During the early 1970's when everybody was waiting in long gas lines, it was assumed by many that this was an indication or sign that oil was running out and that by the 1990's the world would be a vastly different place owing to the almost depleted oil reserves. It turned out that by the 1990's the predictions were proved wrong, and most of the world saw no reason to worry about the reserves, which showed no serious sign of depletion.

MEDIA BIAS

Others predicted that prices of most natural commodities would rise tremendously between 1980 and 1990 due to the growing scarcity of these resources. It turned out that these predictions were wrong and prices actually went down during the decade. There is always a tendency for Democrats to panic this way, because they don't appreciate and understand that the free market continuously adjusts price levels so that new resources or substitute resources are always discovered in sufficient quantity to fully replace the old ones, and to allow a further improvement in the standard of living. No matter what natural resource is thought of: buffalos, beavers, whale oil, coal, or land in Manhattan, the free market was able to orchestrate an orderly and economic transition to the next replacement resource. The free market provides a process that is far superior to the gov't planning process which the Democrats would use to guess at the best way for markets to evolve.

The commonly stated gov't assumption that half the nations 5499 land fill resources will be filled in four years, is designed by Democratic environmentalists to panic America toward recycling. They would really have us believe that in 1995 human history will cease because, all of the sudden, America will have absolutely nothing to do with half of the 160 million tons of garbage it generates each year. Almost any Republican would be willing to bet any Democrat that 1995 will not be the year when human kind faces an ignominious end as it suffocates under its own garbage. It seems that Democrats always use dire predictions to gain political power, and justify further gov't intervention.

To get a look at the problem from the Republican free market point of view, consider that an average American produces 1277 pounds of garbage per year and that it costs $10 per ton to land fill solid waste in the West, where land is plentiful and people scare, and up to $100 per ton in the East, where, by comparison, land is scarce and people are plentiful. With a weighted average price of $27 per ton across America, this means that each of us must bear up under the burden of paying $17.00 per year to land fill our garbage. This seems like a trivial amount to pay for such a socially conscious and environmentally critical thing as land filling garbage, especially when we consider that it is not unusual to pay more than that for just one meal or one book.

NBC WANTS YOU TO RECYCLE

Let's suppose that the price of $17.00, which seems artificially low, was allowed, by the gov't, to rise as the scarcity of land fill space grew, so that the price eventually reached $34.00. Theoretically, with twice the money available for landfill management, it might be possible to have more landfills since you could offer twice the enticement to accept one in any particular area. Or, you would have twice the money with which to learn how to make existing landfills many times more absorbent and environmentally safe. One recent experiment added water to landfills so degradation speed would triple, and the production of energy from the landfill, in the form of methene gas, would increase. Another experiment in composting, seeks to double the amount of land fill space by shredding newspapers and other biodegradables so that they decompose in a month or two, rather than the 15-20 years it now takes. If by chance nothing worked, and prices rose, it would become more and more possible to induce landfills further and further west to accept eastern garbage. Nobody knows exactly what would happen if landfills were part of the free market, but it is known that if there was a genuine shortage of landfill space, the free market would encourage the maximum amount of rational trial and error experimentation to find the most satisfactory solution.

The Republican solution is to get the gov't out of the garbage business so that the market motivated entrepreneurs can evaluate the size and scope of the problem and begin the search for a solution.

When a state gov't passes a recycling law, it does so in a vacuum without regard to the systems affect, and thereby interferes with what would have been a market derived solution. Gov't may be able to force citizens to segregate their newsprint for collection, but it is really difficult for them to force a newspaper to buy the stuff and print newspapers on it. For example, as states over the last three years have jumped on the recycling bandwagon, the amount of newsprint available has gone up tremendously, and the price has gone down. This means that many of the small businesses that got into recycling by themselves, and operated as intermediaries between local govt's, who collected the newsprint, and those who ultimately bought it, have been driven out of business because of the destabilizing affects of gov't intervention on prices. These private and mostly small businesses are precisely the ones that will experiment endlessly, and at their own expense, to find ways to economically and efficiently build a recycling industry.

When McDonalds got into the hamburger business, the age old hamburger was mysteriously transformed, something that may never have happened without McDonalds. The one entrepreneur who gets driven out of the garbage business, due to the government's erratic and heavy handed involvement, may have been the one to solve the garbage problem. The large, clumsy and bureaucratic intervention of gov't turns the industry over to the kind of inefficiency that will ultimately drive up costs in the recycling industry so that growth and development will be slowed to a comparative snails pace. In Rhode Island, where gov't intervention is worst, Victor A. Bell, Chief of the Rhode Island Office of Environmental Coordination, brags that he is displacing the mom and pop facilities with large gov't ones. If he and his Democratic friends believe, in their egocentric way, that gov't can manage the business of recycling well, then he would also believe that gov't could manage all or many businesses, well. This is the basic conclusion that socialist countries have been failing to prove for the last hundred years. It is interesting to note that virtually every new problem that comes up is used as an excuse by Democrats to expand their authority and the size of gov't.

Once the gov't has passed a recycling bill it is often stuck with garbage that it must create a market for. In New York, they have not been able to sell much of their low grade glass so they have processed much of it themselves into asphalt, or glassphalt. The problem is that the price and quality of their glassphalt is higher and worse than commercially available asphalt; this explains why the glassphalt is not produced commercially by businessmen. The people of New York get lower quality, more expensive streets, and they get recycling, but who is to say the tradeoff is a sensible one. Who is to say that by disguising the real cost of recycled low grade glass in NYC asphalt and bureaucracy, that entrepreneurs and would-be entrepreneurs will ever be attracted to the field having then to compete with a gov't subsidized industry.

NBC WANTS YOU TO RECYCLE

If the gov't would largely get out of the garbage business, as good Republicans suggest, most problems pertaining to waste management would have been solved slowly and in an organized, efficient way so that the U.S. wouldn't be facing these dire predictions, silly though they may be, that in four years it will be buried in its own garbage.

Free market Republicans believe garbage collection should be privatized and priced according to the real cost of landfilling, incinerating, and recycling. Each of these methods of waste management would be privately owned or licensed, although regulated by gov't to control pollution and zoning. If this were to happen, the efficacy of waste management would be instantly maximized. A package that didn't quickly decompose in a land fill, burn in an incinerator, or fetch a buyer in the recycle market, would cost a ton to dispose of, and thus discourage anybody from buying in the first place. A package that was made out of readily recyclable clear glass, might actually be sold to garage collectors for a profit or to offset the cost of other less valuable garbage, and thus encourage the use of recyclable materials. There might well be a special higher price for those who didn't want to segregate their garbage into categories, preferring instead to pay a higher cost so that others could segregate the garbage for them.

Once garbage collectors had done their job, they would dispose of the garbage according to the same free market principals. They would sell the garbage to the highest bidder or pay a landfill, incinerator, or recycler enough to make it worthwhile to process the garbage. In this way, the decision about which waste management method to use would be determined daily, according to the actual cost of that method. If a land fill was a cheaper way to dispose of, say, newspaper, then it would be the preferred method. All the costs and social concerns about each method would be reflected in the cost of each approach so that the decision would be made accurately and with consideration paid to all the relevant issues.

If a selfish town or county had a phobia about garbage and pollution, they might elect to ship all their waste out of town to other areas to which they would pay a premium to have it managed by those who were less phobic about, and more inclined to enjoy the profits from, garbage.

MEDIA BIAS

If at some point the non-phobic town decided land was growing scarce and pollution a concern, they might pass a regulation to limit total yearly pollution from their incinerator. To cut usage of the incinerator, prices for use would go up to the phobic town(s) until usage was cut to a point where pollution was at the mandated level., If enough towns felt pollution was a problem, the phobic town(s) would eventually be forced to build their own incinerators, and learn to live with their own pollution. If other towns figured, for whatever reason, that the additional revenue and pollution from the phobic town(s) was worthwhile, then they would be free to accept it. If they chose to meet the mandated pollution levels with new equipment, to increase the purity levels of emissions, they would, of course, have that option too.

If the free market price of incineration and landfilling rose higher and higher over the years, due to unsolved zoning and pollution problems, recycling would become the cost effective alternative. When the cost of recycling became one cent cheaper than landfilling and incineration, the time to recycle would have arrived. To do it sooner is to waste money that would have been better spent on incineration and landfilling; to do it later is to waste money that would have been better spent on recycling than on landfilling and incineration. Only the Republican free market can instruct us, on a daily basis, where money is most effectively spent, and which combination and type of waste management is best, in light of zoning and pollution problems.

The EPA wants the nation to recycle 25% of its garbage by 1992. The extent to which they are successful at encouraging us in this direction is the extent to which they are successful at wasting our money. This would only be a sensible number if by some miracle they guessed the number that the free market would have determined as millions of people bought and sold garbage each day. The EPA could have said 2% or 98%. If they forced us to recycle 98%, the cost would be so high as to probably cut our standard of living in half, but we would save natural resources. Is this a worthwhile tradeoff, and do we want to decide the answer through the free market or

NBC WANTS YOU TO RECYCLE

do we want the gov't to arbitrarily decide for us? If gov't forced us to recycle at only 2%, we would have more pollution, scarcer natural resources and probably more money in our pockets, unless the price of incineration and landfilling went way up. No gov't, think tank, university, or Democrat has the basis on which to adequately predict the complex manifestations which result from waste management. The free market operates on a day by day, sometimes minute by minute basis, adjusting to the real and constantly changing needs of those it serves; it is infinitely more responsive, sensitive and accurate than a Democratic bureaucracy.

In addition to being heavily involved with landfills, incinerators, and more recently, recycling centers, the gov't in 30 states is now offering tax breaks and loans to encourage recycling. All this gov't involvement gets us further and further away from the optimal free market solution which would cost less and better address the zoning\pollution problems.

So you see Mr. Brokaw, you might have had to mention many of these things if you had wanted to explain the Republican position. Instead, you explained your position, the Democratic position, by merely saying that recycling is obviously a good thing, and it is important for the gov't to force us all to do it.

THE DRUG PROBLEM-A FREE MARKET SOLUTION

Dear Rep. Charles Rangel,

In the course of preparing this book, it has been difficult to find elected officials with whom to correspond because most of what they write or speak for public consumption is heavily and understandably influenced by a desire to please their constituencies, rather than by a desire to be straight forward and thorough in the presentation of their position. On the issue of drugs, or drug legalization, you seem to be a refreshing exception in that you have been very bold, honest and thorough by participating in several very public and televised debates in support of the status quo on the drug war; this has encouraged me to respond to the heartfelt arguments you made during those debates. Although the debates often degenerated to a point where people, including yourself, were hollering at one another, it was instructive to note how, as an extremely liberal Democrat, from a NYC district with perhaps the worst drug problem in America, you displayed an abiding faith, that with a little more tinkering from Washington, it would soon be possible to get right on top of the drug problem. Given the tremendous failure of liberal Democratic gov't programs to extirpate illegal drugs over the last 20 years, it is difficult to imagine how such faith in the gov't can persist, even among Democrats such as yourself.

As if to coincide with the increasingly liberal society of the 1960's, drug use became popular, primarily among college students, as a way to confound the establishment and produce an internal "high." The drug culture seemed to stand for the notion that if people could relax enough, sometimes with the help of drugs, to let their real feelings show through, the aggressive impulses that supposedly led toward Vietnam and Racism would be avoided or at least diminished and controlled. Once Vietnam faded, drug use, nevertheless, continued, and at an expanded rate despite constant gov't "get tough" programs. The emphasis did, however, shift as people began to concentrate mostly on the non-political joys and sorrows of drug use.

A FREE MARKET SOLUTION

Today the problem has grown to startlingly serious proportions indeed. About 750,000 people are arrested each year for drug use. If all pushers, not to mention users, were jailed, it would double the size of the U.S. prison population, which is already the largest in the world. Approximately 6000 people die from drug use each year. 40% of all property crime is related to drugs. Approximately 3,000,000 use cocaine regularly; 500,000 use crack, and another 4,000,000 use other drugs. According to DAWN (THE DRUG ABUSE WARNING NETWORK), these numbers are very low. Their research shows 18-35 million regular users of marijuana, 5 million users of heroin, 5-10 million cocaine users, and several million users of other drugs. About 25% of all AIDS cases in the U.S. are contracted through illegal intravenous drug use. Drug related law enforcement on the Federal, State, and Local level, costs about $20 Billion per year. Between 1980 and 1990 the prison population in the U.S. doubled to 1,000,000 people at a cost of $35,000 per person per year, as fear of crime and drugs rose dramatically. According to the FBI, marijuana is the most valuable farm crop in the United States and accounts for 1\3 of all drug arrests.

Democrats and Republicans do not split along any obviously discernable lines on the drug issue. Most Republicans view it as a just another crime for which the individual, as a member of a free society, needs to be held fully accountable. They argue that by improving the criminal justice system so that its features include swift, certain, and harsh punishment for anyone who becomes connected with drugs, the problem can be reduced or at least contained. Democrats tend to treat the individual as a victim of an imperfect society who needs help, education, treatment programs, and enlightened or soft, rehabilitative criminal justice, while society works to perfect itself so that it doesn't produce so many people with drug problems.

Some major cracks are beginning to appear in this neat dichotomy as the successive Wars on Drugs come to look more like the hopeless war in Vietnam or like Russian five year plans to boost industrial and agricultural productivity. Republicans have a problem because they had the opportunity to try the "lock'em up" approach in the 80's and it didn't seem to work,

THE DRUG PROBLEM

although no one can be sure that the problem wouldn't be even worse than it is now if gov't hadn't been so tough. Further, there is conflict within the party in that when you believe in individual liberty as centrally as Republicans do, you are hard pressed to deny an individual the freedom to use drugs, particularly when he has long been free to use chemicals like alcohol and tobacco which, according to one very legitimate school of thought, are many times more widely used and deadly, to both the user and associated people, than drugs. Republicans will often argue that if after 200 years we were able to find a Fifth Amendment privacy right to an abortion buried deep within the Constitution, then it should also be possible to find a privacy right to use drugs. Some Republicans like to point out that cocaine was legally manufactured in many different forms, for sale in the U.S. from 1850 to 1914, with only very minor public health consequences. Social conservatives within the party, however, tend to be much less encumbered by political idealogy; they merely want to turn the clock back to around 1960 when, as Jeffery Hart once said, "the going was good." For them, certain, swift, and harsh punishment is the answer, even if it means the imprisonment of 3,000,000 Americans and the embarrassment of having the highest per capita imprisonment rate in the world, by a factor of 3.

Republicans, many of whom tend to be socially as well as politically conservative, tend to be more alarmed and action oriented about the drug problem, than Democrats. Since the days of Vietnam, when the Democratic Party became the party of protest against the war that Democratic Presidents Kennedy and Johnson started, they have supposedly been the party of social change; the party that gave shelter to virtually all special interests and new ideas as they came along. Jews and Blacks, for example, remain one of the only reliable constituencies that the Democrats have, in the belief that the Democratic embrace of every new, and liberal, special interest group will always include them and thus spare them the exclusion and prejudice they have encountered so often throughout their history. Organizations to promote the legalization of marijuana have long been around and have always anticipated that any political support would come from within the Democratic Party. Little support for these organizations or the 20,000,000 odd marijuana users has been public

A FREE MARKET SOLUTION

though, since around 90% of Americans seem to be solidly and consistently against legalization. Now that the harder drugs of the 80's, cocaine and crack, have been definitely linked to violent crime, no Democrat is likely to publicly support legalization and risk the appearance of being soft on crime or drugs.

This political wall of steadfast opinion on how to deal with drugs is very solid despite the abject failure, but some noted Republican intellectuals, who are not politicians, are beginning to suggest the legalization alternative. As Republicans were called upon to end the Vietnam War that Democrats started, some are now beginning to feel that legalization of the drug culture that Democrats helped foster, is the only practical way to end the drug war, or at best, the only possibility to end the war and stabilize or reduce drug related problems, that has not yet been explored. Some claim that it is time to walk away from the drug war just as the U.S. walked away from the Vietnam War. Others in the Republican Party counter that it is not time to give up. Surrender, they say, is nothing but another capitulation to the Democratic ethos which demands everything from gov't including, condoms, abortions, welfare, health care, social security, international peace, education, civil-rights, and now drugs; all from a Federal Gov't which is seen as the benign and altruistic instrument of collective society.

Legalization proponents from both parties counter that the following essentially good things would happen with legalization: 1) we would have philosophic harmony between our alcohol, tobacco, and drug laws, 2) almost half of all the crime in America would disappear overnight as the enormous profits from illegal drugs disappeared, 3) with jail space, court space, and police time being more abundant; certain, swift, and harsh criminal justice would be possible, 4) the culture which glorifies the quick money and fancy lifestyle of the Columbian drug lord and ghetto pusher would be gone, 5) with drugs in the hands of gov't monopolists, who sold at low prices, new designer drugs like crack, which were innovatively developed as a more potent and more concealable version of cocaine, so it could be priced for ghetto consumption, would not be needed, 6) with users buying from the gov't, they would be known to the gov't; as such, they could be targeted very accurately for education and rehabilitation,

THE DRUG PROBLEM

7) quality and purity could be controlled so that overdoses and grossly self-destructive behavior could be minimized, 8) the banality of waiting in gov't ques for cheap drugs would discourage many people from using them, 9) respect for the law would rise as millions were no longer forced by their habit to break the law and watch the daily disgrace of their gov't fighting a Vietnam style losing war, 10) free needles could greatly control the spread of AIDS, 11) $20 Billion in current Federal, State and Local expenditures could be saved; billions in drug tax revenue could be raised, 12) restrictions on the very important medical uses of drugs would be lifted, 13) police would no longer be forced to divide families and communities against each other as they trade leniency for information, 14) drug enforcement as a threat to civil-liberties would be ended. Police intrusions to discover the victimless and voluntary drug transactions that take place would be eliminated, 15) full time criminal activity would no longer be needed to pay the high cost of illegal drugs; without a criminal record more addicts or moderate abusers could hold jobs, 16) Federal, social welfare expenditures would be used as intended rather than diverted to buy drugs, 17) users would no longer be compelled to associate with and work for criminals in order to indulge their habit, 19) without pushers with a profit and glory motive, drug use might actually decline, particularly since pushers try to sell in a pyramid type scheme to other pusher\users whom they deem to be the most trustworthy or the least likely to be working for the cops, 20) drug use would not go up since drugs are now readily available anyway, 21) many kids would stay in school longer as the possibility of being a drug dealer disappeared, 19) if drug legalization turned out to be a mistake, it could be reversed, just as it was in 1914 by the Harrison Act, which made cocaine illegal after 50 years of production and distribution by the Park-Davis Drug Company.

The major fear is that with legalization, drug use might increase far above what it is now. The arguments against this are as follows: 1) pushers would be gone, and replaced by dreary gov't types who would be generally discouraging, 2) when illegal, drugs are used as if there is no tomorrow; with legalization they could be used in moderation with the knowledge that a variety of drugs would be cheap and available well into the future.

A FREE MARKET SOLUTION

Casual use with a friend would be possible, users would not be forced toward quick, cheap, potent, and concealable drugs as happened, for example, during prohibition when 129-proof alcohol replaced the standard 86-proof variety because it was more compact, 3) Americans are showing a great deal of self-control as alcohol and tobacco use is actually declining; presumable they would show the same restraint if hard drugs were legalized, 4) drugs are already, readily available to anyone who wants them, 5) The billions saved in enforcement and collected in taxes could be used to mount a tremendous education campaign, 6) in the Netherlands, decriminalization has resulted in decreased use, 7) decriminalization would not imply approval any more than the First Amendment implies approval of the KKK, 8) if drug use did go up, it might be a tolerable price to pay for the decrease in crime that would certainly occur, 9) according to the National Institute on Drug Abuse, cocaine and crack are no more addictive than alcohol, 10) the decriminalization of marijuana in 11 of the U.S. States in the 1970's, did not seem to increase drug use in those States, 11) in reality, it may be the criminalization of drug use that has caused the steady increase in usage since the 1960's, 12) the prohibition of alcohol in the 20's seemed to have had little overall affect on consumption; drugs are no more addictive, and presumably will respond in the same manner.

In spite of all the evidence that is piling up about the govt's failure to control drug use, it is amazing, Mr. Rangel, to see you expressing so much faith in the govt's ability to succeed. A walk through the streets of many neighborhoods in your district should convince you that successive drug wars mounted by successive gov't administrations have not worked as intended, and may have had the opposite affect. As with most Democrats, your approach is to simply spend a little more money, try a little harder and hope a little longer. While this approach almost never works in any area of social policy, it is doomed to be even less effective in the drug area, because this war, is truly a war against ourselves. Using drugs is a victimless crime, and a personal choice that 25-50 million Americans make regularly; the problems associated with drugs result primarily from the criminalization of their use. It is the recognition of this that has provoked 11 States to successfully decriminalize the use of marijuana.

THE DRUG PROBLEM

Despite some notable exceptions, like editor William Buckley, economist Milton Friedman, Mayor Kurt Schmoke, and the Libertarian Party (the third largest in the Country) most politicians and most Americans, remain solidly opposed to the legalization of drugs. The debate is really centered around how much to spend to enforce the existing laws. Democrats like yourself, Mr. Rangel, are constantly calling for more money, while Republicans like President Bush seem happy to settle for modest spending increases and improved management.

The current situation is quite preposterous and tragic. Not ten blocks from this authors business address, the police recently busted perhaps the biggest drug dealer in the city. In the middle of the most squalid ghetto street, this dealer always had 4-6 shiny new foreign automobiles lining his place of business, including at least one Mercedes-Benz and BMW. His profession was immediately known to anyone who ever went down his street, but despite several arrests for minor drug offenses, he was never convicted of anything serious enough to land him in jail. When I asked a policeman who was involved in the case, why the dealer didn't go to jail after the last arrest, when he was caught in possession of a substantial quantity of crack, the policeman said, "that's our criminal justice system for you." When I pressed him further about how a major drug dealer avoided jail after several related arrests he said, "to the Department of Correction he's just another number they didn't have room for." When I pressed further, the officer suggested that perhaps he could have been sent to South Dakota where they have excess prison space.

Drug users and pushers know the criminal justice system has no teeth, and that they have little to fear from it. Police officers can be very mean and nasty to arrestees as they feel no other form of punishment is forthcoming. The courts and local jails, where arrestees are held awaiting court appearances, can be cold and foreboding places. Prosecutors and narcotics police officers can threaten to send defendants away forever unless they snitch on every pusher and friend they ever had. Drug treatment programs are forced on those who seem marginally willing, but often this just buys time for the pusher who again beats the system by simply buying black market urine to beat drug testing. In the end, all of

A FREE MARKET SOLUTION

the above turns out to be the worst of it for those unlucky enough to be arrested; the machismo of the ghetto tough drug dealer is tested and often strengthened. He is returned to the street as a better craftsman; more broadly skilled in all the aspects of his profession.

Under the current system there is illegal, but readily available drugs. It is the worst of all possible worlds. It encourages disrespect for the cop, judge, legislator, and society, while driving up usage, price, and a wide range of often violent criminal activity. The Democratic approach, that you favor so loudly, Mr. Rangel, is now more than ever, ridiculously impotent, but, perversely, politically safe. The Republican "get tough" approach may not be practical since it has already filled the system way beyond capacity with the worst 750,000 offenders, without making a dent in the problem. Legalization is the only possible alternative. It is an approach that does not fit well with the idealogy of either political party, and it would now be a political disaster for any politician to support legalization, given that 90% of Americans support the current system, no matter how bad it seems to be. The idea will have to grow a great deal outside the political system before many politicians will dare to embrace it, and when they do, it will have to be a bi-partisan effort so that neither will be burdened with the potentially huge risks from such a bold and innovative approach.

FREE SPEECH-POLITICALLY CORRECT DEMOCRATS

Dear Chris Matthews,

I have recently read your article on campus free speech and the new phrase, "politically correct" (PC). Your article was good as far as it went, but it did not go very far toward putting the subject in perspective so that your readers would know how both Democrats and Republicans view it. I will concede that adding perspective to the subject of politically correct behavior has become very complicated given that there now seems to be at least three different levels to it, as follows: 1) (PC) good manners, 2) (PC) constitutional free speech and 3) (PC) philosophical truth.

This subject is another area in which Democrats are pitted directly against Republicans. As usual, it is the Democrats who are trying to force Republicans to behave themselves in a politically correct way, or in a way that suits Democrats. The issue is an important one since it will be played out mostly on college and university campuses which often are the source of the ideas used to define ourselves, and to determine the direction of our country. Unfortunately, college professors have overwhelmingly tended to be Democratic or worse. They would want us to believe that this is because they are on the side of high intelligence and compassion. In reality, it is because Democrats and professors have a common affinity for big ideas that can save or reshape the world in accordance with their, supposedly, very intellectual prescriptions. For Democratic politicians, big ideas that can dramatically change the world for the better are a way to gain political power and, in many cases, indulge their simplistic belief that new, big ideas can quickly improve the world. For professors, the objective is to explain the way the world works, or better yet, the way it could work if only the world would listen to them. To rely so heavily on ancient wisdom as conservative Republicans do; to assume that individuals

POLITICALLY CORRECT DEMOCRATS

are not evil and, when left largely to their own devices, will work things out at in a civilized and timely manner, would leave professors without the activist, interventionist role they cherish. Republican professors, conversely, tend to be occupied with the comparatively dull job of rediscovering the value of historical wisdom, and finding fault with the new Democratic ideas. The concept of a Republican professor, in some senses, sounds a little boring as it lacks the dramatic possibilities that might come with a hot, new idea. Your article, Mr. Matthews, which ends up by doing little more than gently cautioning the newly aggressive and self-righteous Democratic left, against shutting out the normally calm Republicans, is on track but woefully inadequate.

During the spring of 1991, politically correct behavior on campus became a big issue for the following reasons: 1) hippie professors weaned in the 1960's were now old enough to be making their influence felt on college faculties, 2) Democrats, on and off campus, have grown to be an increasingly embattled minority, particularly as they lost the little chance they had to be part of mainstream politics, by opposing President Bush and the nation on the Gulf War, 3) minority groups (blacks and women primarily) have grown newly intolerant over the growth of conservatism, the success of the Reagan Presidency, and slow minority progress and 4) young Republicans on campus have been emboldened by recent conservative intellectual successes.

The most well known case having to do with campus "PC" behavior had to do with a student who was expelled from Brown university after a drunken celebration of his birthday, during which he acted and spoke in a very impolite way toward blacks, homosexuals, and Jews. There was no physical contact and no threat, but there was action that violated the college's code of conduct by "showing flagrant disrespect for the well being of others or by being reasonably disruptive of the university community." The case might have expanded to a free speech issue except that Brown is a private school and as such, somewhat removed from constitutional restrictions. Many schools have adopted similar codes of conduct with similarly vague language that is subject to a wide range of interpretations.

FREE SPEECH

It seems that universities, where the free exchange of ideas is central, ought to hold the First Amendment in the highest regard, whether they are private institutions or not. The distance between free speech and rude insults has always been very short. During the Vietnam era, for example, it was common for the Democratic left to criticize Republicans as "baby killers." Was this constitutionally protected free speech or just rude behavior?

Secondly, good manners and polite behavior ultimately derive from philosophical interpretations, and definitions of history. In the 50's and 60's conservatives were treated very rudely by Democratic intellectuals; today Republicans win the Nobel Prizes and the situation is very different. For intellectual growth, tolerance has always been very essential. Accordingly, universities should anticipate that 18 year old students will arrive on their doorstep in need of more learning and better manners. Universities should be in the business of separating children from their ignorance; not expelling them for having it.

Other aspects of the "PC" debate focus more exclusively on the free speech issue. Initially the problem on campus was to shout down or otherwise silence Republican speakers, but the situation quickly became more complicated as all political ideas couldn't easily be classified as Democratic or Republican. Simple minded Democrats often portray Republicans as racists, but even blacks run into trouble, as they did on the University Michigan campus when they wanted to support Lewis Farrakhan and his constant, racist anti-semitism. Blacks on that very liberal campus could get away with hating Republicans, but hating Republicans and Jews was going too far. New York University Law school recently canceled a moot court case about the child custody rights of a lesbian parent so as not to be in a position to offend lesbians. Another student in Iowa was corrected with potentially severe disciplinary action for hanging a sign on his door which said that "GAY" stood for - got aids yet. At another university, a student was corrected for expressing his feeling that homosexuality was a disease that could be cured through a clinic he was about to open. No group, it would seem, is very pure for very long. Today's polarized groups seem unwilling to tolerate other groups that too

POLITICALLY CORRECT DEMOCRATS

sharply disagree with them. In the end, the enforcement of (PC) thinking has to be seen as the enforcement of totalitarianism.

In defense of universities, it can be said that something had to be done to stem the sharp rise in incidents of abusive or near abusive behavior. But on the other hand, the universities and the Democrats have conspired together for years to turn down the temperature in the melting pot in favor of disparate multi-culturalism. As a result, individuals will often prefer to identify themselves in terms of the particular group they belong to; not in terms of the single societal group that all Americans were once proud to be part of. It is not surprising that different groups quickly became competing groups.

When Abraham Lincoln committed the country to a bloody civil war "just to save the union" he was telling America that the common values shared by virtue of being American are ultimately more important than the comparatively petty differences between us or between north and south. Since the Civil War Era, from which the modern Republican Party was formed, until today, Republicans have had a lock on the concept of patriotism because the basic and shared Constitutional values of the country were always more important to them than the special interest group values that the Democrats have tried so hard to promote and exploit. University Democrats ought to now realize that patriotism is the only glue that prevents civil war and holds citizens together. Patriotism is a value they should begin to appreciate. "Love it or leave it," is an old slogan, much scoffed at by Democrats, but it accurately implies a recognition that the love and respect we have for our country is the only thing that holds it together. However, to maintain both a patriotic and dynamic society it is necessary to tolerate a wide range of free speech. Not surprisingly, a Republican, Henry Hyde, has introduced a bill to extend the First Amendment to cover colleges and universities.

Besides its lack of respect for the First Amendment, the Politically Correct movement has a growing allegiance to a radical school of thought that is mostly Marxist, but sufficiently different so as to qualify as a leading edge, big idea that can satisfy the PH.D's often Democratic, and sometimes radical thirst to develop a new and improved society.

Religion was the common threat that gave Western Civilization its identity and cohesion. With the development of scientific explanations (after the American Revolution) for so many of the things that had previously been explained by religion, mankind was left more philosophically adrift than at any time in history. This development has been the single most important factor leading to the current disharmony on campus and in the larger general society. Those who haven't been satisfied to merely re-interpret religion in a more general way (i.e., God must have caused the big bang) to accommodate the new scientific knowledge, were left to find their own explanations to give meaning and purpose to life. This led to the development of existentialism, the theory that without God, man, through his own thoughts and actions was free and obligated to design and define his own life. Over the years many variations and extensions developed; ranging from Christian existentialism, developed by Kierkegaard, to Nietzsche's existentialism, which defined man primarily by his inherent desire for power. In all cases, there was the common thread which held that man should define himself in relation to the higher cosmos; not merely through being, but by actions. The actions might have a traditional religious origin; they might be motivated by the pure drama and excitement that comes from dramatic action, or they might be used to support a new and rational political movement. Nietzsche believed that man was defined primarily by his desire for power, and that ultimately all of his thoughts and actions were legitimately and of necessity determined by an interest in pure power which had neither a moral nor immoral dimension. Much German existentialism had an extremely nationalistic aspect to it so that Hitler was able to steal large pieces of the philosophy to justify his use of power, although his National Socialism and existentialism never fit together very well.

The acknowledged central figure of the existentialist movement was Martin Heidegger, a man who had marginal but very definite sympathy for Hitler and anti-semitism. He was to began his career as a phenominalogist,

POLITICALLY CORRECT DEMOCRATS

an area of thought which held that there was no objective knowledge, only illusion based on cultural, historical, and psychological perspectives that were themselves illusions. He refined this perspective into modern existentialism which became, and still remains, the dominant theory of philosophy. Karl Marx, the father of Communism, relied heavily on it to justify the philosophy that almost took over the world. Jean Paul Sartre, the dominate figure of Twentieth Century French literature and philosophy, relied on it as a foundation for his "Critque de la Raison."

Nihilism became an adjunct to existentialism for those who believed that all existing ideas and institutions had to be destroyed before it was possible to build a pure existential world, not polluted by the remnants of religious history. A man afflicted by marital divorce or terminal cancer can understand how possible it is for history to vanish once a new set of underlying assumptions is accepted.

For Karl Marx, God and the very precise history he created, was dead. History was, according to his new discovery, really controlled by economic existentialism. He said, "the method of production in material life determines the general character of the social, political, and spiritual processes of life." It is not the consciousness of man that determines their being, but on the contrary, their social being determines their consciousness." (Marx) 1933, xvi, also 393, n.2.) Hence, group rights, were considered superior to those of the individual, since the individual really experiences life only as a member of the group he or she belongs to.

It is for this broad philosophic tradition that some of American academia has developed a growing sympathy. It is perhaps worse now because radicals from the Ho Chi Minh,1960's are now old enough to be filling the ranks of tenured professors on many campuses. Without a war to coalesce around, this time it is the plight of women and blacks that is their focal point. Today's existentialist, communist, nihilistic professors chant, if you can believe it,"hey hey ho ho Western Culture has got to go." The idea is to nihilistically destroy Western Civilization, or at least any respect students may have for it, so that a brave new world can be formed

FREE SPEECH

in which women and minorities start from a truly equal position that is not corrupted by the fraudulent culture which now treats them so harshly. In the sixties, radicals told America to believe that football represented America at its fascist worst; today they tell us that organized crime is a metaphor for business as usual.

To expose the sexual bias in American society they really do teach a course called, "How To Bring Your Kids Up Gay." To demonstrate that no objective truth exists; that everything is merely a pre-existential product of a fraudulent culture, they would have students believe that the cherished American concept of individual liberty is no more sensible than the concept of the "divine right of kings;" that totalitarianism is intrinsically no better or worse than democracy. Black pride is instilled by teaching that the bedrock of Western Civilization, ancient Greece, really stole its culture from Black Africa. According to the theory, things like mountain bikes and democracy are mere fads based more on cultural conditioning than reason.

Mr. Matthews, you close your article on this entire subject by gently accusing the Democratic left of no longer being protean or flexible because they are so totally intolerant of every point of view except their own; this is like hunting an elephant with a fly swatter. What these friendly Democrats are proposing for America is no less radical than what Hitler proposed for Germany, and Lenin for Russia. As we speak, they have a larger power base than either Hitler or Lenin had when they discovered their new ideas. Perhaps there is no serious cause for real excitement in light of the long and relatively impotent history of Democratic college professors. Nevertheless, children are sent to school primarily to learn an appreciation of their culture; not to destroy it. In the interest of free speech and academic freedom it may not be a bad thing to have radical ideas represented on campus, put there is certainly no reason for gov'ts or parents to support institutions that so badly represent the culture they are supposed to serve.

To gently admonish them for not being protean, is to grossly understate the importance of the problem Democrats are creating on campus. In a very real and practical way our world is defined by the existential choice

POLITICALLY CORRECT DEMOCRATS

we make between Democrats and Republicans each time we enter the voting booth, and virtually 100% of the "Political Correct" professors vote Democratic, unless they can find a candidate even further to the left; this ought to encourage the rest of us to vote Republican.

TAXES - NO END TO DEMOCRATIC TAXES

Dear Jesse Jackson & Isabel Sawhill,

Both of you have just written articles about the level of Federal spending. Republicans and Democrats have always split very evenly on this issue. Republicans believe in less overall spending as part of their philosophy that gov't should be small, while Democrats very much want to maintain or increase Federal spending as part of their philosophy that gov't should be big. Despite the tons of political rhetoric on both sides of this issue, it really is very easy to make sense of the debate by relating it back to the general, but different, principals that motivate both political parties. Both of you, Mr. Jackson and Ms. Sawhill, fail to do this because as liberal Democrats you are running scared; not wanting to reveal too much about your real thinking and motives. At first glance, Mr. Jackson, it is tempting to overlook many of the problems with your article because you are a constant and populist presidential candidate who, publicly at least, is trying to be popular more than logical. But, when your basic sentiments and most of your thoughts are so similar to those of the very scholarly Isabel Sawhill, who published her article in "THE AMERICAN PROSPECT," your thoughts, such as they are, seem much more representative and worthy of comment.

Mr. Jackson, you begin your article by cautioning America that it should not believe its President when he says there is no more money to spend. The President is not to be believed, according to you, because there was plenty of money to spend on the Gulf War ($50-80 Billion), the Savings and Loan Scandal ($500 Billion), and the capital gains tax cut (you didn't cite numbers here).

God knows these are probably the three worst areas you could have picked to make your point, but then again it must be very difficult to prove that the U.S. has lots of money when the Federal deficit is running at $350, 000, 000, 000. Firstly, as you well know, U.S. Allies are

NO END TO DEMOCRATIC TAXES

making good on their promises to pick up most of the tab. Had the U.S. not fought the war and instead allowed Iraq to annex Kuwait, it is likely that the cost in higher energy prices and political instability would have been far greater than the cost of the war itself. All indications were that the sanctions imposed on Iraq were not working; to keep troops in the desert for months or years, and then fight a war, would have been more costly in terms of both lives and money. Hussein's intransigence through the long Iran-Iraq War and then after the Allied bombing began, indicates that war was probably the only alternative. The only way to save our Allies the $50-80 Billion would have been to ignore the situation and risk having both Kuwait and Saudi Arabia (40% of world oil supply) fall into Iraqi hands.

Secondly, you mention that the U.S. had $500 Billion to bail out "buccaneer bankers." You know very well that the money was not used to bail out buccaneer bankers, but rather the little people, the very people you usually claim to speak for, who otherwise would have lost their savings. But still, the gov't did manage to come up with $250 Billion; not $500 Billion as you claim. This money mostly came from selling debt on the strength of the Federal Govt's ability to levy future taxes on all Americans who must, eventually, retire the debt. Had Bush not done this, confidence in the banking system would have been shattered, and economic collapse may well have followed. This was a banking crisis too similar to the banking panics of 1907 and 1929, and it had to be averted at any cost. If you consider that there are around 140,000,000 taxpayers, this means that each will pay around $5,000 in interest plus principal to bail out the failed S & L's; this is, all would agree, a lot of money, but money that had to be spent.

Thirdly, you mention the capital gains tax cut that Bush has proposed, but that has not passed the Congress. This seems like a totally irrelevant way for you to prove that the United States is really holding out on its citizens. I guess you want your readers to think that President Bush's gov't is so rich that it can afford to cut taxes. In truth the gov't wants to cut the capital gains tax to stimulate business and job development for the benefit of everyone, and to enlarge the overall tax base for itself. In 1981, for

TAXES

example, Reagan cut the capital gains rate to 20%, and revenue, from that tax alone, doubled. It is impossible to explain how Bush's proposal for a tax cut means the U.S has extra money; yet you summarize these three examples by saying, "see, I told you so, the money is there; it's just a question of where we choose to spend it."

Would you, Mr. Jackson, be willing to admit that it was the bank customers and not the bankers who got bailed out; that borrowing money to pay for the bailout was a sign of poverty and not excess wealth; that Bush had no choice but to spent the $50 Billion in the Gulf, and that by cutting the capital gains rate, Bush would be raising tax revenue and stimulating the economy; not giving excess Federal money to his rich friends.

Next, you sharply criticize what you call all "the hype" surrounding the budget by saying that Bush, and by implication, Republicans, talk about big spending liberals and then contradictorily propose a $1.17 Trillion budget that is 25% of the Gross National Product. You know very well, Mr. Jackson, that Republicans are for less gov't spending, but that it would not be realistic or politic for them to present, say, a 25% budget reduction plan to a Democratic Congress that would immediately go around to every one of their special interest groups to warn them to beware of Republican spending cuts.

Next, I guess to demonstrate what an independent thinker you are, you criticize your fellow liberal Democrats by noting that they decry Bush's compassion for the wealthy but don't criticize the wealthy management and owners of the bankrupt Savings and Loan Industry. It seems, in reality, that the bankers have been roundly criticized by everybody, and in many cases sent to jail. Even the President's son paid an enormous price. While he is apparently not going to jail, he is broke and in debt $250,000 for legal fees.

You then go on to surmise from all of what you call the Republican bombast, that a phony debate will arise around national health insurance; you say, "buried beneath the bombast, choices are being made about our future; Congress will debate ferociously, don't believe the hype, the real

NO END TO DEMOCRATIC TAXES

choice is not to create a national health care system." Somehow you feel you have demonstrated that there is plenty of money around and that decency should compel us to spend it on national health care. You made a very feeble case that the money was available, and no case that national health insurance was better than what we have now, or better than the reforms that Republicans propose.

Next, in a very inscrutable paragraph, you note that despite a united Europe and the end of the Cold War, military spending is going to go up due to Star Wars, the B-2 Bomber, The Gulf War, and the vagaries of Bush's new world order. You close by saying that Bush thinks military spending is more important than domestic economic strength and security. You didn't address the standard Republican position that a strong military is essential, particularly in this, one of the bloodiest centuries ever, so that the U.S. won't be conquered or defeated as has been the fate of most nations throughout history. Furthermore, the idea of predicting, with any accuracy, how much defense will be needed, is largely futile to sensible Republicans, much like trying to predict the recent rise and fall of the USSR, Iraq, Iran and Nicaragua. The safe and sensible solution is to stay armed to the teeth, rather than gamble with national defense.

You close your article by repeating again that the U.S. can choose national health insurance, and by adding, out of the blue, that the U.S. can dramatically cut pentagon spending by $150 Billion (50%) and still retain the strongest military in the world. You don't say one word to explain how this would be possible. It seems more sensible to Republicans, that the U.S. ought to drastically cut wasteful and senseless domestic spending that has hurt most of the people it has tried to help. Spending the money on the military, so that the U.S. will never again have to worry like it did before the start of the Gulf War, that tens of thousands of young American men and women will be killed by one of the many fanatically anti-American dictators in the world, would be a logical choice. To suggest that we could cut the defense budget by $150 Billion (50%) or more, just after we strained the active military, the reserve military, and the civilian supply system to the limit, just to beat tiny Iraq, is reckless and very irrational. In retrospect, the military fielded in the Gulf, looked very strong, but it would not now look that way if the U.S. hadn't had the fortuitous luxury

TAXES

of having months to move the Allied military machines into place. Similarly the military wouldn't have looked so strong if Iraq had a missile even one generation improved over the World War II era, Scud. Your extreme views, Mr. Jackson, are something of an embarrassment to the Democratic Party, but they are so respectful of your ability to deliver the civil-rights vote, that they can't very well ask you to disappear.

You and Isabel Sawhill are fellow travelers on the left of the Democratic Party, although she is more of an academic type who is not so constrained by politics. For her, the question of where the money will come from is not governed by the "read my lips" no new taxes mentality. She does not feel that there are some general constraints on taxation levels, as you do Mr. Jackson, which would necessitate taking the money from the military so as not to increase overall spending levels. She is not concerned that the U.S. has a $350 Billion deficit that neither Democrats nor Republicans have the nerve to cover with still higher taxes. To Sawhill, the U.S. has gotten itself into a fiscal trap. What she really means is that the Democrats are in a trap and have little reason to exist, and little electoral appeal, now that they can't promise new spending programs. To solve the problem; to get the Democrats back into the game, she wants to force a new way of thinking on the taxpayer. "First and most critical, she says, "it is time to challenge the political taboos against raising taxes." To Sawhill, Democrats need to make paying taxes "fashionable" like dieting, jogging, mineral water, and Ninetendo.

To bolster your claim, Ms. Sawhill, that taxes can be fashionably higher, you note that the U.S. would have to spend another $500 Billion to equal the per capita spending of West Germany. While this is true, if you compare German Federal spending with that of the U.S., it is not true if you compare all of U.S. gov't spending with all of theirs. Since they are a relatively small and highly centralized country, most of their spending is done by the central gov't at a rate of $6854 per person; in the U.S., the Federal spending rate is $4812, but state and local spending is more than 50% higher than Federal spending, so that total gov't spending in the U.S. is actually larger than in your example country, West Germany. This is to say nothing of off-budget items like Social Security ($1331 per person)

NO END TO DEMOCRATIC TAXES

and items like the $500 Billion ($2000 per person) S & L bailout that make U.S. spending still higher. There is virtually no way an honest person can look at the numbers and conclude that the U.S. doesn't have a total tax burden higher than, or comparable to the supposedly more socialized countries of Western Europe.

As a serious Democratic scholar you argue for an ever larger public sector, just as Jesse Jackson, a serious Democratic politician, argues for the same thing. Both of you mysteriously, completely ignore the Republican opposition view that gov't spending is the problem; not the solution. You, Ms. Sawhill, want to raise tax rates to world record levels even though they are there now, Of course, you know that if a politician were to follow your plan and announce to voters that he wanted to tack an additional $2500 per year onto their tax bill, they would be instantly defeated and probably hung. Jackson wants to cut defense spending in half, even though we have just seen, from the Gulf War, how defense spending can save lives and even whole countries. Of course, Jackson doesn't say in public that he would have liked to see the U.S. go into the War with half the military might it had. Your proposal, Rev. Jackson, and your proposal Ms. Sawhill, is reckless and desperate, and reflects a political party that is not capable of even understanding what the debate is about, much less winning it.

VOTING RIGHTS - DEMOCRATIC DECEIT

Dear Messrs. Valelly and Greenberg,

I have read your articles which were published in the new and prestigious, "THE AMERICAN PROSPECT," and it seems that they both rely on basic assumptions that were apparently so obvious to you that you forgot to state them to your readers. In "Vanishing Voters," Mr. Valelly, you devote yourself to detailing the sadly low voter participation levels in the United States. Your very first statement goes as follows: "Electoral participation is vital to political Democracy." From that point on you say nothing about why you feel it is vital to vote, until the last paragraph when you say, "participation can help to turn the subjects of administration into citizens capable of self gov't; it can help create a hardy sense of membership in a political community; and it has great empowering possibilities." This modest, brief, and very vague rationale, stated in just two sentences, in support of voter participation, is woefully inadequate to explain why you devoted a whole article to bemoaning low participation levels. You assume that participation is low, but you say little about the very personal standards you must have used to determine this. It seems that an equal or better case about voter participation being too high, can be made much more easily.

It seems obvious that participation, for the reasons stated above, is almost meaningless given that it says nothing about the primary objective of voting; i.e., getting well qualified people elected. Encouraging participation to impart a sense of empowerment and community is a worthy objective, but certainly not if it forces unqualified voters into the voting booth where they vote for candidates who do not represent their legitimate interests. The U.S. is far better off having fewer, but more knowledgeable people voting, rather than having more, but less knowledgeable people voting. It is very difficult for proud Americans to admit that the

DEMOCRATIC DECEIT

tremendous amount of fluff in the election process is caused by politicians catering to the emotional whims of very poorly qualified voters, but it is obviously true.

It is baffling that at election time, almost any famous person can be persuaded to go on television as a suffragist. It would be against the spirit of our time for famous people to say instead, "voting is a very grave responsibility, it requires much reading and analysis; please don't vote unless or until you think you are well qualified on such matters as foreign and domestic policy." Voting may be the only managerial responsibility in the world that is given out totally without regard to qualifications. In truth, it is not any easier for a voter to represent his interests in a voting booth than for a patient to represent his interests in, say, a hospital. In both cases, the equipment is better left to those who have trained to handle it.

At the beginning of American History, it was common for men like George Washington and Alexander Hamilton, of The Federalist Party, to be very skeptical of the common man's ability to vote intelligently, and yet these men obviously still believed very deeply in Democracy. To them, Democracy was a way of distributing or balancing power so that it would not concentrate in the Federal Gov't; something which they desperately sought to prevent. Only to a small degree was it a way to solicit wisdom from the citizenry. Wisdom was contained in the Constitution, they thought; not in the minds of men (except those who wrote the constitution); that is why they gave America a constitutional democracy, rather than a popular democracy.

One of the major aims of the Constitutional Convention was to severely limit broad scale participation. Hamilton thought Jefferson a contemptible idiot for believing in the common man's ability to vote intelligently. Hamilton felt that Jefferson's preoccupation with concepts like liberty and popular rule would lead to general anarchy. Jefferson himself seemed to agree with Hamilton, at least by the standards of today, which make it practically a crime not to vote, when he said, "Free government is founded on jealousy, and not confidence in man, ...but bind him down from mischief by the chains of the Constitution." Edmund Randolph spoke at

VOTING RIGHTS

length about "the turbulence and folly of Democracy; "James Madison agreed with much more polite language by speaking of "a policy of refining the popular appointments by successive filtration." In the end, only the House of Representatives was elected by the people; the Senate was to be elected by the State Legislatures for long six year terms, and the President was to be elected by an independent electoral college.

It was not until the 1830's, when President Andrew Jackson reportedly encouraged farmers with dirty boots to dance all over White House furniture to celebrate his presidential victory for the common man, that the voting franchise was broadly extended by eliminating property requirements, poll taxes, increasing the number of elected rather than appointed offices, and making all elections more direct. Voter participation reached as high as 74%, up from 25% at the beginning of the 19th Century. The belief that any honest man could vote intelligently was, for the first time, widely promoted by politicians who realized that flattery was an ideal way to win support from the masses who previously had been judged unqualified to vote.

It is not a difficult stretch to see how communists can extrapolate from similar reasoning that they deeply care about their people without being democratic in the Western sense. From their point of view, communist power is distributed, as in a democracy, but only to qualified professional managers who work their way up through the ranks of the Communist Party, somewhat like American corporate managers. Those who aren't in the party have simply to trust that the ruling class is best qualified and will look out for their interests, even when those interests conflict with those of the ruling class.

While Democrats and Republicans generally do not disagree, at least in public, on this issue, as they seem to on most issues, it is a very useful to examine it anyway as it helps to clarify from another perspective how fraudulent the appeal of the Democratic Party is. As a 10 year old growing up in upstate New York, I recall my older 12 year old brother saying to me that Nelson Rockefeller was a man not to be supported because he had just vetoed an education bill. My brother reasoned that since education was

DEMOCRATIC DECEIT

obviously good, a good politician should support education. While I sensed the issue might be more complicated than that, I lost the debate anyway because I couldn't quite put my hands on the words to describe what those complications might be.

Although it is not a polite thing to think about, we ought to be able to face the idea that politics for adults and children is often very much the same. This is how it is possible to explain many of the contradictory patterns that you detail, Mr. Greenberg, in your article, Reconstructing the Democratic Vision, also published in "THE AMERICAN PROSPECT."

You point to a ABC\Washington Post survey which found that 76% of those polled want to increase spending on drug programs, 72% on Medicare, 61% on Medicaid, 68% cancer research, 66% AIDS, 61% day care programs, and 58% Social Security. If something is good, adults, like children, will support it until Republicans come along to point out that the cost is often more than the value of the results. A recent poll by the "New York Times," just prior to the Persian Gulf War, showed how much like children in a candy store we are. When initially asked whether they would support military action to drive Iraq from Kuwait, a very high percentage of respondents indicated that they would. When asked if they would support such action if it would cause 5000 American deaths, a casualty rate thought low by many at the time, the percentage dropped to around half of what it was. The revised number would have been much lower still, accept that many respondents were reluctant to feed into the researchers' hands by contradicting themselves. Similarly, voters often elect Republicans to the White House and then defeat their intentions by sending Democrats to the Congress.

According to the, late, Lee Atwater, and common sense, elections are won and lost by appeals to the swing vote; i.e, those voters who don't have firm party affiliations; who must be persuaded, tricked, or romanced with each new election before they can make up their minds, even though the issues stay the same for decades at a time. It would be a far better thing for the quality of government if the swing vote was discouraged from

VOTING RIGHTS

participating so that more energy would be focused on those who recognize that political ideas matter a great deal and that consistent support of those ideas is essential to sensible gov't policy.

Rather than take a stand on this issue in your article, you simply explain the electorates contradictory behavior by calling it "the enigma of public opinion." Why can't you admit that the enigma is really just ignorance caused by; 1) the Democrats seeking to create and then exploit an electorate, 2) a general failure of the schools and major media to educate voters about the difference between Democrats and Republicans, and 3) the misguided notion that Democracy depends more on the quantity than quality of voters.

Then, as a partisan Democratic strategist you seek to exploit what you call the "enigma" by encouraging "new models and ideas that will enable Democrats to take advantage of popular impulses that favor equity, populism, and national effort." You know full well that these popular impulses which make swing voters susceptible to Democratic spending programs, are the same ones that motivate a child in a toy store.

To exploit the swing vote you propose three projects. The first is the "middle class project." Recognizing that Democrats have lost the support of much of the middle class, you propose a liberal validation of middle class values that will somehow win them back. Your polls show that the middle class is suffering a great deal. Republicans know that this is because Democrats taxed the sox off the middle class to pay for their socialist schemes to help the poor and everybody else. Many Democratic presidential hopefuls are trying to exploit this situation that they themselves created by now getting behind the idea of a tax cut for the middle class. This is a smart strategy since swing voters always will look favorably on a tax cut. But, it shows Democrats at their most desperate and exploitive. To get votes, Democrats now seem willing to cut taxes and apologize to the middle class for past transgressions. But, how can Democrats finance the huge Federal programs that have always been their sole stock in trade and cut taxes at the same time? All of the sudden, the drunk is willing to cut back on his liquor? Don't count on it.

DEMOCRATIC DECEIT

Another project to exploit the swing vote involves national investment. According to your polls, the swing voter recognizes that America is very threatened economically by foreign competition. To answer their concerns you propose, after restoring tax relief and validity to the middle class, new investment across a broad range to put America back on top. The only concrete things you mention are social programs and a "more active role for gov't to encourage productivity growth, to foster technology innovation, to uplift the population and to revive American industry." This is standard Democratic rhetoric under a different banner. Some Democrats want to move toward the center to compensate for past extremes, you want to pursue the risky strategy of going to a further extreme by repackaging socialism, and hawking it to the swing vote. But, if the first project was to cut taxes, how could the second be to increase investment. This is the dilemma the Democrats increasingly face as they clumsily squirm at the end of their rope.

Your third and last project is the "populist project," or the "we hate business project." Accordingly, you want more honest business practices, higher corporate taxes, more active pursuit of new technology, and greater investment in American jobs. On one hand, you are going to regulate them and tax them even more; on the other you are going to help them with new technology and jobs. This is contradictory and socialist micromanagement, in theory; in practice it would be a disaster. Regulations and taxes would certainly hurt, but so would failed, socialist efforts to find new technologies and create new jobs. Plus, you like the idea of a tax hike on those who make over $240,000 per year because 80% of those in your poll supported the idea. Again, the appeal is a standard Democratic one that is not even credibly repackaged. The bold new model designed to manipulate the swing vote is easily seen through. Each proposed action has a cost or consequence which obviates the hoped for benefit. A survey of the popularity of your third project would certainly indicate a 90% approval. Of course, if you mentioned some of the consequences of these ideas, the approval rating would probably drop down to around 10%.

It should be an embarrassment to the Democratic Party that many of their strategists have become obsessed with exploiting the swing vote.

VOTING RIGHTS

This vote is a major distraction to the electoral process and to much of the government policy that later is formed, yet it is the only hope the Democrats have. The swing group is a group whose favor they seek to win, not because they wish to give them a sense of community and empowerment, but because they wish empowerment for themselves and the Democratic Party.

It is true that voting qualifications have been used to deny people political representation, and this undoubtedly accounts for some of the passion that is generated around this issue. But, misuse in the past, in no way implies that misuse will occur in the future. The greater danger comes when the fear of misuse encourages, over-use. If we were afraid to set standards for doctors, for fear that some would be excluded, we would certainly suffer more from too many doctors, than too few. Similarly, college students are denied a voice in determining course curriculums, in the belief that experts will represent students' interests better than they themselves will.

Democrats will always be more inclined and better positioned than Republicans to exploit the unsuspecting swing voter because their Santa Clause like promises to; validate middle class values, make business simultaneously pay more and produce more, generally invest in everything from infrastructure to new technologies, spent more money on: drug programs, Medicare, Medicare, cancer research, aids research, day care, and social security, are often alluring to children and swing voters alike. As a child likes the candyman more than the doctor, a swing voter often likes the Democrat more than the Republican.

Since the days of Andrew Jackson, Democrats have sought to broaden the voting franchise because it was a good way to get elected. Today the job is much more difficult, virtually everyone has been given the vote, and virtually everyone has been given all that can be given by gov't. The question now is whether the habit of exploitation for the sake of political power is more central to the Democrats than the pursuit of legitimate philosophic purposes. An answer is betokened with each new election as the Democrats' strategic ability is verified when virtually any

DEMOCRATIC DECEIT

influential person is willing to be trotted out to urge Americans to vote first, and think some other time. Sadly, for the Republicans, who have a much more complicated message than the Democrats, the Santa Claus like appeal of the Democrats will continue to be a difficult thing to overcome.

RACISM - DEMOCRATS ACCUSE AMERICA

Dear Mr. Raspberry,

I have recently read your article in which you cite a study that, according to you, proves once and for all that America is a racist country, at least as regards discrimination in the work place. One of the most endearing things about Democrats is the way they so easily dismiss and condemn the whole country in their grossly unpatriotic way. Jimmy Carter dismissed the country as suffering from malaise, and regretted it for the rest of his Presidency. Democratic politicians may have learned to be more discreet than President Carter, but Democratic editorial writers have yet to learn, possibly because they are seldom challenged for the things they write.

Your are one of the very few black Democrats who takes a more sophisticated point of view on racial issues than that which is possible by solely relying on 1960's civil-rights rhetoric, and so any criticism of your writing must be undertaken with care and respect. However, when you label the country as racist, you do something that incorrectly describes America's most basic values, as fraudulent. The vast majority of Americans know better than to admit to, to practice, or to feel, racist. They are civilized to the extent that they would feel embarrassed at such a description. Perhaps if you are challenged a little more about your occasional errors, you will finally be pushed that last little bit further so that you will be on the Republican side of the fence, at which point you will be in an improved position to help blacks move forward.

You mention a study which was conducted to show that racism exists in American. From a scientific point of view, your study would automatically be invalidated because it apparently was designed to get the result it got, rather than to seek the truth on an impartial basis. You mention very few details about the study, probably because you regard it as a foregone conclusion that the study was correct, regardless of the

DEMOCRATS ACCUSE AMERICA

methodology employed. Did you check to be sure that the study was conducted on a totally blind basis so that no one participating would know what truths the study was trying to establish. Did you check to see that the number of job applicants in the study was large enough to yield statistically significantly results which could be duplicated if the study was repeated. Blacks are fond of pointing out that I.Q. tests and Scholastic Aptitude Tests are racially or culturally biased; were the materials in this study; i.e., resumes, cover letters, interview techniques, participants etc., biased in a way to get the anticipated results. You don't mention any of these absolutely critical things to your readers, probably because you: 1) had limited space, 2) assumed your readers weren't sophisticated enough to care and 3) didn't think to question a result that, to you, is obvious even without scientific study. None of these is a very good defense.

Let's assume that the old adage about there being lies, damn lies, and statistics isn't true in this case. Let's assume that the studies major statistical finding, that 20% of white applicants and only 7% of "equal" black applicants got to the same level in the employment process, is true and accurate. Does this mean that there really is rampant racism in America?

If this were true, America wouldn't have had the very bloody and protracted Civil War, The Civil-Rights Act of 1965, and The Voting Rights Act of 1965, The War On Poverty, and many other things to numerous to mention. America is a Democracy where the public things that happen must in some way be a very specific reflection of popular will.

If the 20% versus 7% disparity is true and accurate maybe it can be accounted for by what they call the "halo affect," in marketing. This is the affect that enables a beautiful women or star athlete to cast their halo over the products near or around them, and thereby persuade consumers to buy. Consumers seek to improve their situation in life by getting close to the product that is close to the person who has the qualities and characteristics which they find desirable. A businessman does not rely just on a spokesperson, however. A product's packaging is also of critical importance; usually it will have nothing to do with the product itself,

RACISM

but on a more subtle level than the spokesperson, will suggest to a potential buyer that the product is connected to important cultural attributes with which he would want an association. Even after the packaging, there is the product, which is shaped, sized, textured, scented, colored, concentrated, priced and, softened so that it will be attractive to the very subtle psychological needs which consumers all have for cultural or community fulfillment. The young mother might enjoy the purity of Ivory Soap while the more cosmopolitan person might enjoy the scent of Irish Spring Soap, though neither would admit that they are among the millions who, to a small degree, enhance their life through their soap, and the myriad of other goods and services which they buy and use on a daily basis. Everything is relative, in that everything affects everything else, and no one can say exactly which way one thing will affect some other thing.

The "halo affect" is everywhere in life. As a boy, we had a Toro lawnmower that caused tremendous frustration once a week, every week, when it was time to mow the lawn. 30 years later, even though that lawnmower may have been obsoleted with 15 generations of new mowers; all the people who worked at the company then, are now dead or retired, and the company has been sold to different owners-four times, my father will not buy anything with the Toro name on it. A brand name is ideally meant to engender a long term favorable response; in this case there was a reverse "halo affect." Humans make epistemological associations of this type because it provides them with an intellectually and emotionally efficient way to understand and make sense of the world.

The beaches in many East Coast towns have been closed for much of the last two summers due to high fecal coliform counts. Many residents will now not go in the water, no matter how low the bacteria count is. Rightly or wrongly, logically or illogically, a fecal coliform bacteria can cast a broad halo.

The modern day Republican Party was formed in 1854; for a hundred years thereafter white southerners voted Democratic even though Republican views were more similar to their own, again, because mere facts couldn't diminish the halo affect.

DEMOCRATS ACCUSE AMERICA

When a man selects a women he might want to marry he is attracted to a certain look, a certain manner, a certain background, certain qualities and characteristics. Whatever the basis or bases for the attraction it is something that springs from the inscrutable halo deep within his soul that says, "somehow, someway this women fits underneath my particular halo very well." The same process for a women is no more precise or understandable.

If a white couple were to select a neighborhood for a romantic midsummer's night walk, they would probably avoid the black ghetto areas of their town, if there were any, in favor of other areas where they knew they would be safer. Does this mean that they are racist, or that they are wisely paying attention to the ghetto's halo.

I recall, as a high school student, being denied admission to an advanced course by a guidance counselor who advised that in life I would be judged more by what I had done in the past than by what I promised I would do in the future. To this day I have very mixed feelings for the man who doubted my ability; who judged me so harshly; who denied me what I needed most at the time in my life. Sadly for me, I was not able to escape the halo cast by my own inadequate, previous performance.

At one point in my college career a representative from the airline industry visited a class I was attending and explained that even though airline travel is feared by many, the industry knows that it would not be wise to advertise that airline travel is the safest way to travel. Humans feel most essentially like terrestrial beings, his research showed, and the halo cast by the thought of a plane full of human beings falling from the sky to a flattening and fiery death, is far greater than that cast by a head-on automobile crash, on land, at 55 MPH.

A well known Fortune 500 company in my town, knows the history of blacks hasn't prepared them well for employment, and it knows a high percentage of the blacks it has hired, didn't work out as well as they would have wanted. Today, if a black and white apply to that Company for work, the black will certainly suffer from the halo left behind by all the blacks who came before; by all of black history, and by all of human history. The

RACISM

hiring practices of this particular Company, whether consciously undertaken or not, are not an indication of racism, but rather an indication that employers hire according to a much broader set of criterion than those covered by the study you describe, Mr. Raspberry.

Business students are routinely taught that equal products will not sell equally if they are not introduced at the same time. Once consumer loyalty and comfort is established, it takes more than comparable quality to make a consumer change his behavior. This is the way human nature works in most areas; when it happens in the area of hiring, it is not necessarily racism.

On the other hand, the company in question, being located in a ghetto, has done many things beyond its immediate obligation to its stockholders, in terms of job training, housing, and community programs, to help out the people in it's neighborhood, many of whom are black. Certainly any officer in the Company would consider his pride severely assaulted if he were called racist.

This Company in particular, and America in general has done a great deal for blacks to show they aren't racist and that their hearts are in the right place. The halo effect is something that blacks will have to diminish and reverse mostly on their own.

It is well known that short people earn less than tall people owing to, it would seem, both discrimination and diminished self-esteem. While the impact of such a situation can not possibly be much less than the impact of the relatively small amount of racial discrimination your study reported, all of us have an intrinsic understanding that it would be preposterous for the Federal Gov't to mobilize in an effort to eliminate stature discrimination. Similarly, we all know that blonds have more fun, but should we really think ill of ourselves because we may find blond hair and the people attached to it, more employable or attractive than people with ordinary brown hair.

THE DEMOCRATS ACCUSE AMERICA

If you insist that we are racist, I only hope you can persuade your Democratic, politician friends to say so in public. Failing that, maybe they will get together and encourage you to be more polite before the electorate discovers how much fractious Democrats love, in private at least, to label America as racist. For Republicans to stand idly by, as they mostly do when they are called racist, is cowardly.

ELITE DEMOCRATS - INTELLECTUALS PANIC

Dear Mr. Robert Kuttner,

I have just read your book, "THE END OF LAISSEZ-FAIRE," and I found it to be an endorsement of the positions normally taken by the left wing of the Democratic Party, although you never said so directly.

It would seems that there are many liberal Democrats, yourself included, who are quite concerned that the Democratic Party has lost its way, and feel it's high time they found it; before it's too late. Your recent books and your well received new journal, "THE AMERICAN PROSPECT," certainly make you one of most enthusiastic and important intellectuals grasping for a new basis on which the Democratic Party might stand. With Democrats routinely losing Presidential elections, and almost certain to lose the 1992 election, owing to their foreign policy blunders, most recently in the Persian Gulf, and 25 years of failed domestic policies, it is no wonder you are working so hard to find them a new lease on life.

Your book is primarily about economics, as the title would imply, but it does not present any specific economic arguments; so it is very difficult, indeed, to summarize and criticize what you say. You touch on virtually every area of economics in a non-technical way and seem to always come out as a leftist Democrat in favor of a heavily statist, but mixed economy; this would make you something very close to a George McGovern style Democrat, although you never come close to this admission. Your approach in the book is extremely general and vague. While you certainly are a scholarly generalists, I think it is inconceivable, given your approach, that you would ever be asked to write something relatively specific about the actions you would want your party to take should they be given the chance. It seems that Democrats are in such an untenable and discredited position these days that they are often reduced to vagaries and generalities. When they are forced to get specific, they get in trouble very quickly, and

INTELLECTUALS PANIC

are therefore developing a strong interest in avoiding specifics and labels, not because they are too general or inaccurate, but because they call to mind most of the recent Democratic failures. For example, if a Democrat says, "civil-rights," a Republican wins buy saying, "quota," if a Democrat says, "national health insurance," a Republican wins by saying, "budget deficit" or "socialism;" if a Democrat says, "crime," a Republican says, "Willie Horton;" if Democrats bring up their "War on Poverty," Republicans win by pointing out that the war is over because it was resoundingly lost; if Democrats bring up "education" they talk of the status quo while Republicans win by saying "choice;" if Democrats bring up foreign policy, Republicans win by saying, "Persian Gulf."

Toward the end of your book, you finally felt compelled to get a little specific about what you would do if you had to make and implement policy, rather than just philosophize about it. Once you got beyond the intellectual pretence of your initial discussion the positions you took utilized the same old left wing Democratic rhetoric that George McGovern got us very familiar with, plus many of the same ideas and positions.

Firstly, you talk of a competitive work force. You want further gov't control of the educational system, primarily so that more emphasis can be placed on job training; this, you feel, will benefit individual workers and the economy as a whole. Republicans have always countered by maintaining that the current system is an acknowledged failure because of gov't control; that new schemes to perfect it or change it, such as yours, have always failed despite continuous efforts. The solution, Republicans feel, is to make the system private and competitive so that parents will have "choice;" so that schools will have to compete with one another to survive, attract students, and demonstrate the value of and results from the particular academic standards they set. Democrats in gov't have had 150 years to learn how to manage public schools and they have failed miserably; it is long past time for a change away from gov't schools. You did not acknowledge the Republican position, let alone attempt to deflate it.

Secondly, you describe American capital markets as dysfunctional because they require a short term return that makes long term business

ELITE DEMOCRATS

development difficult. Republicans counter that nobody, least of all gov't planners, can say what return, in what time frame, is best. Capital, in a free society, should flow to wherever its owners feel it will earn the highest return. If there is a profit advantage to a relatively long term commitment to a particular industry, then those companies in that industry will be able to attract the capital necessary to realize the profit. As it is demonstrated that high returns can indeed be made by long term commitments in particular areas, it will become easier and easier to attract money toward those long term investments. A Republican free market provides the environment in which this can happen; a few gov't planners can not possible guess correctly at where capital ought to flow and for how long. If you know of some Democratic, socialist planners who have this ability, surely they could prove it by becoming billionaire investors in the private sector first.

Thirdly, you talk of public investment and technology. You point out that Japan and France are successfully investing public funds to develop photovoltaic cells and underground rapid transit. Republicans counter that gov't, without the severe constraints of a competitive free market, can not possible invest money with the same discipline and efficiency as the private sector. If the French and Japanese gov't bureaucrats have made some profitable investments, it must be assumed that it happened by chance. Why don't you prove your thesis by getting together a group of the intellectuals who you claim know when and how to invest public money in valuable new products, and do just that, only privately, either through the stock markets or private start up companies. If by some miracle they were to succeed on a regular basis, you would have a very strong case to make. But, I suppose you already would have done that if you really believed it was possible.

Fourthly, you talk of regulation, saying that the Savings and Loan Scandal is proof that regulation is necessary. Republicans counter that deregulation was necessary so that capital or savings would be free to seek out the highest return for its often middle and lower class owners. The scandal occurred because of gov't intervention as follows: 1) The 1986 Tax

INTELLECTUALS PANIC

Act caused a severe decline in real estate, exactly where the S & L's were heavily invested, 2) savers were conditioned by gov't regulators to trust that their money was safe, and therefore didn't think to put it in the bank(s) where they knew it was safe, 3) the deregulation process was too fast so that bankers were forced to become businessman, sometimes unethical ones, virtually overnight, before they were ready and 4) Democratic regulations created the banks and were causing them to loose money, thus leading to the vain efforts to salvage a sinking ship.

Fifthly, you speak of your desire for universal health insurance. Republicans counter that the basic concept is non- sensical, since the money to pay for it would still have to come from citizen taxpayers, exactly where it comes from now. But, with Federal intervention the pool of money would be diminished by a significant factor due to the mammoth gov't bureaucracy that would be created. And, with the gov't footing the bill, the pressure to hold down the always skyrocketing costs of medical care would be greatly reduced. To get costs down, there must be free market competition in the industry; the way to get this competition is to get the gov't out of the already heavily socialized, American system and rely on some form of gov't imposed self-insurance that will force patients to carefully purchase their own medical care. Besides, if you really believe in national health care, then you must believe in the socialist concept that the gov't must also take care of the other things that are even more important than health care, at least on a daily basis, such as food, clothing, and shelter. Who would believe that Democrats would want to stop at just health care?

Lastly, you mention the need to manipulate a higher savings rate. Republicans counter that while saving money is generally a good thing, especially for retirement and capital investment, it is not for the gov't of a free country to develop policies on the assumption that it knows better than its citizens what they should do with their money.

If your book were to be compared with those written by the four most important economists in history; i.e., Adam Smith, Karl Marx, John Maynard Keynes, and Milton Friedman, a striking difference would emerge in that they were all able to lay out their positions and proposals, and cite their evidence, with infinitely more clarity and detail than you. I

ELITE DEMOCRATS

would bet that this is because they were much more certain about their positions than you, and because in reality, you are more concerned with deceptive, partisan politics than economics. What your book really amounts to is a call for the economy to be placed in your Democratic hands so that you, with your superior wisdom, can make the vast number of decisions that are currently being made by millions who are severely constrained and regulated by the accuracy and discipline of the free market.

You admit with some honesty that your position against capitalism is the minority one, when you say, "The remarkable events in Russia of 1989-90 have been widely heralded as a victory for the free market-a vindication of laissez-faire in general and American-style capitalism in particular." You go on to say, "The Democrats, by and large are without a coherent political philosophy; they have been battered by the recent wave of conservatism and are not yet consistently challenging the continuing vogue for laissez-fare." It seems readily apparent that after your book, the Democrats will be even further from a coherent philosophy. You devote one page, for example, to the subject of savings, and in that page you suggest four different and general methods to increase savings; each one of which would have tremendous ramifications throughout the economy, so much so that it is impossible for the reader, or the most brilliant economist in the world, to guess at what your well planned world would look like.

Undeterred by majority thinking, as you probably should be, you open your book by saying that the major question your book will try to answer is why capitalism came back in favor after WW II, when it had been so thoroughly discredited by the Great Depression, and after so many countries had built their post war economy on the mixed model (part capitalist, part socialist). You close your book by cautioning us, again, that the pursuit of a utopian laissez-faire resulted in one catastrophe, the Great Depression, and that it might well result in a very different sort of accelerated decline in the 1990's.

The middle of your book is filed with absolutely inscrutable talk about how the simultaneous collapse of Communism and American economic hegemony will certainly and inevitable force America, or give America,an

INTELLECTUALS PANIC

opportunity to move toward your promised land of the heavily mixed economy, rather than toward laissez-faire capitalism.

Considering that you opened and closed your book by talking about the Great Depression as the ultimate warning sign that laissez-faire economics can be very deadly, I think it is appropriate to point out that there is no connection between the Great Depression and laissez-faire. It is perhaps the greatest Democratic deception of the Twentieth Century that they go around pretending that capitalism caused the Great Depression. They have gotten a lot of milage out of an argument that is little more than a lie.

It is true that the Depression started during the Republican Hoover administration which believed that automatic market forces (Adam Smith's invisible hand) would correct the problem, prosperity was just around the corner, and relief efforts were to be made only by private charities and local gov'ts. Neither Republicans nor Democrats understood, at the time, that Federal monetary policy had caused the Great Depression; not private capitalism.

As you well know, Mr. Kuttner, by 1929 the American economy had been in the hands of the Federal Reserve for 16 years. The Glass - Owens Federal Reserve Act was signed into law by Woodrow Wilson in 1913, against strong opposition from the Republican banking community. Prior to this, banking was controlled by The National Bank Act of 1863 which limited the supply of currency available to exactly the supply of gov't bonds held by the banks. After numerous bank panics, most notably the Panic of 1907, caused by the inability of the private banking system to expand the supply of currency when needed, the Federal Reserve system was set up to supply an elastic amount of currency and thereby improve the stability of the banking industry and the general economy. Under both systems, the gov't clearly held the power to almost instantly cause recessions and depressions. Although the gov't obviously never intended to interfere with economic growth, it did so several times by inadvertent mismanagement of the monetary system.

Just before the depression set in, Governor Harrison, director of

INTELLECTUALS PANIC

the New York Federal reserve Bank wrote "unless this is done (referring to an expansion of the money supply), after the events of the past weeks, there may be greater danger of a recession in business with consequent depression and unemployment, which we should do all in our power to prevent." It seems that the Fed let the supply of money shrink by an unprecedented 2.6% per year during 1929 when the stock market collapsed; this marked the beginning of the Great Depression. The New York Bank realized the ominous trend but was not able to persuade the other Federal Reserve Banks to go along. The Fed stood by and did not expand the money supply at the appropriate time, as it had done in the past, to correct a badly deteriorating situation. The Depression that ensued would have been avoided if Federal Reserve understanding had been greater.

If you had to give the Fed a political label you would probably call it- Democratic. The Board's formation was opposed by many Republicans; it was signed into law by Wilson, a Democrat, and since Republicans over the years have often wanted to restrict the Fed or eliminate it, in favor of some kind of gold or near gold standard. The Fed represents gov't planning and control over much of the economy; this is something Democrats are much more comfortable with than Republicans, although these days the Fed is generally considered in a non-partisan way. Today, Republicans generally prefer constant, stable long term growth in the money supply, while Democrats prefer a more manipulative use of the money supply in response to changing circumstances.

It is very difficult, Mr. Kuttner, to conceive of how you find even a vague connection between laissez-faire and The Great Depression. You should consider that Milton Friedman, perhaps the greatest living Republican economist, believes that the Great Depression was intimately connected to Federal control of the economy and John Kenneth Galbraith, perhaps one of the greatest living Democratic economists, also believes the Depression was caused by or greatly influenced by Federal Reserve control. It would have to be assumed that once you can come to accept the lack of a connection between capitalism and the Depression, much of the foundation for your book and the Democratic way you think, will be gone.

PHILOSOPHY - DEMOCRATS RUN FOR COVER

Dear Mr. E.J. Dionne, Jr.

Your recent book, "WHY AMERICANS HATE POLITICS," is a book that if taken seriously would, at most, blur the difference between Democrats and Republicans so that people would be voting for the best manager or administrator and not for the candidate with the most rational political philosophy. Good management and administration are, of course, good things, but ultimately meaningless without a guiding philosophy. However, your real purpose, it would seem, was not to encourage Americans to vote for management over idealogy, but rather to blur the poor record Democrats have established so they can still get elected.

Possibly the most important legacy of the Reagan years was the budget deficits that grew so large as to preclude further new spending initiatives. This virtually destroyed the Democrats' reason for existence as they were the instigators of most domestic Federal spending, and totally dependant on it as a reason for being. The Democrats have accordingly undertaken the search for a new reason for being; not because the billions they spent on domestic programs worked well and are no longer needed, but because the billions had very little affect on the problems it was supposed to solve, and because no new money is available to expand old programs or initiate new ones. It would now be almost unthinkable to talk in terms of new domestic spending programs, even if the money was available; this leaves the Democrats without any direction.

Your book, Mr. Dionne, is an attempt to find new directions by declaring the standard political debate in America-dead; dead because the Democratic philosophy has failed despite massive and unprecedented spending in support of that philosophy. You should have considered that if the Republican philosophy had been tried, America would now be socially, politically, and financially sound. In short, your strategy is to

PHILOSOPHY

indict the whole system rather than admit to the failings of your own party.

In 1992 the Democrats are in the throes of a full fledged identity crisis. When it became apparent to old Democrats like Gary Hart and Michael Dukakis that the public didn't like their very liberal Democratic idealogy, they hypocritically tried to rename themselves as competence candidates rather than ideological ones. Hart, used to say, "I'm not ideological because the American people aren't." Lately Paul Tsongas and Jerry Brown, two Democratic presidential candidates, have cautioned fellow Democrats not to sound like Republican wannabes, and that the old solutions (the Democratic ones) no longer work. They fail to say exactly what the new solutions are so that listeners can determine if they are really neither Democratic nor Republican. With a Ph.D from Harvard and Oxford, and a job at the very liberal "WASHINGTON POST," your approach is much more slick and subtle, but it doesn't take long to discover that you too are a thinly disguised Democrat trying to help establish a new identity so Democrats can go on selling the same old philosophy.

You say, for example, "that the central argument of this book is that liberalism and conservatism are framing political issues as a series of false choices; what is required is the creation of a new political center by liberals who do not believe as conservatives do that politics, public life, and government ought to arouse more suspicion than hope." In fact, if you believe as you apparently do, that politics, public life, and gov't is the solution to the U.S.' problems, then you are subscribing to the standard Democratic approach to gov't. Republicans, as you say, generally believe the opposite; i.e, that gov't is the problem. Despite your cloudy intellectual approach it is not difficult to determine that you are a loyal and registered Democrat who is trying hard to help your failed party find some new packaging so it can go on promoting traditional, liberal Democratic approaches to gov't. You say you want a new political center, but you don't even come close to explaining what specific ideas you have that are not exact copies of old Democratic ones. In the end, what your readers learn from your vain effort to become a new style Democrat, is how desperate Democrats must be.

DEMOCRATS RUN FOR COVER

Brian Lamb was exceedingly blunt for a journalist, when on CNN he confronted you with a question that is not often asked, by saying, "are you a liberal?" You grudgingly admitted that you were, but then sought in vain to avoid the commonly denigrated label by responding, "I like to think of myself as a radical centrist." This was a palpable deception designed to prevent viewers from knowing that you are just another registered Democrat who believes gov't is the solution. Perhaps your next book will detail the precise positions of radical centrism and explain how they represent your discovery of a new political philosophy. Jerry Brown recently announced for the presidency with a loose biblical quote by saying, in a very inelegant way, "I vomit out my mouth those who are in the center, because they are passionate about nothing." This is sensible advice that you would be well advised to listen to, Mr. Dionne. Not only are centrists without passion, but they condemn the country to the Democratic status quo at a time when most major trends are negative.

You close your book by saying, "a nation that hates politics will not long survive as a Democracy." This is an interesting statement that seemingly is used to add urgency to your plea for a new center, but unfortunately it has no conceptual support unless you call your brief recital of some of the embarrassing things that have happened lately, like Willie Horton and The Keating Five, as sufficient. Sadly for your theory, the book was probably finished just before The Persian Gulf War, which caused most Americans to fall in love with politics and gov't again, if only for a short time.

If Americans do occasionally hate politics, it might well be because the domestic policy of the last 25 years, which represents the very best of Democratic thinking, is almost universally considered a failure. The recent victories in the cold war and the Gulf War are an absolutely monumental victory for American Foreign Policy (really Republican foreign policy) that virtually ends 45 years of often dramatic tension between East and West and Middle East; this is something that presumably would not make

PHILOSOPHY

Americans hate politics. Despite the domestic failure, and the frustration it engenders, I see no evidence, nor do you present any in your book, that Democracy in America is threatened because of what you describe as hatred of politics. If Americans do occasionally hate politics it is, in part, because the schools, the major media, and people like you, alienate them from gov't as you suffuse the process with new ways to obscure and make meaningless the choice between Democrats and Republicans that they face each time they enter the voting booth. Your approach leads to, at best, divided gov't and stagnation.

Let's assume that two of the most obvious liberal presidential candidates, at least as of this writing, Paul Tsongas and Jerry Brown, follow your advice; declare traditional ideology dead, and attempt to form a new ideological center that will incorporate, as you suggest, the best of both Democratic and Republican thought. Firstly, they would still want to be called Democrats, as you do. Secondly, they would be called moderate Democrats, just like the moderate Democrats who have always been in the party. Thirdly, just as in the past, they would be vulnerable to purists in both parties who naturally have more enthusiasm born on the theory that you can't successfully mix apples and oranges, or in this case, two opposing political philosophies, and get a third, middle of the road and superior philosophy. Fourthly, they would still be opposed by Republicans who would fault them for believing that gov't was the solution rather than the problem. When all was said and done, Mr. Dionne, you did not suggest anything at all new in your book, although the detailed history of American ideology that takes up most of your book is extremely well done, but mostly irrelevant to your basic theme about American's hating politics.

It seemed that you really wanted to write a basic history book, but were forced, maybe by your publisher, to tack on a few pages at the beginning and at the end to give the book contemporary relevance. At one point, in your discussion with Brian Lamb, you mentioned that Alice Mayhew, your editor at Simon and Schuster, was looking for a liberal book like yours. It looks as if you wrote a book about recent American ideological history, and she edited it to be about a new strategy for the Democrats.

DEMOCRATS RUN FOR COVER

As Democrats seek to find a new identity in the age of budget deficits, they will inevitably find that the two party system, as we know it today, is the only realistic choice, because it very thoroughly represents all the essential political knowledge mankind has acquired throughout history. There are no new political ideas under the sun. Your hope to escape past Democratic failures, by finding a new ideology in the center, or by creating a new label for old Democratic ideas, will not allow you to escape the basic conflict between individual responsibility (Republicanism) and gov't responsibility (Democratism) that has defined American politics for so long.

Prior to the American Constitution, world history was shaped by the exercise of governmental power over its own citizenry and that of other citizenries. This power was mostly gained through brute force, although it was often justified as a benefit to humankind on ideological or religious grounds. The American Revolution added the new idea that governmental power should only be justified as a means to protect and promote individual liberty. Today, Americans live in an extreme state of civilization, having learned to restrict political debates to questions regarding how much power individuals can have without becoming self-destructive or tyrannical or, whether the judicious use of governmental power can lead an individual toward the goal of liberty and self-sufficiency.

The dream of a new and radical political center, founded by liberal Democrats, does nothing to advance this historical framework and seems to have no chance to advance the Democrats. To America's Founders, America represented such a thoroughly thought out and constitutionally detailed description of gov't that there seemed no room left for petty squabbles between competing political parties. The idealism of the Founding Fathers, as they failed to anticipate the rise of political parties and ideologies, perhaps is similar to your dream, Mr. Dionne, about a new and unified center that incorporates the best of both worlds, but this is not likely.

PHILOSOPHY

Contrary to the somewhat naive expectation of our Founders, the nation instantly became divided into political parties. The desire to minimize conflict in the new gov't was so strong that George Washington kept the leaders of both competing parties (Hamilton and Jefferson) in his cabinet. In a heroic, non-partisan effort, both Hamilton and Jefferson urged Washington to accept a second term in 1792. By the end of that second term, Jefferson felt compelled to resign because he was constantly outgunned by an increasingly Federalist administration. It seemed that no matter how strong the desire for a non-partisan gov't, divisions quickly arose. The Federalists favored a strong, elitist, aristocratic, central gov't that, it seemed, would favor northern banking and manufacturing interests; Jefferson seemed to favor the common man, southern agrarian interests, and broadly democratic principals. Hamilton thought Jefferson a contemptible idiot for believing ordinary men could play such a major role in gov't. Jefferson believed that Hamilton was trying to centralize gov't to the point where he could set up a European style monarchy. In the end though, it turned out that Hamilton was a truly patriotic American whose primary loyalty was to the Constitution and Bill of Rights, before his Federalist principals.

The inevitable debate about the size and power of the Federal gov't got started immediately and continues today. Despite your partisan desire to avoid conflict, by creating a new center, it seems highly implausible that men of good intention can or should agree on one way of doing things. The competition of different ideas embodied by political parties is a healthy one that continuously asks us to improvement ourselves and our gov't at the fastest rate possible.

The Democrats and you, Mr. Dionne, will have to recognize, 1) Americans don't hate politics in any meaningful way, 2) a move to the center by the Democrats is not ideologically significant, and will not let them escape from the great debate that started long ago under George Washington, and 3) no matter how Democrats squirm, they will still have to answer for their failed foreign and domestic policies of the in last 25 years.

FEDERALISM - WELFARE FOR THE STATES

Dear Mary McGrory and Neal Pierce,

Both of you have just written articles about the Bush Administration plan called "New Federalism." You left so much key information out of your articles that it seemed obvious your intention was to deceive, rather than to explain what the Democratic position really was. Your party is in such an untenable position, now that the Federal Gov't is running a $350 Billion deficit, that reasoning about the wisdom of new or maintained Federal spending is a silly exercise that seems to embarrass you, but nevertheless you persist, much like a labor union picketing a factory long after the factory has closed and moved out of town.

In 1970 the Federal Gov't collected $125 Billion in taxes; in the latest fiscal year the deficit alone will be $350 Billion and spending over $1 Trillion. The Democrats have had the opportunity to spend money beyond their very wildest dreams, but nobody, on either side of the political fence, would claim that much, if any, good has come from this spending that Democrats promised would solve so many of our problems and create "A Great Society."

Bush's "New Federalism" is a plan whereby tax money that is collected by the Federal Gov't is given back, primarily to state and municipal governments. It is a plan that corresponds to Republican thinking about individual liberty and responsibility, in many respects. It does not correspond in all respects, because Republicans would rather have the money stay at the state and local level in the first place, rather than travel to Washington, and then, at tremendous cost, be returned to exactly the place from which it came. They would also be more comfortable if the money were given back to its rightful owners without strings attached, but in the real world, a world divided among Republicans and Democrats, they settle for the best they can get.

FEDERALISM

In this case, the power of the central gov't is diminished in favor of state and local gov't, where money is hopefully spent more carefully under the relatively close scrutiny of the people who earned it and care most about it. Besides, Republicans know that state governments are legally bound to be more responsible with money because their constitutions and laws prevent them from running long term deficits as are common at the national level.

The Democrats are confused or neutral about "New Federalism." They want Federal spending most of all; if it is Federal spending turned over to the states, it is almost as good, but not as fulfilling or comforting as the pure Federal spending they got so used to in the 60's. The Democratic plan is for gov't to spend money to help people; Federal spending is preferred because it naturally involves more money for more people, and seemingly would have the best chance to make a major impact.

The whole point of your article Ms. McGrory was to criticize Washington as a city without problem solvers that seems happy to abdicate power and responsibility to lower levels of gov't. You apparently don't like Bush's "New Federalism" because it turns Federal money and power over to the states. You recall what for you were the glory days, the days when Washington was the breeding ground for wonderful new ideas such as: The New Deal, The New Frontier, The Great Society, Project Head Start, and school busing. These were the ideas for which you indicated a particular fondness. You lament, "the Federal Gov't divesting itself of responsibility for leading the country on social programs." This is all well and good, but for your article to be serious you would have had to deal with two major issues which you ignored completely and totally.

Firstly, with the feds running a $350 Billion deficit it is crazy to dream of new programs, or even maintaining the old ones. What would it take for a Democrat to think responsibly about money; to realize the 1960's are not the 1990's. Secondly, you would have to address the Republican contention that Federal programs, 1) mostly hurt the people they try to help, 2) are enormously wasteful, 3) produce an "entitlement" attitude on the part of recipients, and 4) serve the whims of self-righteous, and ego-centric social

WELFARE FOR THE STATES

engineers. By ignoring the heart of the issue this way you beg not to be taken seriously, but rather as a knee-jerk old fashioned liberal. A Democrat in the 1990's has got to have new ideas that are different from those of the 1960's, because today there is little money to spend, and the money which was previously spent, seems to have been largely wasted. You may criticize Washington for not having any new ideas today, when really you should be wondering if you and your party have any at a time when they are desperately needed for political survival. For all your bluster, it is interesting to note that you could not even present one new idea that would put the feds back in the lead on social issues.

Mr. Pierce, although you are a liberal Democrat, like Mary McGrory, your article on President Bush's New Federalism is very different. Where she was conceptual, you were pragmatic. For you, the idea of money going from Peoria to Washington and then back to Peoria is puzzling. You ask quizzically if it is, "a brilliant breakthrough in federalist sharing, a fiscal shell game, a smoke screen, or a Trojan Horse." In the end you indicate that you don't really care because you have your own program. Without rhyme or reason you announce that you want the feds to be nice to the financially strapped states. Specifically, you want the Federal Gov't to cut back on the $8 Billion the states will have to pay next year in expanded Medicaid coverage. While it certainly is generous of you to want to help the states, at the expense of the Federal Gov't, it would have been nice if you thought to offer some reasons in support of your position.

You did say, although I wouldn't call it a reason, that since the Feds can run huge deficits of $350 Billion, and the states cannot, due to legal restriction, that an additional $8 Billion from Washington "doesn't seem like too much to ask" in these difficult economic times. This is grossly irresponsible and typically Democratic. To many Democrats a budget deficit means nothing; it is merely money somebody else has to pay at some other time; that is why the Democrats have blocked every attempt to pass legislation that would require the feds to balance the budget. In truth, the money borrowed to finance the deficit has to be paid back by future tax payers who will wonder, even more than current taxpayers, why their standard of living does not improve, despite hard work, the passage of

FEDERALISM

time, and constant improvements in the efficiency of production and in the delivery of goods and services. Mr. Pierce, it is this cavalier and Democratic attitude toward another $8 Billion on top of the $350 Billion deficit, that caused the deficit and all the attendant problems that come with it.

You have no need for debate over the concept of federalism. For you, the guiding principal of gov't is: help, help, help, spend, spend, spend. In the old days, Democrats used to be criticized as the tax and spent party; today you seem willing to be criticized as the borrow and spend party. Republicans don't doubt that Democrats are trying to push the party in this direction on the assumption that there might be a lot of political milage in the concept of borrowing rather than taxing. When the gov't taxes to get the money it spends, voters notice; when it borrows, the affect is subtle and well spread out so that it is not nearly as noticeable. Should the Democrats succeed in persuading America that deficits don't matter there will, effectively, be no more economic growth as too much money will be taken out of the productive economy and used to pay passive debts. The Federal Gov't can no more thrive with ever increasing deficits than can an individual.

With the Federal Gov't in virtual bankruptcy, there is little reason for the Democratic Party to exist. To survive, a Democrat must have money to spend; they must shop until they drop. The obvious and only solution for Democrats is to break the barrier of financial responsibility that tenuously restricts gov't to spending only that money which it actually has. If this sounds far fetched, it is only necessary to look around the world and observe that it is commonplace for central governments to destroy any opportunity for future economic growth by wild and irresponsible borrowing, often in the form of currency inflation, that can never be paid back.

"New Federalism" has a convoluted past and present that actually makes it a curious amalgam of ideas from both parties. The relative power of the states vis a vis the Federal Gov't was hotly debated at the constitutional

WELFARE FOR THE STATES

convention and ever since. Teddy Roosevelt called his plan, "New Nationalism;" Lyndon Johnson, "Creative Federalism;"Richard Nixon, "New Federalism or Revenue Sharing;" Jimmy Carter, "New Partnership;" and Ronald Reagan, "New Federalism." Modern Federal aid to cities and states started in the 1960's as Democratic programs to combat specific problems such as health, nutrition, jobs and housing. Strings were attached so the money would generally be spent according to Federal guidelines. Richard Nixon then tried to reshape the programs into something more palatable to Republicans. He said of his plan, "it represents the first major reversal of the trend toward ever more centralization of gov't in Washington, D.C. After power flowing from the people and states to Washington, it is time for a "New Federalism" in which power, funds and responsibility will flow from Washington to the states and people."

In general, the Nixon approach seemed somewhat appealing to Republicans, but it was by no means a pure approach as long as power was in the hands of the feds from where it could be whimsically given to, and taken away from, the states. The purist Republican approach would have been to keep the money and power on the state and local level in the first place, but that would have necessitated more political change than was possible from a Democratic Congress which was, as always, interested in centralizing power in Washington and away from the people.

When Reagan come to power with perhaps more of a purist mandate than any President since George Washington, he was able to make some progress, but still nothing close to what he would have wanted. With the passage of the Omnibus Budget Reconciliation Act of 1981, Reagan began his Republican "power to the people" strategy. Reagan reasoned, exactly the opposite of you, Mr. Pierce, by noting that it made no sense for the Federal Gov't, which at the time was running deficits in the $150-200 Billion range, to give money back to the states who were, by law, breaking even, or, in some cases, running surpluses. Reagan did succeed in cutting revenue sharing funds, but Federal spending kept going up anyway; so it is really not possible to conclude that political power was moved closer to the people owing to this aspect of the Reagan 1981 budget.

A more obviously Republican aspect of the Reagan plan called for the distillation of 54 revenue sharing programs into 9 "block grants" that for

FEDERALISM

the first time would be administered directly by the states without Federal strings attached. The affect was again mixed, because all the money went to the states rather than to states and localities as had been the case previously. Much of the money disappeared into state budgets which at the time were described as "in the worst shape since the great depression" by the National Conference of State Legislatures. Money that once went directly to localities, and then with some certainty to needy individuals, now was swallowed up on the state level and difficult to trace. Nevertheless there was a clear transfer of power to the states from the Federal Gov't; this was an aspect of the program that Republicans had to like.

Reagan had always disliked Aid To Families With Dependant Children (welfare,AFDC), and pushed as hard as he could against the omnipresent Democrats to relinquish all Federal responsibility in this area to the states. While he was not particularly successful, he made his intentions clear; money should be spent as close to the people who earn it as possible, because in this way it would be spent more carefully under the close supervision of those who earned it and cared most about it. When money and power disappears hundreds of miles away in Washington, taxpayers can't easily trace it, or maintain an interest in it. This is why Federal revenue sharing money that theoretically was earmarked for needy people, instead often went to well healed towns like Greenwich, CT., Vail, CO., and Palm Springs, CA. In fact, at one point, 25% of the money went to cities in the 10 wealthiest states. It is axiomatic that Federal programs are simply too large to be fairly and efficiently administered; Republican revenue sharing, was no exception.

While revenue sharing is conceptually a plausible way for Republicans to approach some of their goals in a divided gov't, it is by no means a certain program since state and local gov't can be almost as abusive and irresponsible as the Federal Gov't. Perhaps the most famous example of this was John Lindsay of New York City who promised to diminish welfare dependency when he ran for mayor in 1965 but instead put 1 out of every 7 New Yorkers on welfare.

Many other states are heavily controlled by Democrats who have exercised what power they have in a way to make Republicans cringe.

WELFARE FOR THE STATES

For example, 20 states and 93 localities are taking action on "comparable worth," 10 states have raised the minimum wage, 15 states provide for parental leave, and 1 state, Massachusetts, forces employers to provide health care. Still, Republicans counter that this experimentation on the state and local level may provide helpful information about the futility of gov't programs in general, and certainly be far less harmful than a bad program administered by the feds over the whole nation. Republican, anti-federalist efforts to return federal tax dollars to their rightful owners have been moderately successful at best in an era of huge budget deficits and divided gov't, but it does provide testimony to the essential spirit within the party.

What ever the pros and cons about "New Federalism" it is certain that Mary McGrory's dream of returning to the 1960's when Democrats had the money and political power to tax and spend as they chose, and Neal Pierce's idea to continue spending anyway without regard for the deficit, is senseless and typical of Democrats in the 1990's who are absolutely unable to think responsibly given the new realities created by their huge and wasted spending in the past.

CONSUMERISM - DEMOCRATIC CONTEMPT

Dear Mr. Will,

Thank you very much for your article in which you defended consumerism against liberal scorn. On balance I think you were correct on all points, although not terribly specific about the exact relationship between liberals, conservatives, and consumers.

More importantly though, I wish you wouldn't use the terms liberal and conservative instead of Democrat and Republican. Voters are very confused; that is why they elect Republican Presidents and Democratic Congressmen. Since we have a two party system, isn't it better to talk about the issues in terms that relate directly to the choice voters face when they enter the voting booth. I recognize that you are perhaps the most intellectual of all the widely read columnist and may feel the task of really spelling things out to voters is better left to others, but nevertheless, you might broaden your already ubiquitous presence and value by making this change. Would ABC News be very upset if you and Sam Donaldson labeled yourselves as Republican and Democrat and then really debated issues in terms of the philosophy of each party. An informal poll that I have taken indicates that 80% of those who watch the two of you on Sunday morning, don't know your party affiliations and consequently aren't listening to you in any meaningful context.

Most of your article is spent detailing the intellectual origins of Democratic scorn for the consumer. You close, happily noting that a new Democratic journal, "THE AMERICAN PROSPECT," has, a generation late, noted that contempt for consumers is not wise, and perhaps will no longer be part of the Democratic agenda. There was very little said about why the Republicans feel very comfortable with consumers, and the Democrats, very uncomfortable. If you had the time and inclination, you might have said the following things:

DEMOCRATIC CONTEMPT

The Democrats have historically been the party of big government, the party which believes that if major problems are to be solved, the gov't must be actively involved. To a Democrat, citizens, consumers, or voters, acting freely, will be alternately greedy, sexist, racist, imperialist, and generally vulgar. Their power to act independently must be taken away and given to Democrats in Washington, who by virtue of their intellectual and moral superiority will wield that power in a more benignant and Judeo/Christian way.

Republicans counter that the major lesson of history is that central governments, from Mesopotamia to Nazi Germany to Communist Russia, were not likely to be populated with the most virtuous people; that when corruption does inevitably find its way into gov't, if it was not there in the first place, it is infinitely more damaging and difficult to control when asserted by a powerful central gov't, rather than by a weak central gov't. The corruption of many individuals or small groups, with power that otherwise might have been in the hands of one central gov't, is far less damaging, and is naturally neutralized by other individuals or small groups with a similar amount of power.

Further, Republicans will argue, no matter how totalitarian and clever a gov't is, individual liberty is not something easily manipulated. Any attempt to do so will likely incur the long term enmity of the manipulated population, rather than the desired allegiance. A look at the very recent history of East Germany, Nicaragua, and The Baltics, makes everyone doubt how deeply into a man's soul, even the most thorough totalitarian gov't can reach. Individual liberty and capitalism (the economic counterpart) has moved mountains because it is most consistent with human nature, unlike socialism or authoritarianism which never get anywhere because they are at odds with the critical aspect of human nature which seeks independence and freedom.

A Democrat's criticism of capitalism rests to an important degree on the perception that people or consumers, when left to themselves, are vulgar in the choices they make, and easily manipulated by the marketplace in

CONSUMERISM

general, and advertising in particular. It seems to them that capitalism is ultimately driven by the capitalists' ability to produce, often frivolous products, and then to trick dumb consumers, mostly with Madison Avenue advertising, into buying them, even when they really don't need them. The solution is always the same, it is to take away power from both businesses and consumers and give it to Democrats in Washington who would limit production and consumption to a civilized level so that precious physical, psychological, and spiritual resources, wouldn't be wasted on a continuous, and spiritually meaningless cycle of producing, advertising, and consuming.

Some Democrats now know this thinking is simply not consistent with the basic American interest in individual liberty, as you point out Mr. Will. But, it should be remembered that the Democrats are the majority party because many have still not come to the realization that Democrats are equally contemptuous of both consumers and businessmen. Most Democrats don't know that advertising has very little power to manipulate. For example, some large supermarkets have 20,000 items, but only a small fraction of those items are advertised. If advertising had power, each item would be advertised and sell by the ton. Sadly, for the Democrats' theory, there is only a limited amount of money available for consumption, and all the advertising in the world won't make artichoke hearts, for instance, sell as well as laundry soap. Every consumer products marketing executive knows that a fast way to lose his job is to persuade his boss to spend $10,000,000 advertising in one of the many product categories that isn't naturally big enough to pay back the advertising dollars.

Someone once said to a businessman, as he was about to market a product, that it ought to be easy since even pet rocks could be sold if smartly advertised. This is mostly false. Pet rocks sold well only for a short time. Toothpaste, conversely, sells well all the time, because it is a necessary product. All the advertising in the world won't make pet rocks sell well, because the consumer is not as dumb as the Democrats would like to think. It seems that people are responsible enough to still spend most of their money on food, clothing, shelter, medical care, transportation, education and infrastructure, despite the advertisers wish to sell pet rocks

DEMOCRATIC CONTEMPT

and other frivolous goods and services which are far less costly to produce and have far higher profit margins.

The Proctor and Gamble Corporation is the largest consumer products company in the U.S. and the one, Democrats would say, most skilled at manipulation through advertising. Their products are, after all, frivolous commodity type items like, soap, shampoo, and toothpaste. Advertising, Democrats would say, is the only way to create demand for Pert Shampoo over Head & Shoulders Shampoo, isn't it?

The answer is a resounding-no. The Proctor & Gamble Co., like any company, has a corporate culture, and at P & G the culture does not teach them to think of themselves as slick marketeers and advertisers; rather, they think of themselves as ingenious scientists who dominate most of the categories they compete in because they produce superior products. There is ample evidence to support them. For example, in 1946, after decades of research and millions of dollars, P&G produced the first general purpose synthetic detergent, and called it Tide. Due to the obvious superiority of synthetic detergent, it became the number one seller in a huge market category. All the advertising in the world, from competitors, could not shake Tide from the number one spot because it truly was the first and best product. This single innovation and the imitations it spawned did more to improve humankind's standard of living than all the Democratic economists in the world.

In 1955, P & G introduced a very "frivolous" brand called Crest; it became the number one toothpaste in the world because P & G scientists had developed something called, fluoristat, which was the first ingredient to be added to toothpaste that could successfully help control cavities. The brand became number one, and all the competitive advertising in the world couldn't stop the first and best product from selling more than all the others.

In 1989 P & G scientists brought to market the first hair care product to legitimately combine a shampoo and conditioner; it very quickly became the number one seller despite an advertising budget no bigger than the brands

CONSUMERISM

with which it competed. It was cheaper and more convenient than the normal regime of shampoo and conditioner that most women, and a lot of men endured. Again, advertising could not interfere with the consumers' ability to almost instantly spot a superior product and reward the company that produced it.

Tide, Crest, and Pert are three of the major products at P & G, and each represents a brilliant and long term effort to satisfy the consumers' need for high quality and inexpensive products. These products certainly do not represent the creation of a want by a greedy capitalist who must be quickly controlled by a powerful Democratic gov't which is simultaneously contemptuous of both business and consumer freedom.

Advertising, while not nearly as powerful as Democrats would have us believe, is still very powerful. It has the power to reduce the cost of things purchased by about 80%. Advertising can inform the world, virtually overnight, of the existence of a product, thereby creating an instant market in the millions of units, assuming the product is good, of course. Without advertising, market growth would be very slow; product cost and prices very high due to small scale production and distribution. With advertising comes high demand, big factories and big production runs; this means big economies of scale, lower cost production and lower consumer prices. Investment in plant and equipment, overhead, R & D, etc., is recouped faster and enables lower costs and prices, which in turn leads to a higher standard of living. MBA students are routinely taught that the best competitive strategy is to produce as much as possible, as cheaply as possible, as soon as possible, so that competitors can never get the same unit volume and market share and thereby never have the same low production costs and consumer prices. Advertising is essential toward this very desirable goal.

Additionally, advertising has acquired a bad reputation among many Democrats who may be watching too much TV. TV is often watched by people who aren't in the market for the product being advertised. For example, research shows that if your life is inextricably tied to that of a cat's, probably because you own one, you are apt to find the commercials

DEMOCRATIC CONTEMPT

showing Morris (a famous advertising cat) doing things that cats do, as very cute and precious; if you find cats objectionable, as many people do, then the commercials are at best boring, and most likely, obnoxious. Sadly for advertising, most Americans watch commercials that are designed to be pleasing and inspiring to other people, owing to the large number of products advertised versus the small number actually purchased. This, however, does not mean that advertising and business should be controlled by Democrats.

John Kenneth Galbraith, the famous Democratic father of consumer contempt and, for that matter, socialism in America, says "production only fills a void that it has itself created; production of goods creates the wants that the goods are presumed to satisfy; consumer wants can have bizarre, frivolous, and even immoral origins; all would be regarded as elementary by the most retarded student in the nations most primitive school of business administration in the country." This kind of arrogance and self-assurance is difficult to fathom when it is so absolutely mistaken, and yet it is a concept still at the heart of the Democratic Party as they continue their war against consumers and business. Perhaps there should be a constitutional amendment forbidding anyone from voting Democratic until John Kenneth Galbraith has produced a pet rock, created a want for it, and presented the case history to the most primitive business school in the country.

When Galbraith tries to get serious in his old book, "The Affluent Society," he mentions breakfast cereal and soap as his best examples of capitalist manipulation. He expects us to believe that the people at Kelloggs cause us to grow fatter and fatter as they trick consumers, with advertising, to consume more and more cereal each morning to satisfy production capacity. In truth, the amount of breakfast cereal Americans buy is very constrained by the size of their stomachs, something that the people at Kelloggs have very little control over. Galbraith further expected us to believe that Colgate Palmolive forces us do our laundry more and more often so they can sell us more and more soap, when actually we obviously exercise a great deal of control over how much laundry we do, owing mostly to the natural limit on how many clothes we want to wear and soil

CONSUMERISM

in the course of a day. What Mr. Galbraith and the Democrats really demonstrate is how contemptuous they are of consumers and business alike, and how desperate they are to socialize all aspects of our lives.

Over the years Democratic intellectuals have come up with a vast array of arguments to justify their desire to limit individual freedom and enhance the size of gov't; these particular arguments about consumer docility and vulgarity are not the current vogue with the more modern Democratic editors, like those at, for example, "THE AMERICAN PROSPECT," but new arguments are being advanced with exactly the same intent. These are some of the things you would have said if you had had the space, Mr. Will.

QUOTAS-AFFIRMATIVE ACTION & DEMOCRATS

Dear Mr. Carl Rowan

I have just read your article on the Reagan-Bush judiciary. It is a very simple article in which you as a Democrat express your disappointment that Reagan and Bush, both Republicans, have appointed only Republican judges to the bench. You worry that these judges have made and will continue to make decisions in harmony with the Reagan\Bush conservative political philosophy. In particular, you note how the Republican judges have opposed affirmative action, a policy by which a black person is given, say, a job or university admission even though his qualifications are less than those of others who had applied for the same position. Your only additional comment, or reason in opposition to the Reagan\Bush appointments, is that most of the appointments are wealthy white men, some of whom (30%) belong to clubs that once practiced racial discrimination in choosing their members. You feel that, "A judiciary that fails to reflect the diversity of our society is that much more hard pressed to mete out equal justice."

As more and more data comes in reflecting the failure of the 1960's civil-rights ethic, Republicans increasingly have less and less sympathy for affirmative action. Despite a cautious initial acquiescence about affirmative action, Republicans have never had any sympathy for packing the court with poor black judges (as you apparently would want), anymore than they have had sympathy for packing it with poor or middle class, white judges, in order to reflect the diversity of society. A Republican President will always nominate a Republican judge who thinks similarly. A Democrat obviously will do the same thing. Politicians don't generally care which branch of gov't promotes their point of view, and they are not likely to be interfered with by your notions of affirmative action as they apply to judicial appointments. There is no debate about judicial affirmative action, let alone the mechanism by which it might be implemented. If someone,

QUOTAS

besides you, should mysteriously take an interest, the two of you would certainly have an uphill and lonely battle to fight. Moreover, consider the case of Clarence Thomas, he is, or was, a poor black man, and you certainly do not want him on the Court. What you really mean when you complain about the rich, white men on the court has nothing to do to with skin color or money. Your real concern is to simply get judges who agree with you on the Court, but saying so directly would make you seem petty.

Rather than worry about how much money a man has, or what the color of his skin is, why don't you focus on whether he thinks rationally. Your interest in side tracking the debate at a time when many, including black neo-conservatives, are skeptical about affirmative action, must reflect your fear of a debate whose outcome would not be helpful to your cause.

In the next election, Republicans will be generally opposed to the idea of "quotas" or affirmative action, and Democrats generally supportive. Democrats believe that affirmative action is a good way to reverse the affects of slavery and racism. Republicans believe that it does not work, no matter how well intentioned, and that it is not fair to whites and other non-blacks.

From the Civil-Rights Act of 1964 and The Voting Rights Act of 1965, until today, the Democrats have gotten essentially everything they every dreamed of on behalf of blacks and other minorities. When historians write the history of this brief period, Democrats will have little to fear; the programs and policies may have been an abject failure, but just as importantly, they provided new knowledge and showed that American hearts were in the right place. The "Great Society" period was easily the most significant and dramatic period in black history since the Civil War, but the results were not impressive. All the statistics presented today point to a very, very tragic plight for blacks, despite, or because of, all the things Democrats have tried to do for them. 31% live in poverty; 25% are in jail, on probation or parole; 60% of black children are born to mothers without husbands; a man in Bangladesh is more likely to reach age forty than a black man in Harlem; there are more black men in prison than in college;

AFFIRMATIVE ACTION AND DEMOCRATS

the best day to push drugs or get a bed in a homeless shelter is the day Welfare checks and Food Stamps are issued. A ghetto culture has evolved that glorifies bad English, violence toward women, one hundred dollar sneakers, drugs, and outlandish hair and clothing. Educational achievement has remained about the same. The few successes, like the increase in black elected officials from 300 to 7000, have not been translated into concrete gains.

The most frequent Democratic response to all this is that more of the same is necessary. We simply need, they will say, more orchestration from Washington, another Civil-Rights bill, more affirmative action, and the problems will begin to recede, even though they have only gotten worse over the last 25 years with such medicine. Both parties have eagerly looked for the light at the end of this tunnel, and it has never appeared. At their worst, Democrats describe Republicans, particularly Reagan, who publicly said that welfare was a kind of slavery, as racist. At their most practical and harmless, they often now ignore the issue owing to the govt's lack of remaining resources and\or a suspicion that maybe they don't know what to do after all, even though they retain an emotional attachment and loyalty to a failed social welfare policy that they were once heavily committed to.

Modern Republicans no longer accept much guilt for slavery and its aftermath; this is not to say that they are uncaring, but rather to say that if everything from the Civil War to the modern Welfare State didn't help, then neither can they. The help must now come mostly from other blacks. Economic times are tough and guilt is not as affordable; if a white or asian loses a job, through affirmative action, to a black who was less qualified, he will probably object, and loudly. This is an issue that appeals to the rank and file as well as party theoreticians. It crosses many issues; not just race, and highlights the general idea of fairness.

For example, Republicans generally oppose the Small Business Administration whose main purpose is to help secure loans for people who want to start or expand small businesses. They reasoned that it was not fair of the gov't to help one guy get into business and compete against another

QUOTAS

who did not have the same help. Similarly, capital gains incentives and other tax measures are not fair to those competitors who do not qualify for them. A massive subsidy to Amtrack was great for the people who worked for the train industry but not at all fair to the people who worked for other industries which competed with the train industry. The Republicans were always opposed to a wide range of gov't actions which were not fair. To Republicans it is not fair for gov't to recognize and support labor unions so that its members get higher wages, while everybody else then pays higher prices for the goods and services produced by the unions. It is not fair to raise the taxes of poor people so rich people can use tax deductible home equity loans to buy yachts.

The gov't doesn't produce anything; so all it can do is divide things others have produced; eventually, if the gov't becomes powerful, everybody becomes a special interest group using the gov't to steal from other groups. Affirmative action was possible for a while because blacks were considered a very special, special interest group. Today the climate has changed, affirmative action and the other programs, whether targeted at blacks or other minorities, seem not to have worked and perhaps even did harm. The number of special interest groups the Democrats began assembling in the 30's has proliferated to a point where different groups often end up competing with each other rather than with a privileged majority which no longer exists. Today, Republicans can say, without guilt, that the concept of affirmative action, in all its many variations, has been thoroughly tried by the Democrats; it did not work, and it was not fair.

In California, recent studies have shown that affirmative action for blacks in the university system has shut out Asians more than Whites, since there are large numbers of well qualified Asians in that state. Does the U.S. really want to create a society in which every special interest group, from a person to a large institution, devotes himself or itself to, and becomes dependant on, a whimsical gov't bureaucracy to gain that which must be taken from somebody else.

On a more conceptual level, it is necessary to ask Democrats whether it really makes sense to conclude that people will benefit if the gov't artificially lowers standards for them. If a medical school and business lower their standards for students and workers, won't they theoretically

AFFIRMATIVE ACTION AND DEMOCRATS

produce worse doctors and products? Is there a net benefit in this process, or just a short term political gain because a new student or employee is easier to see and measure today, than a slightly substandard doctor or product tomorrow? Will lowering a standard today cause it to be to raised tomorrow or lowered still further? Does lowering standards lead to a point at which beneficiaries catch up and become equal, or does it really cause the development of both lower standards and self-expectations?

In a very real way, affirmative action naturally exists for all Americans. If, for example, a student cannot get into Harvard; society will make an allowance; he can apply to Yale. In fact, there are thousands of educational standards to compensate for each ability level. It is beyond reason to understand why the gov't would waste enormous amounts of money and energy forcing every organization in America to have duplicate standards and programs, when they exist naturally for all Americans.

Suppose there was non-affirmative action? Might it work better? I recall a high school football coach who used to say that by practicing twice a day before the semester began, while many competitors were only practicing once, his team would have an increased probability of winning. Similarly, I recall a track coach who said, "always practice your event by running the next higher event. If you run the quarter mile, practice by running the half mile." These it seems, were good models for success, models that leave a participant with a realization of where real and sustainable progress comes from, as opposed to the kind that is artificially created by gov't policy, and just as easily destroyed by a new election, different policy or real world competition. Suppose Jesse Jackson had changed his famous exhortation to black children to say, "I may be poor, I may be black, but I am somebody...., because I can work twice as hard as anybody I know."

For a host of reasons, Republicans are generally opposed to affirmative action, quotas, race norming and set-asides; if Democrats like you, Mr. Rowen, want to get back in the debate, you will have to come up with a better reason than: it seemed like it was worth trying back in the sixties. In the 90's, America has 25 years of experience with affirmative action; it is

QUOTAS

necessary to present at least some analysis from that experience if you want your position taken seriously. That someone as steeped in civil-rights politics as you, can do no better, must be testimony to the difficulty faced by Democrats who would hope to justify continued affirmative action.

PACIFISM - THE DEMOCRATIC SOUL

Dear Mr. Colman McCarthy,

It is difficult to know whether you expect your article on pacifism to be taken seriously. As a pacifist you have found a home in the Democratic Party; how comfortable they are with you and you with them is not certain, but it is certain that while you and the Democrats are not a perfectly matched pair you do have many things in common. Certainly you always vote with the Democrats since they are much closer to pacifism than the Republicans who have frequently regarded war as a legitimate, last resort, foreign policy tool. Most Democrats won't publicly identify themselves as pacifists; this may be because they really are willing to fight and die in some situations, or just because it may not be politically popular in many situations, even for a Democrat, to identify himself as a pacifist. What ever the case, you are at the very least courageous for identifying your position, labeling it, and never missing a chance to encourage those in your party to move closer to your position.

Within the Democratic Party there are many indications of how deep the desire is to avoid war through the use of pacifism. If pacifism is the avoidance of war through the refusal to participate, then the Democrats have become very close to pacifism. George McGovern, who worked so hard against the development of the Patriot Missile, which is purely defensive, is considering another run for the presidency with the encouragement of some major players in the Democratic Party. Sen. Kennedy is captivated by the thought of a peace dividend as the Communist Party in Russia crumbles, even though there have been two world wars this Century that had nothing to do with communism, and even though he doesn't know whose finger will ultimately end up on the world's mightiest nuclear arsenal after the dust settles in Russia. Saddam Hussein, a tiny third world despot, quickly taught many Democrats a lesson when he started what could have been a very deadly and large war, just as the Soviet threat seemed to be diminishing. The demise of Russian Communism gave the Democrats an excuse to let down America's guard, and they quickly jumped on it, but Hussein quickly reminded them that war existed long before communism. Democrats don't want to think about war, they don't want to plan for it, and they certainly don't want to participate in it. Whether they would be outwardly pacifist, as you are Mr. McCarthy, if they didn't have to dilute their public positions in order to seem more in step with and be elected by mainstream America, is not certain.

PACIFISM

Democrats an excuse to let down America's guard, and they quickly jumped on it, but Hussein quickly reminded them that war existed long before communism. Democrats don't want to think about war, they don't want to plan for it, and they certainly don't want to participate in it. Whether they would be outwardly pacifist, as you are Mr. McCarthy, if they didn't have to dilute their public positions in order to seem more in step with and be elected by mainstream America, is not certain.

A specific look at the arguments you use in support of pacifism make it very clear just how difficult the road you have chosen is. The buzz word in you area of scholarship seems to be conflict management. You say that it is a technique being used successfully, all over America, but not in the White House or in the house of Saddam Hussein. The implication of what you say is that, if only Bush and Hussein would adopt your techniques for conflict management, a war could be avoided. Interestingly, you mention that the techniques are used all over the U.S., but your silence about their use in Iraq implies that they are not being used there. Already the forces of peace are in trouble. Pacifism is popular in America, except in the White House, but not popular anywhere in Iraq. You can't introduce this evidence, Mr. McCarthy, and then pretend that both sides of the conflict have an equal commitment and desire for peace. If Iraq could be expected to be a partner in the search for peace, then peace would be somewhere evident in their gov't or somewhere in their recent culture.

Let's be serious, Saddam was raised under very tragic circumstances by a mad dog uncle who taught him from a very early age that God made three mistakes; he created Jews, Persians, and flies. That Saddam wound up killing Kurds and Kuwaitis was merely incidental, as they were small but important obstacles blocking the Persian\Israeli road, on which the mother of all wars was eventually to be fought. Saddam rose to power by knowing how to simultaneously slit a man's throat and keep him so quiet as to not make a sound loud enough for the man in the next seat to hear. He is once said to have boasted that he knew who was being disloyal before the disloyal person knew. I suppose you might call his approach a kind of

THE DEMOCRATIC SOUL

conflict management, although not exactly the kind you may have had in mind. For you to suggest that there is a similarity between Bush and Hussein; that they are both equally unskilled in conflict management, is a preposterous insult to America. Do you really believe that the two men are morally neutral and equal; just two guys with an honest disagreement. It denigrates even the little value that can be derived from pacifism, which at its best, asks us to always look even harder for a alternative to violence.

When a Hussein, Hitler, Mussolini, Tojo, Khadafy, or Bonaparte attack; if you are truly pacifist, you are truly dead. Pacifism is not a theory that we want to rely on too seriously; yet it is a theory you seriously present to us.

You describe the Allied bombing of Iraq as, "a campaign of slaughter and destruction against Iraqi soldiers and citizens." You do not describe the Iraqi bombing of Kuwait. How would you describe the Allied fire bombing of Nazi Germany. When Churchill described the bombing by saying, "let he who sows the wind, reap the whirlwind," he bespoke a sad truth about the way civilization grew. Violence begot violence, and civilization grew. Morality, it often turned out, as Bonaparte said, was on the side of the mightiest artillery. Who dares to think what would have been, had men not been willing to die for Judeo\Christian ideals? How do you describe it when a violent murder\rapist is thrown in jail? Is this violence toward the murderer, or pacifism toward the victim, and would-be victims. Republicans are stridently pacifist, as long as the bad guys will permit it. Democrats seem to be pacifist all the time, or almost all the time, regardless of what the bad guys are doing. You might say that Americans have always been willing to die for their ideas. The Pilgrims and Puritans came here despite the near certainty of death. The Revolutionary War was fought against impossible odds. The bloody Civil War to save the Union was fought brother against brother. World War I was fought on distant shores, to end all wars, and for not much more. Ideas and principles were king; human flesh seemed to matter little. Today is different, a mother won't quickly sacrifice her child to war, life has gotten very pleasant; many essential principals have been realized for so long that not many new ones are deemed worth dying for. Old principals are now securely

PACIFISM

useful tool to manage the kind of conflict created by Saddam Hussein.

As if to lose your readers completely, you go on to speak admiringly of Rep. Jeanette Rankin, the famous hero of the pacifist movement who voted against American participation in both world wars. She supposedly said "you can't win a war any more than you can win an earthquake." On the subject of this perverse Representative, Republicans are all pacifists. It is just not possible to find the patience to fight about the value of winning a World War against Nazi Germany. Just remind us one more time, Mr. McCarthy, that you are one of the most widely read Democratic columnists in the country.

On the positive side though, you do not represent the queerest of the Democratic special interest groups. Gloria Steinem of N.O.W is campaigning for Bill Clinton despite her statements: "children should be raised to believe in human potential; not God, and over-throwing capitalism is to small for us. We must over-throw the whole fucking patriarchy." When Ms. Steinem was asked to explain the furor over N.O.W. president Pat Ireland's heterosexual marriage and homosexual social life she said, "I think everybody is just jealous." Hollywood types Martin Sheen and Harry Belafonte support Castro one day and the next are asked to host major Democratic political functions in NYC. Democratic Sen. Al Gore describes the greenhouse effect as "the most serious threat that we have ever faced" even though nobody has ever died from it. What about war, famine, disease, and auto accidents? Suppose we allocated our resources as Gore would want? Moreover, scientists have not even established that the effect is real. The Democrats don't stand for anything sensible and so every weird idea can fit under their umbrella. The Republicans do stand for something; this is why David Duke is kicked out when he tries to join.

ATOM BOMBS-DEMOCRATS TOO SCARED TO THINK

DEAR MARY MCGRORY

Your article on the upcoming U.N. conference to promote a complete ban on nuclear weapon testing was curious in that as a liberal Democrat you are opposed to American nuclear bombs and the testing of those bombs, and generally in favor of the Complete and Partial Test Ban Treaties. But why didn't you think to present any reasons in your article to support your positions?

This is something that Democrats often do because their feelings about an issue are so strong as to often preclude an ability to think and reason. It is so emotionally obvious to you that nuclear bombs, and weapons in general, are evil, that it completely slips your mind that a sound rationale may also be necessary to promote agreement with your position. The burden falls on Republicans to show the discipline and maturity to recognize that even though weapons and wars may be horrible, they are often necessary to save lives.

The best effort you made in support of your position was to point out that Gerald Smith, an expert, and Paul Warnke, also an expert wrote a letter to the President which said, "the test ban is the single strongest measure available for stemming the spread of the atomic scourge." This is interesting, but of no value since there are loads of people on both sides, expert and non-expert, who are writing letters for and against the treaty. Without any explanation, you anoint this letter as heaven sent and then say in mock surprise, "It has had no visible affect." Good grief, why did you think one letter would have such a great affect when you know full well that Republicans never listen to letters that describe Democratic feelings, anymore than Democrats listen to letters that describe Republican thoughts. Your article made no further reference to the letter.

ATOM BOMBS

Your next angle of attack suggested that the recent crisis in the Persian Gulf, and Saddam Hussein's reputed possession of a nuclear bomb, should offer the perfect opportunity to think new thoughts. Staying in character, you didn't say what new thoughts you had in mind. Probably you meant that if all nations had signed the test ban treaty, lived up to it, and then all the nuclear weapons (due to some unknown cause) disappeared, Saddam Hussein's Iraq would have been much less menacing. It would seem that the above scenario makes no sense since Hussein, like all the people who you would really want to sign the treaty, wouldn't; even if he or they did, he would feel no compunction about breaking it when the time finally came to demonstrate the weapon with which he might destroy Israel or Iran. Lastly, if he did have a nuclear weapon, it obviously would only be wise, militarily speaking, for Hussein to test it directly on Israel or Iran; so the subject of a test ban treaty is irrelevant in this case which you think should serve to encourage us to think new thoughts.

You go on to imply a criticism of Republicans because they still want to test nuclear weapons despite the protestations of our former enemy-Russia. You then imply that Republicans get too excited as they think about who will be the next rulers of Russia. If you were to try to reason your way beyond these feelings, you would merely have to assure us of exactly what is going to happen next in Russia, and that it poses no threat to us, but of course you can't do that because you have no clue as to whether the future rulers of Russia will more closely resemble Jesus Christ or Adolf Hitler. If you would again study the last two year period of mankind's history, paying particular attention to Russia, China, Eastern Europe, Iran, Iraq, and Nicaragua you would reasonably conclude that it is extremely unwise to attempt to predict history. A study of the previous 10,000 years would reveal more of the same unpredictability. How is it, Ms. McGrory, that you are so confident about predicting history? Did you know that the U.S. developed the bomb to use on Japan, but that, Russia, our ally at the time, became the target at which the U.S. aimed all of its subsequent bombs? Did you know that the U.S. and its allies sold weapons to Iraq less than a year before it went to war against them?

Republicans, are aware of the horror a nuclear bomb can cause,

DEMOCRATS TOO SCARED TO THINK

but they are equally aware of the horror it can prevent. The bomb was developed to end World War II and used to save, perhaps, about 1 million American soldiers who otherwise might have died as they invaded the Japanese mainland; it killed about 250,000 people in Hiroshima and Nagasaki but it saved, perhaps, 15 million Japanese who might have died defending their homeland. Prior to the bomb's development about 10,000,000 people per year were being killed by World War II. This killing stopped almost instantly after the bomb was dropped. It is not sensible to talk about the morality of the bomb as separate from the morality of the war, since they both occur simultaneously. Moreover, to date the bomb has been more good than bad, it ended World War II, and helped, or possibly assured that the peace would be kept for the following 40 years.

After WW II, Russia developed its own bomb and it has been used ever since primarily to impose a balance of terror. Both sides went on to develop bigger and better bombs and delivery systems while voluntarily limiting with anti-ballistic missile treaties their defensive capability against such weapons. It would not be unreasonable to conclude that this conscious creation of a balance of terror may well have prevented WW III. This is no small feat when you consider that both Russia and the U.S. have had long and active military histories and that seldom, if ever, in history were two countries so meaningfully and diametrically opposed as the U.S. and Russia. That countries with such diametrically opposed ideologies would end up resolving their differences peacefully, may be a good indication that the bomb has been a good thing, indeed.

The Reagan Presidency changed the nature of the balance of terror. Republicans never liked a balance of terror with a country they considered to be a moral and economic midget. Reagan announced the Star Wars defense system (opposed by Democrats) which was to end the terror, at least on the U.S. side, by giving America a thorough defense against a Russian nuclear attack. Technologically, it was going to be infinitely more complex than an offensive systems; this was something the Russians feared immensely because they knew their struggling economy, which turned out to be less than one fourth the size of the U.S.', couldn't match it. Russia's

ATOM BOMBS

inability to match the West in this area, and the growing realization that it couldn't match the West in any area, led to its collapse. Their inability to match our bomb and our defenses against it, was the most significant element in the collapse. Again, the bomb was a positive force in history; something that was always very central to the U.S.' relationship with Russia.

Republicans believe as Ronald Reagan said, "America is the last best chance the world has to preserve freedom;" consequently, they don't feel it is a contradiction for us to keep nuclear weapons while strongly discouraging others from keeping and developing theirs. The others don't need the weapons, they reason, as long as the U.S. has them. When President Bush says, as you point out Ms. McGrory, that "the growth of nuclear weapons is one of the greatest threats to the survival of mankind," he is referring mostly to the growth in other countries, particularly all those dictatorships ruled by people who may be like Saddam Hussein, and to the 15-24 new countries that will develop a nuclear capability in the next ten years. Republicans are not about to leave the last best hope for freedom, under-defended. This is very difficult for most Democrats to swallow as they neither comprehend what American values have meant to the world, nor acknowledge the leadership responsibility thereby conferred.

Much of the world, and many of the Democrats, won't allow the U.S. this moral high ground, and so the U.S. may have to simply ignore the test ban treaties, as President Bush is currently doing, until such time as Democrats like you, Ms. McGrory, are able to recognize the role the U.S. is heavily and rightfully obligated to play. Nuclear non-proliferation, among other countries, is very important to the U.S. Perhaps the most pragmatic and politic way to make this seemingly arrogant position palatable is to offer guaranteed international borders to those countries which agree not to develop and test nuclear weapons. Failing this giant political step, the U.S. must maintain and improve its intelligence \ reconnaissance capability, its ABM system (anti-ballistic missile) and its conventional first strike capability so that it can deal with potential nuclear adversaries as handily as it did, Hussein.

DEMOCRATS TOO SCARED TO THINK

Finally, the U.S. and the Republicans must resist the Democratic thinking of Mary McGrory. The simplistic notion of the U.S. participating in a test ban treaty is kind-hearted and soft-headed, something that would appeal only to a Democrat.

RALPH NADER-CONSUMER ADVOCATE AND DEMOCRAT

Dear Mr. Rowen,

I read your article about how wonderful Ralph Nader is for "making the American System live up to its own stated ideals." On the whole, your article was very well balanced as you devoted almost half the space to detailing the positions of Mr. Nader's detractors. However, two major problems do exist with the article. Firstly, you wait until the very last three sentences to say, in effect, "I love Ralph Nader," but you never even evidence any need to present a rationale for your feeling that the arguments in support of Nader are better than those against.

Secondly, your article is badly out of context. You mention FDR, right wing think tanks, Nixon, Carter, Reagan, and Forbes Magazine, but you mysteriously never make your article actionable by going the next step to say that those who are Republican, generally don't like Nader; while those who are Democratic, generally do. In the end, all Americans must walk into the voting booth and be confronted with the only governmental choice that has boiled down from the last 10,000 years of human history: Democrat vs. Republican. Why not help them with this choice?

To put Mr. Nader in context, as you discussed the book "Unsafe At Any Speed," which launched his career as a consumer activist, 25 years ago, you might have started with a quick look at his childhood. It seems he was raised by an incredibly precise, 1 in 500,000, mother who had very precise ways to handle every one of lifes little problems and situations. Her detailed formulas for standing, sitting, cooking, thinking, and eating, probably were a little wiser than most, and certainly well intended, but more importantly, they were certainly a lot more controlling and dictatorial than most; this probably is what motivates Mr. Nader, who responded with gentle compliance to his childhood, to seek so much control over everyone else's life and to promote the Democrats, who similarly seek to control and regulate the whole country. Perhaps if Mr. Nader had had his own family, the way his mother had her own, he would have been content to recreate is own childhood there, rather than impose it on his country.

RALPH NADER

Certainly, no one could have criticized Mr. Nader if "Unsafe At Any Speed" had been written to warn consumers that the General Motors-Corvair was a relatively dangerous car, but it wasn't written for that reason; it was written more to describe how evil business is; how willing Detroit is to kill people in the name of profit, and, most importantly, how in need Detroit and the country is of Mr. Nader's maternal and very Democratic regulation.

The question of automobile safety is an infinitely more complex one than Mr. Nader would have us believe. For example, should we say, "the 140,000,000 automobiles now in use in America are so safe that only about 30,000 people get killed each year." Or should it be stated as follows: "the automobiles in America are such outrageous death traps that 30,000 people are senselessly slaughtered each year," about the same number as were killed during the entire Vietnam War that so badly traumatized the whole country. How do we decide which perspective is the most sensible?

If America decided that 30,000 deaths was insanely high, and it wanted to reduce them to zero, it would be very nearly possible. Congress could reduce the speed limit to 35 mph, make four airbags per vehicle mandatory, add front, rear, and side bumpers so that each car could survive a 35 mph crash from any direction, and ration the number of miles that each car could be driven. The cost of this would be enormous, but maybe not so enormous to someone who saw a loved one mangled and killed in a car accident.

If, on the other hand, America decided that 50,000 deaths was what realistically had to be expected from two trillion passenger miles per year, it wouldn't have to do anything but leave the present system alone.

The kind of gov't intervention that would reduce auto deaths to zero or some other arbitrary but lower number, is the approach that Mr. Nader and the Democrats would prefer, while Republicans would generally prefer the current system which allows each citizen to vote his choice with dollars as he selects the car, the number of airbags, and other safety features that appeal to his own values. The difference is that Democrats want to decide

RALPH NADER

for everybody what the correct target number is, while the Republicans are content to let everybody live freely and decide for themselves. Only with free choice, they argue, will the most accurate safety number emerge. If people occasionally make dumb choices, it is not a cause for panic since they will probably make fewer dumb choices than Democrats in Washington. Besides, the freedom to make dumb choices and to learn from those choices is the thing that gives greater knowledge to free people, a Republican would argue.

Chrysler has been advertising the wider availability of air bags in its cars than in the competitions; yet the company is currently doing very poorly, apparently because the added safety of airbags, rightly or wrongly, has only a limited appeal. Volvo, has devoted a great deal to the idea of safety and has nevertheless not become a major factor in the U.S. market, although it does satisfy, if only psychologically, many people who trust that they are safer in a Volvo.

If the Democrats set the safety standard, or any other standard, for such things as price, quality, features, and appearance, it is not possible to know whether that standard would be higher or lower, better or worse, than the standard the free market would have set. What is know is that it would be their standard; the arbitrary Democratic standard, based on their belief that they are wiser and gentler than you are.

Let's say Mr. Nader got his way, and it cost each American $1000 more per year to pay for reducing auto deaths to 25,000 per year. The money would have to come from somewhere; if the $1000 came out of money that would have been spent on some combination of medical care, education, recreation, and food, is it possible to conclude that the trade off was a good one? Women want to spend money on clothes at a rate 10 times more than men, even though this may seem to some, like the obsessive and acetic Mr. Nader, who is proud to never waste a nickel in his personal life, to be a frivolous endeavor. Is it possible for the Democrats to know that women would be better off putting this money into something like safety features on their cars? When women voluntarily spend money on clothes that they could choose to spent elsewhere they are very precisely describing a ratio between the two that they prefer. What presumption gives a Democratic gov't the right to object to these numerous and highly individualistic expressions of free will.

CONSUMER ADVOCATE AND DEMOCRAT

Women and men do not live by bread alone, as the Bible correctly instructs, but only the Democrats presume to instruct us about how much bread versus how much non-bread, consumers should buy. If somebody buys an energy efficient, inexpensive small car, and forgoes the expense and safety of a large car, are they doing the wrong thing according to Mr. Nader's metaphysical judgements. If a sybarite likes beer, whole milk, buttered pop-corn, and bungi jumping, do we punish his lack of discipline, or reward his free and high spirits? Should Democrats preserve life so it can be boring; can a bored person be spirited and productive?

A person who has terminal cancer might ask, "why don't we mobilize the world in a war against cancer the way we mobilized the world in a war against Hitler and Tojo." Many would support such an effort, that way maybe they wouldn't have to see loved ones suffer and die with cancer, or worse, consider the possibility of their children suffering from cancer. Such people would be in the minority, it would seem, as there never has been any significant sentiment around the country to mount a World War II size effort to cure cancer, even though it is a disease that will kill one third to one half of the worlds population. Who is to say that the view of those who want an all out war on cancer should be imposed on a world that currently prefers to put a little more of its money into having fun today than preserving life tomorrow? Republicans respect what the wisdom of a free people has wrought, or to be less charitable, they recognize the futility of dictating to the descendants of self-willed Pilgrims and Puritans. Democrats are, as a matter of philosophy, contemptuous of people and all the mistaken judgements and decisions they will make in the absence of gov't guidance; that is why a Ralph Nader never doubts that all of his very specific prescription for Americans are exactly right. Not only does he want the gov't to mandate his safety standards for cars, but he wants gov't to socialize America so that it can regulate everything in accordance with his compulsions.

Ralph Nader, has always spoken highly of "Consumer Reports" magazine. Presumably it should have been enough to almost satisfy him, because it gave Americans a perfect opportunity to really find out from an impartial source, which products were really cheap, safe, reliable and

RALPH NADER

effective. As it turns out, not many people buy the magazine. Not many find it convenient to hunt around in their local stores for the particular model numbers the magazine recommends; not many find the standards used to evaluate products to be relevant, and many of the recommendations are scoffed at because of their sheer arrogance. "Consumer Reports" will, for example, tell its readers which beans taste best, and what number from "their scale" describes the sound quality from a high-fidelity system. Rather than learn from this about how heavily nuanced free market choices can be, Nader is more inclined to scold us by saying, in effect, if you won't pay attention voluntarily, I'm going to create a socialist gov't that will make you pay attention. This contempt for consumers, can be traced back to the famous socialist economist, John Kenneth Galbraith, who wrote at length in his book, "The Affluent Society," about the vulgar choices which freedom loving consumers will make when not properly regulated by Democrats.

The split between the Democrats and Republicans on this issue is absolutely straight forward and total. You acknowledge, Mr. Rowen, that Reagan, the right wing think tanks, Forbes, and a few other factors have caused Nader to lose popularity and influence, and then in your last inexplicable paragraph you say, "Nader's ideas are now generally excepted as prudent around the world." What you must have meant to say is that Nader's ideas are widely accepted as prudent only by Democrats and their friends around the world.

In your last sentence you say that Nader has "set out to save the American system by making it live up to its own stated ideals." Only God knows where these ideals you speak of are stated. They are certainly not in the Constitution which is devoted to promoting individual liberty and freedom from gov't. Moreover, it is hard to think of Nader saving the system, since he is opposed to it in the first place; preferring instead, a Democratic version of socialist regulation, to individual liberty and free choice.

THE FREE PRESS-REPUBLICAN GENERALS IN THE GULF

Dear Mr. Wicker,

In your recent column you spent all of your time informing your readers how sad it is that the Pentagon got to regulate the press during the Persian Gulf War. Strangely, you never mentioned why the whole country seemed perfectly content with this, or how the situation evolved from the drastically different one that existed during past wars when the press had the freedom you seem to covet so much.

When a journalist so obviously avoids listing and deflating the opposing point of view he becomes closer to a lobbyist than a journalist. A lobbyist represents a special interest group from within a vacuum, which is to say he promotes his interest with little or no regard for the other interests that may be affected. A journalist should have a somewhat broader perspective owing to the idea that his readers are likely to be of varying perspectives and thereby may lose interest if their position, whether similar or opposed, isn't supported or intelligently denied. To look at it another way, a lobbyist is paid to promote one point of view, while a journalist, even and editorial journalist, is paid to reconcile competing points of view, although he may rightfully end up supporting one view.

Your editorial is very close to a lobby, a liberal Democratic lobby, as is much of the work you do, and this may well explain why the Pentagon, the Republican Gov't, and the public, were very happy not to have you and the press underfoot during the Gulf War. To look at it another way, 85% of those in the major media are registered Democrats, while only 25% of Americans are now willing to describe themselves as Democrats. Is it a no wonder that the country didn't really want the minority point of view from the Democratic press as it was trying to marshal all of its emotional resources for use in the impending war.

In the case of the Vietnam War, it was the Democrats (Kennedy and Johnson), who got America slowly involved, and the Republicans who

FREE PRESS

got America uninvolved; yet it was the Republicans and the troops who took the heat, the heat that was often delivered by the press. In the Gulf War, the very real silent majority that Democrats have always been so contemptuous of, got organized very quickly, yellow ribbons and all, and paid back the Vietnam era troops and the national psyche. This time was going to be different, they weren't going to wait for years to discover how badly they hurt so many of their own by abandoning them on a Vietnam-like battle field. They were going to support them now, through a quick, decisive and powerful military campaign; no cowardly Democrat was going to turn this into another Vietnam.

Based on the little reporting that you, Mr. Wicker, and your Democratic friends got to do from and about the Persian Gulf, it is fairly certain what track you were on. There was one report that Bob Simon did in the early days of the build up, before press restrictions were tightened up, with a group of American soldiers who while practicing night maneuvers got lost in the Saudi Arabian Dessert. It was indeed very pathetic to see American troops wandering lost in the desert. Simon could have shown any one of a million successful practice sessions, but he chose that one, the one that might breed discontent; make us doubt ourselves, and put us back on the Vietnam road. There was another story done with a light infantry group that was practicing with a battery of four, tube launched, wire guided missiles. As it turned out, on that day and at that time, three out of four of the missiles misfired and fell, almost humorously, a few feet in front of their launch tubes. The group's leader grumbled to the eager newsman that had it been a real combat situation, his position would have been fully illuminated by the ignition of the misfiring rockets, and he and his crew would undoubtedly have been killed.

Those stories were just what the Democrats and the press wanted, precisely because they undermined the war which they were generally opposed to. The hopelessness and futility of war, and self-righteous compassion, has become the stock in trade of the Democratic press since the middle of the Vietnam War. To them, The Gulf War was a war America couldn't win; a war that would cause tens of thousands of causalities, not

REPUBLICAN GENERALS IN THE GULF

withstanding that the Allied cause was just, and that Iraq was a third world country with only 17 million people aligned against the whole of Western Civilization. Geraldo Rivera, a very influential Democrat by virtue of his daily, national TV show, asked in a very pious way, "why is the Pentagon sending 60,000 body bags to Saudi Arabia?" All of the Democratic machinery was fully mobilized to tell America that if it dared to fight Saddam, it would lose more troops than it could bear.

It is not difficult to imagine the kind of inspiration the Iraqi Republican Guard might have gotten from these newscasts; the joy in seeing their enemies' ineptness, and the confidence that comes from knowing how frightened their opponent was. The military has long known, and re-learned from the Iraqi regulars as they surrendered in droves during the war, that morale is important, perhaps the most important thing a soldier has as he enters combat. High morale enables a soldier to maintain exact performance levels, and ideals of duty, honor, and country, even as death may be a spilt second away. Fear, or low morale, caused by a lack of confidence in yourself, your country's support, your equipment, or the righteousness of your cause, can cripple and kill a soldier in combat. Whether in combat, in football, or golf, fear cripples, but it nevertheless was what these newsman sought to create in an effort to prevent the war that they were opposed to from starting. The Democratic press had no business around troops or a nation that may have been moments away from battle. Even in a democratic country, the debating has to stop at a logical point; in this case the point was in the sands of Saudi Arabia.

The military quickly saw what the press was up to; thereafter reporters were required to meet in pools, from which they would be escorted to areas or situations where they could report on things that, in the military's view, would be innocuous or helpful to the war effort. A loyal opposition is a wonderful component of democracy; just not on the battlefield.

One of the other psychological tactics that the Democratic press used was to ask the same old question they got so much milage out of during the Vietnam period; namely, why are we there? This was a question that President Bush and the Administration spoke and wrote about a 1000 times, including a cover story in "Newsweek" magazine; yet the Democrats figured if they kept asking the question, people would be finally be tricked into

FREE PRESS

believing that no one had yet been able to come up with a satisfactory answer, and therefore the effort against Hussein should be abandoned. It got to be very silly, when one day Secretary Baker said we were there for "jobs." This was all the Democrats needed to hear. The Administration had not put it exactly that way before. Previously, the administration had spoken about "oil;" now they were speaking about "jobs;" The Democratic press wanted everyone to believe that the administration had flip-flopped about the rationale for the war because it used what were really, synonyms, to explain our primary interest in Kuwait. The press knew very well that oil was necessary to create and maintain jobs in the U.S., but they also knew that the press has an emotional hold on many people that is often more powerful than rational debate, or accurate reporting.

Mike Royko, a widely read Democratic journalist for 27 years, wrote, "if those who are over there don't know why they're over there, and those who are back here don't know why we're over there, it appears that Bush hasn't done a very good selling job." In truth the Persian Gulf War was one of the simplest wars in history to figure out, and everyone, no matter where they were, had it figured out. Mr. Royko may not have, but then again he probably has not yet figured out why we were in World Wars I and II. Certainly South Korea and South Vietnam are too complicated for him to figure out. When really complex foreign policy issues like Panama, Grenada, and Lebanon, come up, Mr. Royko would certainly have to defer to others with minds sufficient to grasp these obviously more complex issues. Playing dumb has become something of a stock in trade for Democrats as regards foreign policy. Conversely, they are more ingenious than children when it comes to dreaming up excuses for things they want to participate in, such as more and more gov't involvement in domestic affairs.

At one point during the war, Carl Rowan, a dean among Democratic journalists, said, apparently in frustration at the Saudi Arabian press core's inability to come up with a really damaging story, "I know most of them and they couldn't cover a fire in Baltimore." Now that the war is over, Mr. Wicker, I hope you and Mr. Rowan and Mr. Royko and your Democratic friends can put out the fires within your own party caused by your misguided lobbing efforts against the War. It is no wonder that no one wanted you guys covering the War.

RACISM - DEMOCRATS REMIND REPUBLICANS

Mr. Les Payne

In a recent article you strongly supported the notion that the army the U.S. was sending to Saudi Arabia is racked with racism. You mentioned how very proud the reporter, Derek Davis, made you by putting President Bush on the spot by asking him about why a disproportionate number of minorities will serve, and in all probability, die, on the front lines of the Persian Gulf War.

You quite correctly observed that President Bush was not able to provide a logical answer to this question as he stumbled to point out, mainly, that since everybody volunteered, right up to the black Chairman of the Joint Chiefs of Staff, no racism could be involved. You countered this argument from Bush by saying, "so what, everybody knows that blacks join to escape economic racism on the outside of the military."

When the obligatory time came to quote an expert, you laid your cards on the table and quoted the famed Swedish economist and sociologist, Gunnar Myrdal. You did not mention that Mr. Myrdal was equally noted as a socialist who desperately longed to remake the entire world in harmony with his grandiose and well meaning proclamations. If he were alive and voting in the United States he would certainly find the George McGovern wing of the Democratic Party too conservative for his very liberal, socialist agenda. Undoubtedly you share his political persuasion, that the central gov't needs to take massive steps to exorcise the nation's easily defined ills, although you seem reluctant to specifically point this out. It seems that if you did point out exactly what plan of action you would want; those who would want to support you would then know exactly which political party to vote for. Or, perhaps you have no plan of action; it is just a rude habit of yours to accuse the President and the country of racism, and to encourage others to do the same.

One of the very nicest things that Democrats do for Republicans is to generally indict the whole country as evil, in this case, because of racism. If the country as a whole weren't evil, there wouldn't be anything for

RACISM

central gov't minded Democrats to fix with their fountain of wisdom and sensitivity, and they would be out of business. Republicans, conversely, believe the country and its military is essentially good; that the slow, steady progress it has made toward a fair and just society is the major phenomenon of world history which cannot be matched anywhere in the world. Accordingly, the Republicans are the feel good, patriotic party, while the Democrats always must make a hypocritical spectacle of themselves as they try to catch up in this area at election time. During the last presidential election, candidate Bush scored heavily against the Democratic opponent because he was able to symbolically wrap himself in the American Flag. When the Democratic candidate, Dukakis, tried to do they same thing, he felt and looked hypocritical; something that was very transparent to the voting public.

No one, it seems, will ever believe that Democrats are patriotic as long as they would have us believe that as a country we are evil, racist, and imperialist. Believing as they do about America, it is not surprising that Democrats are very meek about asserting any foreign policy, since that policy would be evil like the nation that authored it. With this in mind, particularly as manifested by the Democrats' reticence to use a racist military to support Operation Desert Storm, it is unlikely that the electorate will soon envision a Democrat as Commander in Chief. Fortunately, for our survival, the greatest nation in the history of the world chooses not to be negative about itself; this is something that the psychologically depressed Democrats can not understand.

If Mr. Payne believes America is racist after all it has tried to do for blacks: including, fighting The Civil War in which 10 times as many people died as in Vietnam, at a time when the country's population was less than half of what it was during the Vietnam period, it must be really difficult for him to defend Saudi Arabia, a country whose gov't got around to eliminating slavery only 35 years ago. The Democrats like history to move at a certain pace; certainly not the pace of Saudi Arabia; not even the rapid pace of America, but rather the pace of some fiction that only they can imagine. The specific charge of racism, whether in the military or anywhere else, that Democrats love to level at America is preposterous in a practical

DEMOCRATS REMIND REPUBLICANS

sense; a mere fiction that keeps the Democrats chortling, and may actually be responsible for the recent lack of progress in minority development.

Jews, Japanese, and mainland Asians are all different from European Americans, and have all been easily identified and discriminated against in their recent pasts, and yet they are the three most successful minorities in America. In fact, they are more successful than European Americans themselves; this doesn't sound like racism, but rather, like the melting pot that America was so proud of in the 1950's before the Democrats and Lyndon Johnson's "Great Society" came to power in the 1960's. Who really wonders what would have happened to blacks if the Democrats hadn't sold them the big gov't, socialist, civil-rights ethos, but instead had encouraged them to turn inward and develop the same kind of personal qualities and characteristics that Jews, Japanese, and mainland Asians have.

There is good data around to measure the progress blacks were making before the 1960's as compared to what they have made thereafter, and it shows a slowing of progress to coincide with the massive and very well intentioned Federal Gov't intervention. Most Americans are now familiar with the statistics about blacks as they pertain to: family instability, education, employment, drug use, murder, and infant mortality, all of which show very negative trends. America wanted so badly not to be racist, and was so sensitive to the charge of racism, that it tried every program it could think of, and every program Black America could think of, but nothing worked. To this day, you can turn on the evening news and hear reports about how some governor or some county or some city has found a promising new program to turn failed minorities into productive taxpaying citizens, but the program never seems to catch on nationally, and the trends keep getting worse. The worse it gets the more traditional black leaders like you, Mr. Payne, and your cohort Carl Rowen, charge racism. There is no doubt that you are a very decent and well intentioned man, but nevertheless, you are sadly misguided if you think you can help blacks by portraying them as victims who helplessly suffer at the hands of racist Americans who discriminate against Blacks, but not Jews, Japanese and main land Asians. According to some noted Black intellectuals, like Clarence Thomas and Thomas Sowell, who you would be well advised to pay some attention to,

RACISM

Blacks are significantly different from other minorities only in that they were unfortunately singled out by Democrats in Washington to benefit from gov't programs, while other immigrant groups were allowed or forced to develop themselves from within. The revolutionary enlightenment that Malcolm X and Martin Luther King brought to both Black and White America would have had tremendous benefits if only it had been used to encourage good personal habits more than good governmental habits.

Sure there is racism, and even hunger, in America, and all of us should feel badly about it, but oddly enough we can be proud to suffer more from the misguided attempts to eliminate racism than from racism itself. Similarly, we can be proud to live in a country where over-eating is more of a problem than under-eating. It is a peculiar irony that old-fashioned Democrats, like you Mr. Payne, are too proud to admit that their medicine is worse than the illness it purports to cure.

These are the facts, Mr. Payne, the ones that Mr. Bush couldn't provide to your friend Derek Davis; not because he didn't know them, but because he couldn't play partisan politics as he was rallying the country toward war, and because being President of all the people; not just those who elected him, often requires of a President, politeness more than honesty.

SOCIALISM - THE MANY FACES OF TSONGAS

Dear Mr. Raspberry,

I read your article in which you supported a major new booklet from Presidential contender Sen. Paul Tsongas. You will recall that the paper's major proposal was for an industrial policy to assist domestic manufacturers, and thus rescue the economy and its workers. Your approach was to pay lip service to the Democratic Plan, (industrial policy, i.e., socialism) and the Republican plan (capitalism) and then say, in effect, to hell with the complexities of serious economic thought, the Democratic plan is "just plain good sense." You apparently felt no need to offer up even one reason for your endorsement; this is something very uncharacteristic of you, but increasingly common among Democrats.

At one point you did mentioned that the shift in jobs from manufacturing to services "inevitably means a cataclysmic decline in our standard of living" because, 1) non-union service jobs pay less, and 2) a decline in manufacturing causes a decline in the financial industry. Most can see the problem with this line of reasoning without having to pull out an Economics 101 textbook.

Firstly, if unions can create national wealth by demanding higher wages, with the threat of a strike, then the hour of our redemption is indeed at hand. Congress would merely pass a Federal law unionizing all workers and granting them a 50% pay raise without even having them waste their time and energy organizing unions and threatening strikes. In truth, absolutely no good does come or could come from unions or the scheme described above; what happens in a union environment is that management raises prices exactly enough to compensate for unionized wage increases. Wage increases become just another expense that is passed on to consumers. To be sure, when only one portion of the work force is unionized, that portion does benefit; it gets higher wages, but those wages are paid by the mostly non-union people who buy the expensive union made goods. Non-union wage earners pay higher prices; i.e., lower their standard of living to pay the higher cost of union produced products. It is a simple case of union people stealing from non-union people, or to put it another way, a case of the Democrats, who created and supported unions, playing a trick on unions to

SOCIALISM

get their votes, and hoping that those who pay the bill won't catch on.

Secondly, please consider that every good manager is trying to reduce the cost of what he makes so that more people can afford his product. He will eliminate union jobs as their cost goes up, in exchange for equipment or capital (which includes everything from screw drivers to robots) that becomes relatively less expensive as union wages go up. Additionally, to avoid union workers, sub-assemblies and complete assemblies will be produced in non-union shops and even in non-union countries. As the unions encourage this trend with their expensive labor, they have actually decimated their own ranks. It is almost impossible to believe that the Democrats would support such an obviously fraudulent and self-destructive process.

Lastly, since unions raise the costs of what they make, consumers are more inclined to buy, for example, non-union Japanese cars. To be sure, unions are only one factor operating against American Manufacturing, but who is to say how bad their affect is. Perhaps if the price differential between U.S. and Japanese cars was slightly less, people might flock to them in droves, out of loyalty; who is to say what the real cost is of structuring a huge manufacturing operation to satisfy and avoid 500,000 or so of its own unionized employees.

You then mention, Mr. Raspberry, that with a decline in manufacturing (something unions clearly encourage) it is not possible to maintain a financial industry. This is quite an enormous conclusion that you have made and it is proffered without any rationale. It would seem that the correct mix of various industries provided by any economy is something about which it is almost impossible to speculate. Adam Smith, perhaps the most important economist in history, instructed us long ago that even the simplest task, like the manufacturing of a pin, involves the coordination of literally thousands of people from all around the world; all in a miraculous effort to get one little item made and on a retail shelf at a cost of one cent. This is the capitalist miracle of efficiency and organization that produced the high American standard of living. It is something that could not be duplicated in a million years by gov't planners. In its communist heyday, the Soviet economy produced about 25% of what the U.S. economy did; had they not

THE MANY FACES OF TSONGAS

been able to steal ideas from the West about what to make and how to make it, their real output would have been about 10% of the U.S.' The Chinese are still 90% farmers because they are too smug to steal products, much less idealogy from the West.

The American economy has shifted from a point at which all were involved in agriculture, to a point at which 97% have moved on to numerous other industries, from electronics to entertainment. The creation, size, importance, and number of these industries represents the result of economic activity, mostly governed by the free market, in a process literally millions of times more complex than the manufacture of a pin. The gov't should not even dream of attempting to manage the ratio of manufacturing to financing to servicing, or be concerned about whether manufacturing or agriculture or finance is the real foundation of the economy. They must leave the economy alone to allow it the process that made it the strongest in the world, while recognizing that the more they tinker with it from Washington, the more it will falter as it is directed in ways different from those that would have been encouraged by the free market.

The electorate must also recognize that a Democrat is a Democrat, whether he calls for new taxes, Industrial Policy, Socialism, or increased regulation. Your Senator Tsongas, Mr. Raspberry, describes George McGovern's main economic advisor, Lester Thurow, as his favorite. McGovern, as you will recall, was the most liberal Democrat to run for President since the 1940's. McGovern supported the communist, Henry Wallace, when he ran for President in 1948, and he supported a guaranteed minimum income for all Americans in the 1970's. The deceptive call from Tsongas for an Industrial Policy is an indication of the lengths to which a Democrat will go to disguise and repackage his standard rhetoric to make it appealing to voters. If Tsongas had said, "when you get to the heart of the matter, all I really want is what George McGovern and Lester Thurow wanted," would you have endorsed him with the same enthusiasm, Mr. Raspberry? Lately, Tsongas has shrewdly been emphasizing a simple capital gains tax cut, but if he should get the nomination he will not be able to escape the much more socialist emphasis of his campaign booklet which was written before he knew the recession would linger.

A NEW TERM - DEMOCRATS RENAME SOCIALISM

Dear Mr. Chancellor,

I heard your commentary tonight and found it very irrational on several different levels. You advocated gov't\business cooperation and called it- Industrial Policy. You did not point out that this is just another variation of liberalism or socialism, something the Democrats have always wanted, or at least what they have always pushed us toward.

Something like 85% of you in the media are registered Democrats; so it is not surprising to hear you advocating their policies. This is very deceptive though, especially for those in your audience who can't put what you say in a Democratic / Republican context. I suppose what you anticipate is that swing voters, those who flip back and forth between Democrats and Republicans, will hear a Democrat talking about "Industrial Policy," at some point during the campaign, and then go out and vote Democratic.

Since America is governed exclusively by Democrats and Republicans, and since the electorate's huge responsibility is to distinguish between them, why don't you "do the right thing" and label your agenda so people can act on it in the voting booth.

The electorate almost always splits their vote between the two parties because they are very confused about what the parties represent. Is this because the electorate is dumb or because you in the media are dumb about the way you present the news to them? Is it difficult to understand the difference between Democrats and Republicans, or is it something you in the media have chosen never to deal with on a consistent basis?

If the gov't can help, as you seem to believe, why didn't it do so in Russia, China, N. Korea, E. Germany, Cuba. If the Japanese are so successful as you claim, could it be in spite of their govt's Industrial Policy; not because of it, as you so cavalierly assumed. The Japanese are often sexist, Buddhist, Communist and extremely authoritarian, although democratic. Should we adopt these characteristics too, as the cultural foundation of business success.

DEMOCRATS RENAME SOCIALISM

Further, you spoke glowingly of Bobby Inman, who is undoubtedly an academic\bureaucratic genius, as someone who could be one of the socialist wizards who could plan our economy. But you did so without recognizing that someone with those qualities is often totally befuddled by the rigors of an often random and intuitive marketplace. It took a kid in his garage (Steve Jobs) to but a mainframe on every desk; not Bobby Inman or IBM. It took IBM to introduce computers; not RCA and General Electric, the electronic giants of the time. The computer world has been exploding in a million different directions at once for the last 20 years; it would be incredibly preposterous for Bobby Inman and the Federal Gov't to guess at which of the new explosions was correct, and then back that guess with taxpayer money.

When Xerox invented the first copy machines, they had no idea whether the product had any value or not. They hired consultants who estimated that total placements would be about 3000 units. No expert on earth had any idea that millions and millions of units could be sold. Many new products develop amid the same confusion. Would Bobby Inman and the Democrats have been able to guess correctly at what the Xerox machine was to become. It turns out that many young entrepreneurs succeed because their inexperience and youthful self-confidence encourages them to do things that older, more knowledgeable folks are not inclined to do, and they often do these things with a kind of religious zeal or personal passion that no one else can match, least of all, stodgy Democratic bureaucrats.

Republicans believe in experimental free enterprise (capitalism) because the history of business seems to suggest very clearly that new products and technologies come from places where they are least expected. The people who made locomotives laughed at those who thought the automobile was practical; those who made the automobile laughed at those who thought the airplane would be successful. It is natural for those who should know best, to often know least. Moreover, products and services are often brought to market and made profitable by people other than those who originally invent them, and these people are equally unanticipated. The Democrats somehow believe in gov't planning (socialism), or Industrial Policy, as you call

A NEW TERM

it Mr. Chancellor, while Republicans know from a study of American capitalism that new products and technologies appear only according to a random process that no one, least of all, Democratic bureaucrats, can figure out. If the gov't tries, it will be doing, to one degree or another, what they try to do in Russia or China, and they will get essentially the same results.

If you want to give the forthcoming debate some context and meaning, Mr. Chancellor, you will need to apply some accurate labels and explain the difference between the way Democrats and Republicans view Industrial Policy. To pretend that Industrial Policy is something new and wise, and not directly connected to standard Democratic thinking, is very deceptive.

POVERTY - DEMOCRATS ENLIST REPUBLICAN

Dear Mr. Elliott,

I read your "Newsweek" article "March on Washington" dated April 8, 1991 and was appalled at how deceptive and naive it was.

In sum, your purpose was to encourage Americans to mount an epic march on Washington for the purpose of encouraging the Federal Gov't to give the cities money with which to confront what you called their "Clockwork Orange" like problems.

At no point in the article did it occur to you to explain why or how Washington's money was or could be the solution to the cities' plight. The Feds now run a huge deficit, the reduction of which is central to the economy's long term recovery and stability. The notion that Washington might somewhere find additional billions for some sort of massive subsidy to urban America is so remote as to be silly.

Further, the whole idea of Federal help, even if it were possible, and even though it would be well intentioned, is fraudulent given that the money, whether it came from selling debt, printing money, or taxation, would ultimately be billed to precisely those people it came from in the first place. Mr. Elliott, you seem to believe that the Feds somehow create money by miraculous conception and then simply spend it so as to help people, and make problems disappear. Does it make sense, for example, to tax the people of New York City, send the money to Washington; then bestow it back on the people of New York as if it wasn't theirs in the first place. The concept is an insult, and of course, the Federal Gov't, well known for its legendary inefficiency and waste, charges a high price for handling the money on the round trip from NY to Washington to NY.

Even stranger though, is the deceptive way in which you call for both Democrats and Republicans to join this epic march. Presumably, you know full well that Republicans generally regard gov't as the problem; not the solution, and accordingly, would not be remotely inclined to blister their feet at your summons to Federal action. By encouraging Republicans to participate, you are showing the desperate straits in which Democrats

DEMOCRATS ENLIST REPUBLICANS

now find themselves, and, more importantly, you are deliberately blurring the notion of a two party system, a system that is the only possible vehicle through which your leftist political philosophy might again gain popular identification and support. As a journalism professor, Mr. Elliott, you must surely appreciate that without political parties to embrace and embody coherent philosophies, the work of journalism has no context; no coherent thread for voters to decipher, and is unlikely to result in a voting pattern from which national movement, rather than national paralysis, might emerge.

It is a minor sin, and something of a practical necessity in the current climate, for journalists to often pretend that they are neutral, but a major sin or joke to openly encourage, as you do, the notion that Democrats and Republicans should abandon their parties and join together to do the things that only Democrats believe in.

To be a helpful journalist you must first crisply define what each party stands for; then publicly encourage an allegiance to the party of your choice. What you have done through your article in "Newsweek" is to deceptively promote the Democrats, in perhaps the only way possible, given that only 29% of voters are now willing to identify themselves as Democrats. Nevertheless, it would have been honorable to be straight forward about it, and smart, to have recognized the long established disrepute of the very old fashioned political ideas you are still clinging to.

H. ROSS PEROT-MANAGEMENT WITHOUT PRINCIPLE

Dear Mr. Perot,

You recently did a ninety minute, C-Span interview with Brian Lamb. That interview should have finally been enough to convince you that your understanding of gov't is simply not sufficient to enable you to rescue America from its very complex problems, or from the Democrats and Republicans, although your strategy of waiting until after the election to reveal your positions is a stroke of contemptuous political genius.

When Mr. Lamb asked you to respond to the commentators who have compared you to strongman dictators like Juan Peron and Benito Mussolini your response was that these writers didn't know you, had never met you, and would think differently if only they knew what a nice man you really were. As the evening progressed many got to know you better and they were certainly not reassured. For example, when you were asked what function the Congress of the United States would have in a Perot Administration that favored a popular democracy voting with the use of an electronic town hall, you said, "I don't know all the details yet but Congress could vote too." In one instant you resisted the comparison to a dictator and in the next you offered no thoughts on your support for the existence or role of the U.S. Congress.

Actually, the role of Congress is described in precise detail by the Constitution. America's ingenious founding fathers turned their brilliant minds to a detailed study of history before they composed the Constitution which reversed all of human history in an instant. It is an understatement to say that what you may be thinking of proposing is grossly unconstitutional. You seem to have no capacity to understand how potentially dangerous it is to tamper with fragile democratic processes and institutions. Oh well, I guess America will just have to wait until after your election to see whether your ongoing analysis lands you closer to the side of George Washington or Benito Mussolini. In the mean time, some of us will pray that your status as the teflon billionaire does not last long enough for us to find out.

It would seem apparent that you are uniquely qualified by virtue of your indecision on all of the major issues, not to be President. When Jesse Jackson asked you how you would stop free trade, you said you'd explain to the Congress that free trade must be stopped in order to preserve

H. ROSS PEROT

American jobs; then you said,"it would be interesting to hear their response." It would be more interesting if you already knew the response to this age old question. When you were asked to explain how you have the audacity to be a candidate without any positions, you alternated between saying that you were going to develop positions soon or that Americans didn't care about positions because they were insightful enough to be seeking leadership. This borders on the subversive given that it is obviously possible and very desirable for a President to be both a strong leader and have principles too. In fact, leadership without direction or principle is not possible; yet it is exactly what you seem proud to propose.

You are getting an unprecedented, wide berth from the press for the time being because much of America is very wounded and confused by its new status as a declining country. Although your candidacy seems to be without rationale, many have turned to you as they would turn to John Wayne or the Lone Ranger. No one can say how you became the alternative, rather than, say, the Libertarian Party which is the third largest Party in America and has a legitimate agenda. The need for an alternative candidate or Party comes from a fundamental mistake that both you and those who support you have made. Your rationale is that since the gov't is failing and the country declining, it must be the fault of the Democrats and Republicans who jointly manage the gov't. This analysis, which sustains the Perot minions, ignores the possibility that the decline of America arises not from both Parties but from the non-synergistic effect created as both parties develop a homogeneous appearance due only to their physical proximity in Washington. Isn't it necessary to distinguish between convicts and guards in a prison in order to determine who the bad guys are? To assume that Democrats and Republicans are the same, is a gross mistake given that they pursue opposite approaches to gov't. Sadly though, it takes more study than you and your supporters are willing to undertake before this can be seen.

There are many ways to demonstrate this for those who insist that both Parties are the same and equally negligent. It turns out that in 1991 "The American Conservative Union" gave Republican Senators an average rating of 72.8%; they gave Democrat Senators an average rating of 21.9%. "The American Security Council" which is concerned with maintaining a strong military defense of America gave Republicans a 88.7% rating; Democrats only a 36.3%. The "Americans for Democratic Action"(ADA), a liberal organization, gave Republicans a 20.3% rating; Democrats a 73.9%. COPE

MANAGEMENT WITHOUT PRINCIPLE

which is the liberal, political action arm of the AFL-CIO gave Republicans a 24.1% ratings; Democrats a 77.4%. All of this serves to demonstrate that serious groups with no connection to one another who know what to look for, find major and opposing differences between Democrats and Republicans. The numerical differences described above would be greater still if politicians weren't always moderating their positions in order to build a consensus for both electoral and legislative purposes.

The Republicans are the party of traditional American values. They believe as our founding fathers did that America is about freedom, i.e., freedom from gov't, individual responsibility and voluntary economic relationships. This is the tradition from which Reagan/Bush draw when they say,"read my lips, no new taxes - gov't is the problem; not the solution - isn't welfare a form of slavery." The Democrats believe that big gov't is a marvelous tool with which to confer freedom from all problems, especially those problems which disproportionately effect the disadvantaged. This is why they are for national health insurance and against balanced budget amendments. To a Democrat, a person is the creation of the society or gov't he lives under; to a Republican a human is his own creation or, if you prefer, the creation of God.

While U.S. Senators seem to be very certain of what philosophical tradition they prefer, the electorate, being much less sophisticated, is very confused. According to a recent "Congressional Quarterly" study, 47% of Republican voters would prefer more rather than less gov't spending. And 42% of Democrats would prefer less rather than more spending. This sad and unbelievable confusion from the electorate is what causes them to split their vote and send what appears to be divided gov'ts to Washington. It is no wonder that an electorate that can not distinguish Democrats from Republicans is so willing to blame both for the country's decline. In fact, most trends in America began to level off and turn down in the 1960's; this is precisely the period when we began to have divided gov't. Prior to 1956 we had 42 elections and only 3 divided gov'ts; since 1956 we have had 9 elections and 6 divided gov'ts.

Just as important is that the divided gov'ts which presided over our decline were not divided evenly, but instead were heavily skewed toward the Democrats who became increasingly big-gov't oriented in the 60's. As Democratic, big gov't influence grew, America declined. For example, in

H. ROSS PEROT

1960 Federal spending was only 10% of GNP; today it is 25%. Social welfare outlays were only $52.2 Billion in 1960; $834.4 Billion in 1987. But, today we have more social welfare problems than in 1960. Economic growth after 1960 slowed to the lowest rate in American history, averaging only 2.5% despite tremendous technological growth. Mr. Perot, your candidacy is designed to exploit the sad situation in America which has led you and your supporters to believe both parties are the same and equally responsible for America's decline. In truth, divided, Democratically controlled gov't has caused the decline of America. If you really are as concerned and patriotic as I'm sure you like to think, you should drop your demagogic campaign and devote your prodigious money and energy toward helping yourself and the electorate understand the very large and real differences that exist between the parties.

When you were asked whether you were liberal or conservative you said, "I don't fit in either pocket." Your claim to be independent of both the Democrats and Republicans is purely a function of your inability to understand either Party. If you were to ask Republicans to provide a basis for their thinking about freedom from gov't, they might draw a long historical line from Socrates to Jefferson. Similarly, Democratic thinking about big, benevolent gov't might draw a line from Plato to Hamilton. Perhaps you will tell us on which intellectual traditions independants rely. When you legitimize indecision and lack of education with a candidacy built around it, you accomplish little besides distracting America.

I suppose if you were pressed hard you might say something like, "cut out all the academic stuff, I'm for leadership; for getting things done; for common sense management." This is a trick answer because it implies that there are people for no sense, bad management and poor leadership. Will leadership alone solve the budget deficit crisis which you often identify as our most significant problem? Democrats generally like deficits, and oppose balanced budget amendments because those deficits provide a painless and insidious way for gov't to grow without new taxes. Republicans oppose deficits and support balanced budget amendments because they want to reduce the size of gov't. Once you choose a solution, Mr. Perot, either raising taxes, or cutting spending, you will be squabbling just like Democrats and Republicans. The only honest solution is to build a large majority for one Party and hold that Party accountable for the good or evil that then happens, but first you have to decide which Party, Mr. Perot.